HUNT/KILL SELLING

Sales Secrets of the Professional Persuaders

HUNT/KILL SELLING

Sales Secrets of the Professional Persuaders

Jack L. Matthews

SHAPOLSKY PUBLISHERS, INC.
NEW YORK

A Shapolsky Book

Copyright © 1991 by Jack L. Matthews

For any additional information, contact:
Shapolsky Publishers, Inc.
136 West 22nd Street
New York, NY 10011
(212) 633-2022

10 9 8 7 6 5 4 3 2 1

Library of Congress Cataloging-in-Publication Data

Matthews, Jack L., 1924–
   Hunt/kill selling: sales secrets of the professional persuaders/Jack L. Matthews
     p.   cm.
ISBN 0-944007-78-3
1. Selling. 2. Sales presentations. I. Title
HF5438.25.M377   1990
659.1′0688—dc20   90-37100

Design and Typography by The Bartlett Press, Inc.,
Somerset, New Jersey

Printed and bound by Graficromo s.a., Cordoba, Spain

This book is dedicated to my best friend . . .

Charlotte Matthews
. . . whom I love, like and respect.

Its value is due to her inspiration, motivation, objectivity, cooperation, direction, instruction, critique, encouragement, efforts, labor, guidance, evaluation, analysis, services, advice, counsel, expertise, training, discipline, knowledge, inspection, examination, skill, observation, assessment, judgment, standards, assistance, recommendations, decisions, consultation, perception, ability, participation, understanding, cognition, principles, patience, intelligence, scrutiny, appraisal, interrogation, competence, aptitude, authority, reasoning, opinions, discernment, taste, suggestions, support, proposals, determination, conclusions, deliberation, consideration, probing, research, industriousness, insight, stimulation, TLC, comprehension, dedication, thoroughness, vision, talent, involvement, tolerance, sympathy, objectives, goals, devotion, loyalty, effectiveness, adroitness, ideas, forbearance, adeptness, strength, approbation, sanction, rationality, esteem, convictions, belief, acumen, thoughts, attitude, endurance, interest, advocacy, comfort, exertion, profundity, contemplation, investigation, exploration, practicality, diligence, ingeniousness, intuition, clairvoyance, imagination, revelations, creativity, energy, indulgence . . . and other contributions too numerous to enumerate.

Contents

Introduction

Why This Book Is for You

This book is written for all those who work for, with, and against Advertising Agencies. (Throw in all the other experts on selling, and this includes practically everybody.) Specifically, it is for those whose purpose is winning the business they want—faster.

As a scenario, the frame of reference is Ad Agency–oriented, because the strategy and techniques of Ad Agencies have set the pace for all those in the communications industry. Here's why. An Ad Agency is expected to have the greatest power to persuade. So, to sell most productively, it is a shrewd move to emulate its operation.

To create and maintain this reputation among clients and prospects, it must consistently evidence success. Thus, an Ad Agency is a grow-or-die business. Despite this, there has never been a single source that has dealt with every conceivable matter that determines whether they win or come in second. To fulfill this need, you have it now. It's in your hand.

Beyond Ad Agency people, this book is also "must" reading for those in marketing/advertising departments, the media (TV, radio, magazines, newspapers, outdoor), sales promotion agencies, public relations firms and direct response agencies. Because the book's insights can take the gamble out of *their* new business crapshoot, too.

Matthews' New Business "Smarts"

To make good on this heavy claim requires exceptional qualifications.

The author, Jack Matthews, has them—with plenty to spare. His "selling smarts" were gained from a potent combination of experiences: the type that gave him the scars to which you can relate.

To begin with, he has paid his dues, being a 25-year veteran of Agency wars. He has served as a vice president at major shops, managing multi-million-dollar accounts. Matthews was also vitally involved in new business activity—assuming key responsibility for the development of strategy and conduct of over 150 full-scale presentations.

Eighteen years ago, he established a management consulting firm to concentrate on the critical area of Advertiser/Agency Relations, or as it can also be described, What Happens When the Lion Lies Down with the Lamb. (It's up to you to decide who's who in this relationship.)

Seriously, part of his operation consists of counseling advertisers on selecting Agencies. In this unique position, he has flushed out what they *really* think—and the difference between what they say and what they mean.

This consulting had provided an enviable insight into advertisers' subjective expectations of an Agency, their actual reaction to new business solicitation—and what turns them on or off. The importance of this insight becomes evident when considering the vastness of the market that exists and their range of its attitudes:

- Fifteen percent of advertisers intend to fire their Agencies.

- Sixty-five percent claim to be satisfied with them—but then detail a laundry list of complaints.

- the remaining 20 percent are unqualifiedly happy.

Therefore, the objective of this book is to furnish tested ideas to convince the 80 percent of advertisers who are willing and vulnerable to change the reasons why why *your Agency* is best for them. Especially now.

Correspondingly, on the other side of the street, Jack conducts shirt-sleeve sessions for Agencies on pitching new business. Having consulted for 382 individual Agencies, he can reveal with reasonable certainty whether what they are discovering succeeds or fails—the hard way. Because at each of these, he usually gets two good ideas and two bad ones. And sometimes the latter are more valuable than the former.

Thus, with his input being entirely case-history-oriented, he can tell you what works or doesn't, thereby saving you the time and effort of having to reinvent the wheel.

This behind-the-scenes experience exposes how the professional persuaders sell for themselves. Obviously, their strategies would also be of considerable value to anyone involved in sales. Thus, the hunt/kill procedure detailed in this book contains gems for everybody.

And, as this extensive track record continues to grow, Jack becomes an even firmer believer in the priceless advice: "It's what you learn *after* you think you know it all that counts."

Matthews' Revelations

The reason for this book is to make more money for both of us. Any questions so far?

Further, this book is going to be a worthwhile experience, because I am going to provide you with the insight that will enable you to control your Agency's future and improve your individual security, income, and opportunity.

Does this seem like too much to hope for? Well, all that's what you *want*. Then, why not operate on a basis so as to make it happen?

To accomplish this, I am going to give you a top-of-the-line set of clubs. But remember: You still have to play them. So start taking your practice swings now. Then, when it comes time to tee off, you will be all warmed up and ready to go. Also loose and confident.

While getting in shape, here is what you can expect. . . .

Fortunately, I have been running into just about whatever situation in selling occurs when going for the jugular. It ranges from the outstanding to the disastrous. Whatever your concern, it is very possible that I came across it recently in New York, Chicago, Los Angeles, or your city. So try me. I feel just as responsible for the worth of the input furnished as I would if my name were on your door.

In doing so, I can be objective and uninhibited, since I'm not emotionally involved. In order to level with you, I can risk terminal candor. I would be derelict in my responsibility if I told you only what you *want* to hear. Where required, you will find this book provocative—and sometimes not very ingratiating. However, in taking this lattitude, I can clue you in to what is less apparent.

To capture and hold reader interest beyond its how-to appeal, the book is liberally salted with solicitation war stories, especially those illustrating what works or doesn't. And it is written in "people talk" so that the tactics furnished can be easily understood and applied. The aim is to deliver the missing link for scoring: confidence.

For openers, not mincing words, here is why this book is so necessary: In my cross-pollinating, I have found that much Agency new-business activity is based on the assumption of having some mystical intuition as to what goes on inside the advertiser's head. Yet the advertiser believes that a certain amount of holding back is his prerogative. He/she believes that what he/she knows—that *you* don't—forms his/her power base. And knowledge is power. So I'll also be revealing to you what the advertiser withholds for tactful or tactical reasons.

Why they do this requires an understanding of the advertisers' frame of mind. Regardless of the degree of sophistication of any of them, they all have the same thing in common: *self-interest*. And your new-business approach is only as appealing as the prospect perceives it will serve his/her individual purpose. For this reason: You're not dealing with a corporate logo or bricks and mortar, but rather with a person's ambition and security.

For the record, what I will be reporting to you doesn't represent any pet philosophies of my own. However, where Advertiser or Agency input has inspired direction, ideas, or solutions, these will be offered for your benefit. Further, since my business *is* giving the store away, I am not going to presume that any idea is too big or too small for you. Rather, I'm going to supply *all* the worthwhile information I have accumulated. Then, let it be *your* judgment call as to if and when its use would be appropriate.

Granted, I'll be giving you:

- some things you already know—but might not be as familiar with the amount of emphasis or importance that advertisers attach to them

- matters that you know—but may have forgotten . . .

- or things that you know—but aren't doing anything about

For that matter, you may consider some of these so fundamental as to take them for granted. Well, Mike Ditka never takes blocking or tackling for granted.

Finally, there are a number of factors detailed that are new—which will be revelations to you, as they were to me.

In total, this book contains 276 key subjects. However, as one of your peers put it, "Jack, I'm looking for just one gem. One that will trigger landing an account we want. If I can find that one, I'll concede you the other 275."

So join the search. You'll make out—because I'm going to show you where these gems are hidden. You have my credentials. And now, the premise for this book. It's been said to me, "You must have to be very bright." And I can answer, with justifiable modesty, "No, just a good sponge." So use this depth and breadth of knowledge compiled to take the gamble out of *your* new-business crapshoot.

What's in a Title?

This book's title is the most realistic description of an Ad Agency's new-business operation. But it didn't come easy. Nor did the subtitle defining what can be expected. How these two revelations occurred can be revealed by tracking the evolution of both.

My first impulse was to use the title to establish my qualifications for writing this book. This resulted in: *What I Learned About Landing New Business in Working with 382 Advertising Agencies*. This was judged to be rather heavy. Not a grabber. Although it might be worth considering as a subtitle.

Then it was decided that the name should identify the subject matter—and offer a benefit. By contrast, the objective became brevity, with strong buyer appeal. Thus, I came up with: *How to Get More New Business—Faster*." This seemed to say it all in the quickest, most compelling manner. Upon closer scrutiny, though, this wasn't literal enough. Namely, an Agency doesn't "get" new business. It must win new business. Further, the concept was wrong. Your goal is not to land "more" new business. Rather, it should be to win the *right* kind of accounts. Applying these two requirements, the revised version became: *How to Win the Business You Want—Faster*.

This latest approach best communicated the message desired. And the original statement, as a subtitle, validated this offer.

Yet, I still had a nagging doubt about the title's impact. Although strategically correct, it doesn't go for the jugular. Also, it doesn't reflect the uncertainty that exists in new-business solicitation. Regardless of how dynamic the presentation, and how convincingly it is delivered, there is still a substantial risk. For instance, there may be a hidden agenda in which the selection process is rigged in favor of a wired-in Agency. Or unforeseen chemistry may dominate.

So I went back to square one. This began with redefining the functions of the title and subtitle. The upshot was that the title would identify what the Agency new-business activity *is*—provocatively. And the subtitle would convey the unique insight it reveals—irresistibly. Further, they would be conceived to work together. Finally, it was realized that all these criteria could only be achieved if there weren't any restraints.

Combining discipline with lack of inhibition, this produced the title *The Ad Agency Crapshoot*. Then to take the gamble out of it, the subtitle contained the payoff: *Sales Secrets of the Professional Persuaders*.

Seemingly after all this effort, I was finally finished, right? Nope. The publisher's 18 sales reps felt that this title restricted the market.

They wanted the same gutsy approach—but with broader appeal. This challenge inspired identifying what today's solicitation activity must be: *HUNT/KILL SELLING*. (However, I couldn't top myself on the subtitle. That stayed).

Apparently, it worked. You bought the book.

Chapter 1

Developments Profoundly Affecting You

A. Perspective
B. Grow-or-Die
C. Reason for Success or Failure
D. Advertiser Attitude

A. Perspective

As you will notice, I am evangelistic on the matter of going after new business. For two reasons.

First, the size of the market is mind-boggling. In 1987, advertisers switched $1.2 billion in billings. Therefore, if your growth wasn't significant, it sure wasn't due to lack of potential.

Second, in my extensive cross-pollinating among Agencies, I see such a pedestrian job being done. Not bad—or they wouldn't be in business. Rather, just sort of blah.

For example, so many new business presentations consist of the Agency sitting on the side of the bed telling the prospect how great it is going to be. And in their eagerness, the Agency fails to notice that the prospect has either fallen asleep or gotten up and gone home.

You can be a mile ahead of the pack and score by just taking 16 steps. If you know what they are—and how to do so. These are the 16 areas in which an Agency's performance determines whether it wins or comes in second. Yet, Agencies are surprisingly unaware of how to function most productively in these areas. And of advertiser reaction to their efforts.

I'm going to furnish the insight needed in both respects. But to begin with, I have good news and *good* news for you. The good news is that I'm not going to tout any blue-sky, off-the-wall ideas and suggest that you experiment with them. The *good* news, though, is that I can clue you in on what works or doesn't in new business activity. Here's why.

- In the shirtsleeve seminars I have conducted for 385 Agencies on this subject, what I learned from their specific new business experiences has proved extremely valuable.
- I work with a couple of Agencies per month who phone saying, "We have a major new business presentation coming up. Come on in, spend a day with us in rehearsal, and cut us up."

In this hands-on involvement, I've found there are definite reasons why Agencies score—or don't.

In reporting this to you, though, I am not going to do so based on your present level. You're already there. Rather, I'm going to challenge you to reach out to where you should be—and provide the best route for getting there. The purpose is to achieve the kind of Agency growth that will make it possible for you to realize the personal growth desired.

Therefore, this book will be as worthwhile as the extent to which you get involved. So read it on the basis of how you can apply its input to your operation—and how soon.

To get you started, I promise you will land the most important client your Agency will ever have before you are one-third through this book. In case you miss it, I'll remind you of who it is at the end.

B.   Grow-or-Die

To maintain objectivity throughout this book, let's bring the role of new business into sharp focus.

But first, who is your most important client? The usual answer I get is whoever is the Agency's largest client. Or most profitable or popular client. *Wrong!*

Your most important client is your Agency. Because if you lose that one, it's terminal.

This was a fatal lesson to Agencies who thought their sole purpose was servicing existing clients. Or figured they were safe and could get by with the accounts they had. Then they blame their demise on not having had time to go after new business. Actually, the truth of the matter is that it seemed like too much work.

It needn't be. I can take the gamble out of your new business crap-shoot, because my insight is based on what turns advertisers on or off in new business solicitations—and what Agencies are discovering succeeds or fails . . . the hard way. These "street smarts" will save you considerable time since you won't have to await the occurrence of winning ideas. I have them for you now.

To succeed, though, this input needs to be matched by realizing what is at stake: *an Advertising Agency is a grow-or-die business*. For the two most important reasons:

- Advertisers want more than a survivor. They want an Agency that is success-driven.

- Personnel want to be with an Agency that is on a roll. Because they translate being hot into raises and promotions.

Yet, despite this grow-or-die truism, Agencies use a variety of lame excuses to rationalize their lethargy.

- Like, "We'd become active in the new business area, but we don't want to risk antagonizing our clients." Let's put this fallacy to rest. As long as a client continues to be satisfied with the amount and quality of attention received, he is *pleased* with your new business success. Because it confirms the soundness of his judgment in having selected your Agency and continuing to retain it.

  Even so, when landing a major account, some suspicious client might needle you with, "Does this mean we will get less service?" You can honestly reply, "Actually, you'll be getting *more* service. Because this new business will enable us to hire additional people who will serve as a source of further ideas for you. Also, we can now afford to add more functions and increase our computerization. Thus, this growth will make us of greater value to you."

- Another fallacy is that soliciting the accounts of others is immoral. (The first time I heard that was in Salt Lake City.) This, too, is a copout—ignoring reality. Your client roster forms the new business list for a number of other Agencies. Therefore, you can expect some attrition for which you have to compensate.

  So, it's not a matter of whether you should compete—only *how* you conduct this operation. That is what determines whether it is moral or otherwise. If you function on a strictly positive and constructive basis—forgoing any devious devices—then you are as righteous as you want to be.

- Still another weak rationale is that you are just too busy. This doesn't wash either. Because you establish your new business program and its application in advance. Then it is only a matter of customizing the strategy and materials for the prospect. So don't lose out on a great opportunity because of lacking the foresight or ambition to prepare for a successful future.

- Finally, not quite as inflexible as this "stuck in neutral" category of Agencies, are those who are a little bit pregnant. They severely handicap themselves with holier-than-thou policies based on two other excuses: "We never make spec presentations" or "We only pitch accounts who have announced their intentions to switch."

Yet, how are these Agencies going to convince prospects that they can help them compete more effectively if they believe in only restricted activity? As an advertiser, which type Agency would most appeal to you: the one who believes in a total selling concept—or the type who might be available on its own limiting terms?

Therefore, your new business effort should be your best shot—or else reconcile yourself to account attrition eventually closing your shop.

C. Reason for Success or Failure

Due to my constant networking among Agencies, I am frequently asked, "How is the Agency business shaping up today?" My answer in this economic climate: "It seems to be polarizing into two distinct types—those who believe what they tell their clients and the others who don't."

Here is what's happening. The late '70s recession provided the first documented evidence that if advertisers just maintain their level of marketing activity during a recession, they will actually increase their share of market. Correspondingly, the faint of heart who cut back suffer disproportionately. This experience is proving to be every bit as applicable to the Agency field. Despite client budget cuts and the profit crunch, those shops which maintain an adequate new business program are doing very well. And increasingly so.

By contrast, the other group of Agencies responds to these circumstances by instituting an austerity program. And the first function affected by this belt-tightening masochism is soliciting new accounts. As a result of just trying to tread water during an undertow, these myopic Agencies are hurting badly—with their income continuing to spiral downward.

Further, by dropping out of contention, they are conceding prospects to those who realize that the new business function is an ongoing, integral part of the Agency operation.

Thus, current conditions have spawned the Agency business's own version of "the haves-and-have-nots." The key difference in the case of the latter, though, is they can't stay at the poverty level for very long.

D.   Advertiser Attitude

And now for what your program is all about: the advertiser.

Even though they are becoming increasingly restless, the greater accountability being required of them is causing them to be more calculating regarding the decision to change Agencies—and more diligent in the selection process.

Thus, greater quality and effectiveness of new business activity has become necessary. This has resulted in a general upgrading of performance. In fact, as is being said by advertisers, the efforts of many Agencies are even approaching the level of mediocrity.

The first time I heard that, I thought, "Now that's a smart-ass remark!" But after cooling off, it become apparent to me that with the existence of this attitude, if you treat the new business function as more than a spare-time activity, you'll be in an elite group of Agencies.

Yet, even after getting into this league, recognize that there is only one new business game being played now: hardball. And you have to be willing to compete with the intensity required. Remember: You don't make much money sitting on the bench.

Chapter 2

The Attitude It Takes to Win

A. Perspective

Success begins with *commitment*. Dedication to an aggressive new business plan, consistently applied.

Not a sporadic quick-fix when an account is lost. Rather, ongoing activity accorded as much importance as client service.

This amounts to *you* taking control of your Agency's future. Rather than relying on news of loose accounts, *you* make things happen. Decide on what advertisers you *want* to work with—based on profitability and desirability. Then take whatever action is necessary to score—for as long as it takes.

This isn't just a matter of your devotion to landing new business being desirable. Because, as stressed, an Ad Agency is a grow-or-die business. If you're not a winner, you're a loser.

B. Management Dedication

There are two *functional* reasons why an Agency doesn't score in pitching new accounts. It is due to ineptness in either strategy or conduct.

More insidious, and a less apparent cause of new business failure, though, is the matter of *attitude*. Specifically, if the Agency principals are no longer hungry enough.

This is reflected in their reduced concern about growth and the minimal effort they are willing to expend for this purpose. They paid their dues and now feel entitled to a less frantic pace. This frame of mind isn't the result of age, or having become burned out, but, rather, of having arrived. It is due to loss of desire. And then this personal success stifles Agency success.

If any of you in top Management have lost the drive to be more successful, then get out of the way. As normal attrition takes its toll, the Agency won't be able to afford to provide you with the comfortable income you've become accustomed to. Because complacency begets atrophy.

And your employees will not tolerate this stagnation for long. They know they are not going to progress any more than the Agency does. Sooner rather than later, they will opt for a shop still committed to growth.

Therefore, go back to the original appeal of this business: the excitement of winning. Instead of settling for holding your own, rededicate yourself to the fulfillment of greater accomplishment.

Its importance transcends the accompanying exhilarating feeling. Rather, there is the cold hard fact of reality. If you don't stay aggressive on new business, your competition will take not only your employees—but also your accounts. Due to your inertia, your Agency will no longer be considered a force to be reckoned with. And when this cavalier activity becomes evident, the vultures won't circle for too long.

Any Agency principal who no longer enjoys the hunt/kill function had better make room for someone who is turned on by this challenge. Otherwise, your last executive act will consist of presiding over the wake for your Agency.

C. Effect of Creative Director

A successful new business program requires a *total* Agency commitment. For this to occur, top Management has to provide the necessary direction and inspiration.

Among this key group, the person having the greatest *influence* on results is the Creative Director. Is yours Agency- or function-oriented? One who considers himself/herself as an integral force in the entire Agency operation—or a prima donna who feels the business end is dirty and anyway—it's not his/her job.

I now have enough evidence to conclude that there is a direct correlation between the Creative Director's outlook toward new business activity and the Agency's rate of scoring. If you have a person who is gung-ho in this respect, your Agency is blessed. Otherwise, you're carrying just a craftsman—which isn't enough for today's Agency.

Therefore, objectively analyze your Creative Director's attitude and initiative in this arena. And take whatever action that will assure your getting the maximum contribution from this vital source.

D.   Constructive Dissatisfaction

Hardly ever is one single idea responsible for an Agency scoring.

Sure, you might luck out with an occasional miracle. But realistically, it is the application of every conceivable advantage that results in winning. And the more thorough, the greater the likelihood of getting lucky.

However, to win bigger—and more consistently—it takes an attitude of *constructive dissatisfaction* with your program. Namely, continuously suspect that something was overlooked—or could be improved. Then play: "Beat the Devil's Advocate."

Summing up, you know the *routine* components of a new business operation. So do your competitors. The winners, though, are those who compound the basics by constantly assuming they can do better—and following through.

E.   Agency Location

When I'm at an Agency in a city other than New York or Chicago, I'm sometimes asked, "Are we at a disadvantage in soliciting new business because of being out of the mainstream?" And they seem somewhat reconciled to this assumed handicap.

I won't commiserate with these Agencies. Acknowledging this factor as being a problem would be a grave disservice. Because if there is a lack of achievement, location would be used as a scapegoat—obscuring the issue. And having this excuse provides an out for not finding the *real* cause. Thus, they don't need sympathy. Rather, perspective.

The most convincing rebuttal to this negative thinking is the enviable success achieved by those in very unlikely locations. For instance, ask any of the following how badly they are hurting due to being off the beaten path:

- Ralph Callahan—HENDERSON, Greenville, SC
  ($75,000,000)

- Steve Gurasich—G.S.D.M., Austin, TX
  ($124,000,000)

- Bill Biggs—BIGGS/GILMORE, Kalamazoo, MI
  ($62,800,000)

- Tom Smythe—KELLER CRESCENT, Evansville, IN
  ($110,254,000)

- Chick McKinney—McKINNEY & SILVER, Raleigh, NC
  ($121,000,000)

- Bob Noble—NOBLE, Springfield, MO
  ($75,000,000)

- Janet Muhleman—GROUP 243, Ann Arbor, MI
  ($75,000,000 est.)

- Tom Ferguson—THOMAS FERGUSON, Parsippany, NJ
  ($102,000,000)

- Smoot Fahlgren—FAHLGREN & SWINK, Parkersburg, WV
  ($134,500,000)

- Bernie Schramm—WILLIAM COOK, Jacksonville, FL
  ($76,500,000)

- Don Adams—LONG HAYNES CARR, Winston-Salem, NC
  ($110,000,000)

- Buzz Baker—C.M.F.&Z., Cedar Rapids, IA
  ($89,500,000)

As can be seen, you can hardly get to any of these places from anywhere; but a benefit won't have to be held for any of these entrepreneurs.

It didn't occur to them that they were hindered by location. Rather, they set out to sell the only two factors that matter: *quality of performance* and *compatibility of relationship*. Based on their track records, apparently it works.

So don't get hung up on not having a Madison Avenue or Michigan Avenue address. Usually, all advertisers care about is *what* you deliver—not from *where*.

F. Selection Rigged?

One of an Agency's first concerns when an advertiser decides to switch is whether the selection is rigged. Agencies are cynical. And justifiably so. Because too often, intentional or otherwise, there is a hidden Agenda. The upshot is that you develop a sour attitude which translates into less effort and impact in soliciting new business.

If you ever become bitter to this extent, forgo new business competition. However, the alternative to this will be for normal attrition to eventually close your shop. And at the present rate, this would statistically take only $6\frac{2}{3}$ years.

Or if you suspect that a given solicitation is a loaded beauty contest: Skip it. Because to convince a prospect that your Agency is best for them, *you* need be obviously convinced of this yourself.

Yet, don't second-guess yourself out of a very desirable account. This lesson was learned the hardest way by an Arizona Agency when the state instituted a lottery. This Agency felt eminently qualified to handle this account. But, at that time, with Governor Babbitt being an Elder in the Church of the Latter-Day Saints, they assumed it would be awarded to a Mormon-owned Agency.

So they decided to spare themselves this ritual in which they didn't have a prayer—literally or figuratively. How perceptive was this analysis of the situation? The lottery account went to a Jewish-owned Agency. Therefore, for God's sake—and yours—keep the faith.

Instead of being in a position of suspecting you are at a disadvantage because there is a possibility of the choice being predestined, shoot for the flip side of the situation. *Why couldn't the wired-in Agency be yours?* What would it take? If it's too late to create bias in your favor this time, decide on what action to take to set up future prospects. And give *yourself* the competitive edge.

Therefore, in going after an account, preparing your strategy should begin with becoming the rigger rather than the riggee.

G.   Why Y&R Wins

Young & Rubicam's consistent success in landing new accounts is a constant source of amazement. Even greater is the curiosity as to *how* they do it.

We will have to concede their having considerable know-how, but not necessarily any more than you—or than could be obtained. That's the reason for the baffling question, "Then why do they score so well?"

What's their secret? The secret is that there isn't any. In fact, Y&R would probably be proud to reveal why they are so tough to beat.

It is simply *because they have such a compelling urge to succeed*— matched by equally dedicated work. Trite as it may seem, it's their New

York Yankees/Notre Dame complex. Not only do they earnestly *believe* they can win—but they are willing to get their hands dirty enough to *make* it happen.

Although much of the credit for Y&R's exceptional track record on new business was attributed to Ed Ney's and now Alex Kroll's personal charisma, more significant is their having instilled an obsessed *desire to win* in their people—across the board. Including the pride to be willing to pay the price.

Here, too, it's not a matter of a magical quickie inspiration. Rather, it has been a cumulative effect. For instance, let's go back to when they were pitching on Kentucky Fried Chicken. As you know, during the summer, Manhattan empties out on Friday at noon. And those in the Agency business plan on beating the rush. For that matter, throw in a holiday and stand back.

As it happened, Y&R was coming down to the wire in wrapping up the presentation—with the only time left being the Labor Day weekend. However, while you could have fired a cannon down deserted Madison Ave., there were thirty-four (34) staffers at the Y&R office over this long, sacred weekend putting the final touches on the KFC pitch. (It's history: They made the necessary effort to win—and did.)

As some frustrated Agencies have put it, "How are you going to fight that kind of dedication?" Easy. Instead of cursing the darkness, light a candle. Motivation isn't some God-given gift awarded exclusively to Young & Rubicam. It's available to any Agency that wants to take advantage of it. The only way you can compete against Y&R— or whomever—is to compound your ability and experience with an achievement/action-oriented attitude.

It's a wry gag that one of the ways to tell whether a client is in jeopardy is if you see Alex Kroll's name in their guest register. This needn't strike fear—if your entire Agency is also as determined and psyched to succeed.

Sorry I couldn't divulge some esoteric answer for Y&R's winning ways. However, you now know the actual reasons—and what it takes to win as they do. An Agency must become a gung-ho entity—with the staff realizing that their individual interests can best be served by the *total* Agency's success.

Chapter 3

The Only Policies Needed

A. Perspective
B. Accounts: Type
C. Accounts: Size
D. Accounts: Upgrading
E. Spec Presentations
F. Compensation

A. Perspective

Agencies have a tendency to try and develop pat formulae for whatever the new business function. Then, for any situation, they have an established modus operandi. The procedure is broadly accepted because it is based on empirical solutions—and its existence saves time and effort.

However, while that approach was appropriate under previous circumstances, it can't be pertinent enough the next time. So sure, learn from past experience. But don't use this as a substitute for bringing to bear the most relevant strategy the next time.

Nevertheless, from an overall operational standpoint, there are certain basics that have universal application. The following, as distinguished from one-time ideas, can provide the direction necessary for the success desired.

B.   Accounts: Type

Some agencies will boast about being able to get all the new business they want. Then, as evidence of their prowess in this area, they will announce the number of accounts and employees added.

And it's true. Their kill ratio has been very good among accounts such as used car dealers, political candidates and real estate developers. All volatile and labor intensive. So much for *quantity*.

Admittedly, when an Agency is born, it has to chase down whatever accounts it can get to provide cash flow. But sooner rather than later, it has to grow up and go after the *quality* of clients that are preferable. They are the type who(m):

- you want to work with
- are satisfactorily profitable
- are marketing-oriented
- will be conducive to attracting and keeping desirable employees
- will showcase your Agency
- have good growth potential
- are interesting, fun and exciting
- improve your image
- enhance your appeal to prospects

How do those on your client roster stack up according to the above descriptions? A perfect 10 is too much to hope for. But a general upgrading in their level of value would be wonderful. There are two means by which this can be accomplished:

- Set higher standards for the prospects solicited.
- As you attract more preferred clients, weed out those you romanced for expedience.

Summing up, it's not the number of accounts—but *who* they are. And it's not the amount of billing—but how *profitable*.

Thus, if your Agency is at the stage whereby it is no longer necessary to pass the hat each month to pay the rent, then it's time to progress from being a new business scavenger to a class act. Because you have now earned working with advertisers who would be fulfilling—both professionally and financially.

C. Accounts: Size

It is understandable that Agencies will set a minimum size for accounts they will solicit or accept. This establishes a goal for quality—and rules out unrealistic or undesirable business.

This policy is *not* valid, though, when the criterion is based on billing. Because this figure could be a smokescreen for labor- or time-intensive accounts that could cause you to lose by winning. Instead, there is only one basis for qualifying a prospect: *profit.*

There can be enough indication of an account's viability according to estimated income and projected workload. Although inexact, it is still more reliable than the other umbrella number. Therefore, judge a prospect's budget according to its *worth*—not what it seems. Then, distinguish between gross and net income. The payoff isn't in what they spend. It's in what you keep.

In this context, what do you do when approached by an advertiser whose business is too small to handle?

You never refuse per se. The advertiser feels they are bestowing a great honor on your Agency—and it is inconceivable that you wouldn't covet their account.

Backing off due to its being economically unfeasible is not enough justification. It still nets down to your having rejected them. And after experiencing this perceived humiliation, you're wiped out forever as far as this account is concerned. Then what if their budget increases to a size whereby they become desirable?

You can salvage this tacky situation for now and if significant growth occurs. Use the following strategy employed by Bob Bloom from the Agency of the same name in Dallas.

When offered an account whose billing is less than the established minimum, he tactfully informs the advertiser that his Agency would not be appropriate for them—*at this time.* Then he promises to call back within one day with his recommendation of the three Agencies that could best serve their interests (again, at this time) and who to contact.

Bob Bloom did the prospect a favor—and made a friend. And you can bet the ranch that if and when any of these advertisers become big enough, Mr. Nice Guy will be there to harvest the seeds he planted—because the time is *now* right.

D.   Accounts: Upgrading

For both financial and possibly moral reasons, I'm asked with some frequency about the advisability of upgrading clients. Namely, going after competitive accounts that are bigger than existing clients.

The first consideration is whether the prospect would be so much more *profitable*, and its *growth potential* that appealing, as to be worth the risk of losing your present smaller client. Is that conflicting prospect so desirable as to justify this crapshoot?

If you can rationalize this gamble from a business standpoint (with no regrets), then it's a judgmental decision: immediate gain and opportunity versus the hopeful security of existing revenue.

Now let's deal with the matter of morality. With all due respect to the righteousness factor, the final criterion needs to be based on *what is in your Agency's best interest*. Period. Sounds callous? Cynical? Try realistic. Because clients have all the characteristics of a dog—except loyalty, and many can be bitches.

Therefore, whether you should try to parlay a smaller client into a larger one begins with your responsibility to the Agency. After this priority is satisfied, you can then be as dedicated to the present clients as circumstances and income warrant.

E.   Spec Presentations

Should your policy be for or against spec? Neither. Your position should be one of flexibility.

As it is controversial, we had better first define "spec." It is *any* attempt to solicit an account. *Any* action whatsoever.

Based on this truism, let's take on the purists, those Agencies who righteously claim they *never* do spec. I've asked them, "How about when you write and/or phone a prospect?" And I'm told, "That's different. We're just showing interest." So I'll follow through with, "Then what about when you research them?" This time the answer is, "We're just showing that we care." *Aw c'mon!*

This hypocrisy is justified because spec Creative isn't done. Apparently becoming a little bit pregnant is okay. As long as you don't deliver.

The hard truth is that *every* Agency specs to *some* extent. It is just that there are those who won't admit it. Least of all to themselves.

Having this perspective, we can now deal more realistically with this new business device. Actually, this is a gray area, a matter of degree. Yet, for some reason, Agencies feel compelled to take a black-or-white stand on this matter. But on what? The term "Spec Creative" can cover a multitude of sins.

Thus, your interest can best be served by hearing out the prospect's terms. This enables basing your judgment on firsthand impression rather than assumption.

In this way you can determine whether their presentation requisites are compatible or conflict with your method of operation. If acceptable, you can then decide if the cost and effort involved can be justified. This positive approach will preclude taking your Agency out of contention for a desirable account because you settled for rumor or gossip.

Therefore, don't base your new business operation on old bromides, ranging from "Even prostitutes don't give away free samples" to "If they're worth going after, they're worth the family jewels." Instead of arbitrarily ruling out or plunging ahead, evaluate each opportunity on its own merits—then decide whether the game is worth the ante.

This isn't a matter of passing judgment on what degree of spec is right or wrong—morally or financially. Rather it is recognizing that advertisers are increasingly using "Creative shootouts" as a key consideration in the selection process. And like it or not, you will be increasingly confronted with this tactic.

So instead of resentfully *reacting* to this request when made, anticipate whether you want to initiate the effort. Or whether to comply with it afterwards.

If you conclude this prospect is worth going after, then your only approach consists of whatever it will take to win—because, the most expensive presentation is a half-ass one. By contrast, if going the full route is too steep a price to pay, forgo it. Either way, whatever the prospect's requirements, *you* control the situation.

F.   Compensation

Agency compensation is rarely given enough attention when pitching an account. It's assumed that if we knock their socks off with our Creative, all else will fall into line.

However, when soliciting new business, don't ever forget why. It is to create *profitable income* as well as you create advertising. On this basis, the hand plays itself. Either the compensation will enable you to realize the amount of dollar profit to which you are entitled, or you fold.

Thus, there should be an ongoing conscious awareness of the compensation factor from initial prospect contact to post-presentation activity. Essentially, how much you will be paid, by what method and when?

So don't invest heavily in time and money in an attempt to impress, and leave the subject of payment as an afterthought. Because it may be discovered after all this effort and expense that the prospect is economically unfeasible. As vital as is compatibility from a performance and relationship standpoint, if there isn't *financial* compatibility, it's academic.

This concern is especially appropriate now with compensation becoming an increasingly important influence in Agency selection. Granted, this isn't the only criterion. However, the financial consideration shouldn't come as a rude awakening—to either party. Particularly, once the prospect romance is progressing well, the mechanics of money shouldn't get in the way.

In the final analysis, you are seeking to enter into a business arrangement that will be satisfactorily rewarding for your contribution to their success. There isn't anything crass about making your intentions known to the prospect. Because selling their product or service at a profit is their ultimate objective, too.

Chapter 4

What Advertisers Now Expect of an Agency

A. Perspective
B. Greater Balance
C. Fastest Payout
D. Exceptional Adaptability
E. Strong Internal Leadership
F. Involvement by Top Management
G. Acknowledge Their Growing Sophistication
H. Receptive to Contribution
I. Willing to Listen
J. Belief in Fieldwork
K. Summary

A. Perspective

The most frequent question asked me regarding the development of a new business program is, "Where do we begin?" To be meaningful, it has to start with a knowledge of advertiser expectations. Particularly, those they don't tell you about. If you seem oblivious to these nine requisites, no amount of fancy footwork will redeem you.

You won't read about these elsewhere. Or be told about them. But the following nine factors form the foundation for the advertiser's confidence and comfort in an Agency. If you don't register having this understanding of their expectations, you'll be building on sand.

B.   Greater Balance

The advertiser is expecting greater balance of an Agency. By this they mean: total marketing capacity. They want assurance that all your functions are at par with Creative. Obviously then, it would behoove you to feature the scope of your Agency—and its high level strength across the board.

Granted, a prospect will invariably state that what they want of their new Agency is cutting-edge Creative work; breakthrough Creativity. In fact, they may give the impression that this function is their only concern. Yet, even though that is what's said, it is not entirely what's meant. For example, I was retained recently by an advertiser who specified creative superiority exclusively in their Agency search. Afterwards, in the selection meeting, one Agency clearly emerged as having the most dynamic evidence. This was so apparent, I assumed the choice was a foregone conclusion.

Not so. While the advertiser admitted that this Agency's Creative "Knocked our socks off, we wonder if their Media operation is strong enough. And we can't afford to have our budget invested in anything less than the shrewdest, most economical manner."

Since this hot Creative shop took the prospect *too literally*, they came off as being a boutique. Because no reference was made to the value of their other services, which would have dispelled this misconception of inadequacy.

Was this Agency deceived? Undoubtedly there was a sin of omission by the prospect. Their direction was incomplete. The advertiser told the candidates what function they considered most important. But *not* to the exclusion of the others.

Therefore, the presentation should have been *Creative-oriented*. Specifically, the Agency opening with and emphasizing Creative superiority. And then further enticing the prospect with why their other services were as desirable. Plus: how their contribution would increase the value of Creative. In this way, the advertiser is assured of receiving the outstanding Creative wanted—and all the support for it deemed necessary.

This case history had an unhappy ending for the heads-on favorite. The prospect compromised and opted for another Agency who demonstrated having ample strength in *all* areas.

So, remember: an advertiser's stated wishes may not be their only wants. Actually, they would prefer to buy a **total** Agency. Of course, they will have greater interest in some services, but they want the synergism of each enhancing the effect of the others—thereby compounding Agency productivity.

C. Fastest Payout

They also want the fastest payout for their money and efforts.

To be considered, an Agency need demonstrate that it understands and appreciates this strategy—and is especially qualified to apply it.

D. Exceptional Adaptability

Because of rapidly changing economic conditions, and the accompanying uncertainty, advertisers are expecting exceptional adaptability of an Agency.

Position your Agency as being a can-do operation—that is geared more so to producing on a crash basis when necessary. Sure—so what else is new? That's standard operating procedure at your place.

Capitalize on your having this *flexibility*. And for instance, not being restricted by the typical Agency practice of requiring six weeks lead time for any Creative assignment.

It's possible that the prospect you're pitching believes that their present Agency is so rigidly systematized that trying to accomplish anything through them is damn frustrating. Therefore, the prospect would be very receptive to any reference to your being able to turn on a dime. In fact, they *want* to hear it. Verbalize this and it will be a strong plus in your favor.

E. Strong Internal Leadership

A prospect is perceptive to, and highly respects, strong internal Agency leadership.

They shouldn't have to discover this about your shop. It should be amply evident in your solicitation activity.

This particularly applies to the presentation, where your C.E.O's authority should be made apparent by his/her control of the program—however, not dominate it.   Because the prospect assumes that this involvement is indicative of the amount of attention they will receive from this person. Thus, his/her function should be that of a Quarterback or M.C. so the prospect won't get a false impression.

F. Involvement by Top Management

Advertisers understandably assume that Agency top Management is its ultimate talent and expect that if awarded their business, your principals will give it reasonable attention. However, don't promise an unrealistic share of Management contact time as bait. Most advertisers are fairly calloused to this transparent ruse. Besides, it could prove disastrous.

For example, there is an Agency President in Chicago who is such a spellbinder that he is frequently interrupted during his portion of the presentation by the prospect asking: "If we were to award your Agency our business, what percent of your time could we hope for?" He had his reply rehearsed to a gnat's eyelash.

First, he would close his eyes to give the impression he was thinking. Then, he would place his hands in a pious position to symbolize truth for his reply. And finally, after a suspenseful pause, he would authoritatively state, "49%." (Obviously, promising one-half or more would be unbelievable since the C.E.O. also has an Agency to run.)

They were scoring quite well for about a year—until these new clients began to meet each other. And then they discovered he had allocated 336% of his time. After that, at the first indication of friction, they had no compunction about leaving. Because they were deceived in presentation.

Actually, constant personal contact isn't expected. What the prospect really wants is the assurance that Agency top Management will have a direct interest in their account. This concern can be satisfied by pointedly informing them that your Management will be involved with the planning and approval of what is developed—*to whatever extent necessary*.

So in your eagerness to score, don't trap yourself by promising a definite percent of top Management time. Or a specific number of hours. Rather, more believably, represent their involvement as being based on *need*.

Nevertheless, to the prospect who has read "The Art of Negotiating," this explanation may not suffice. For instance, how about when they are smitten with your Creative Director. And zap you with, "We'll award you our account on the condition that we get 50% of Bruce's time." However,

Agency workload makes fulfilling this request impossible. Besides, they deserve only 10%.

Acquiescing and making a promise that can't be kept could backfire. Instead, here is how a C.D. who was fast on his feet dealt with this situation. He countered with, "Don't restrict me to 50%. There may be circumstances when I'll want to devote more time to your account. Let me determine how I can be of most value to you."

The prospect bought it; the Agency landed the account—and didn't risk deceit.

G.   Acknowledge Their Growing Sophistication

Advertiser people have increasing belief in themselves as being at parity with those at Agencies.

Thus, it would be a shrewd move to make a point of acknowledging their growing sophistication—and taking it into account in your relationship.

H.   Receptive to Contribution

Today's client wants the opportunity to contribute—with the Agency being receptive to and respecting their efforts.

Cite recognition of this situation—and your willingness to operate on this basis.

I.   Willing to Listen

Advertisers especially want an Agency that will hear them out—so their expectations will have a better chance of being fulfilled. Inform and show them that you use your senses in accordance with how they were provided: having two ears and one mouth.

J.   Belief in Fieldwork

Finally, the advertiser's ultimate concern is where the action is: where their sales can be made.

Register your earnest belief in getting involved out there—and desire to get your hands dirty with them. And cite that this doesn't mean sporadic trips. Rather, planned periodic fieldwork, flushing out what is happening, what can be improved, and recommending how.

In fact, as evidence of your sincerity, provide the prospect with a procedure and timetable for this purpose.

K. Summary

Don't be fooled by these nine advertiser desires seeming to be pedestrian. These are what they now expect, yet, Agencies soliciting their business are not playing these desires back to them. You can distinguish your shop by pointedly registering what they want confirmed. Most Agencies take for granted that the prospect knows this. But they don't. Not unless you verbalize these nine key matters. And they want to hear them.

Chapter 5

How Advertisers Judge Agency People

A. Perspective

From a performance standpoint, of course an advertiser wants:

- the most persuasive Creative work
- the shrewdest Media buying
- Research whose integrity is beyond reproach
- an accurate, prompt Billing operation
- the same level of professionalism for other services offered (Marketing, P.R., Sales Promotion, Collateral, etc.)

Regarding your interaction, they expect:

- an open relationship
- planned communications

- involvement by Agency top Management
- functional familiarity with their Company, industry and market
- objective Contact person(s) who will be accountable for Agency performance

In order for an Agency to convince a prospect it can deliver in all respects though, you need to demonstrate having the characteristics they are looking for. We'd better examine these traits because they must be consciously applied to satisfy the above advertiser desires.

B. Impression Necessary

Despite a prospect's pious declarations of objectivity, claiming that their judgment of the Agency is based entirely on the content of the presentation, *their impression of you is the deciding factor*. What turns them on or off? This can best be answered by the key question they ask each other after meeting you: "Are they our kind of people?"

Advertisers know that upon selecting the finalists, they could probably get in bed with any one of them. The decision then comes down to which one they want to marry. Therefore, their judgment of you: "Are they our kind of people?" is the bottom line in Agency selection.

Thus, your first consideration is not *what* you present. It is to *whom*. So it is imperative that you know each prospect audience—and appeal to them accordingly.

Here's why. An Agency President recently asked me in because he was fed up with always being a bridesmaid on new business presentations. He said, "I want to start throwing the bouquet—instead of settling for trying to catch it." He then continued with, "And I'm confident we must have a damn good pitch because we never come in worse than second." (Have you ever heard of an Agency coming in third?)

At this point, he gave me the script for a recent presentation to a retail chain and asked, "Take a look at this and tell me where we went wrong." I didn't have to get past the Table of Contents to discover why they blew it. It began with:

A. Modular Marketing

B. Critical Marketing Path

And it kept getting heavier. Plus more esoteric.

That may have been great for an M.B.A. Brand Manager at P & G. But the selection team was comprised of store managers—who were looking for shirtsleeve ideas and solutions. Not scholarly Profundities. Therefore, even if the content was brilliant, it was doomed to failure because of not being appropriate to their audience.

Actually, there is nothing wrong in being academic—if you use the right set of three R's. And for a new business presentation—which includes any prospect contact made—these are:

- the prospect being able to favorably *relate* to your people
- the content of the presentation being *relevant* to their interests and needs
- and the *results* promised being believable—and better than they could get elsewhere

So do your homework and you'll graduate with honors—and the account.

C. Four Attributes Sought

Even with your efforts directly targeted, though, their *effect* depends on the vitality of your people. This is indicated by the following four attributes which the advertiser believes forms the substance of an Agency.

1. Although loath to admit it, a client wants **leadership**. Maybe discreetly exercised in the guise of direction, but nevertheless, leadership. Here is a dramatic, yet actual example. I was told by the Ad V.P. of a major insurance company that "We have a controlled relationship with our Agency. We dictate to them precisely what is expected. Then, they comply with that or they are fired."

   He then went on to say, "In fact, we just got a new Agency." So I asked, "How come?" And he looked me right in the eye and said, "Because the old one never provided any leadership."

   The crux of the matter is that no client wants to get caught playing "catch-up marketing." They are looking for an Agency who will anticipate conditions—and can recommend adjusting course as necessary.

   Of particular importance, this aptitude provides the client with the security desired.

   In addition, there is another key reason for their increased expectations of you. Since they too are operating with far fewer personnel, the Agency is expected to compensate for the information and ideas previously furnished by ex-staff members.

2. An advertiser also wants an Agency that is **decision-oriented**. Not gofers. Or more concerned with playing it safe than getting the job

done. Rather, the type who, upon receiving approval, has the drive to follow through without having to be spoon-fed.

3. Another characteristic highly regarded is **initiative**. Sounds like 101A? I hear this word repeated too often at advertisers to be taken for granted.

They know they can get implementers anywhere. Instead, they want an Agency that will challenge them to more productive, profitable activity. A shop that can do more than put out fires. Today's client wants one who can also start fires.

4. Another attribute that crops up frequently is **innovation**. Because they want more innovation than imitation.

Clients are becoming very concerned about the growing buyer attitude that there are insignificant differences between brands. And about the inroads being made by private labels and generic products.

Thus, advertisers are increasingly anxious for your freshness, uniqueness across the board. They are no longer willing to settle for Creative being the sole source.

Advertisers know that Agencies have substantially upgraded the caliber of their staffs. Operating with half as many people per $million billing as ten years ago—but paying them over twice as much.

Accordingly, *all* are expected to contribute—thereby compounding Agency productivity.

Therefore, your Marketing, Media, Research, P.R. and Production services need also be dynamic—and represented as such. As much so as Creative—with their value not restricted by their function.

These four words are particularly meaningful to advertisers—and they will be impressed according to the degree of Agency evidence of these attributes. Thus, the combination of your capacity for leadership, your being decision-oriented, plus your dedication to initiative and innovation, could be stressed as the basis of your operation.

Chapter 6

Foundation Necessary for a New Business Program to Succeed

A. Perspective
B. Identify Agency Market
C. Select New Business Manager
D. Composition of New Business Team
E. Develop Marketing Plan
F. Set Goal for Growth
G. Stature of New Business Program
H. Use Weekly Traffic Report
I. Create Unique Selling Proposition
J. Treatment of Agency Philosophy
K. Document Advantages
L. Generate Employee Involvement
M. Institute Employee Incentive Plan
N. Finding Additional Time

A. Perspective

This operation begins with *attitude*.

When an Agency gets the reputation of being hot, it didn't just happen. They made it happen. Their success is due to a compelling urge to succeed—matched by equally dedicated work.

Also, the hot Agency's attitude is that the new business function is an integral part of the Agency operation—with projects for prospects scheduled right along with those for clients. And neither new business solicitation nor client service is performed at the expense of the other.

B. Identify Agency Market

Eventually, in an Agency's development, an identity crisis occurs. What type operation should it become?

General: To enjoy variety, broaden opportunities and protect against economic vicissitudes

Market-Oriented: To capitalize on a segment of the economy which offers substantial potential (Healthcare, High-Tech, Agbusiness, Financial, Business-to-Business, Travel/Leisure)

Ethnic: To appeal to a market in which a racial or nationalistic loyalty exists (Black, Hispanic)

Type: To concentrate on an individual advertising need (Direct Response, Recruitment)

Specialized Function: To provide a particular service (Sales Promotion, Creative Boutique, Media Buying)

Which is best? That depends on your qualifications and desires. Is your talent and experience especially marketable in one of these areas? More important, though, which of these opportunities are most appealing to you?

Yet, after targeting on where you are worth most, and what you particularly want to do, this needn't be restrictive. If you do that great a creative or marketing job for a client in a certain field, it could attract advertisers with broader interests. And then you have the best of both worlds. So set your course—with the understanding that there is no limit to how far you can go.

C.   Select New Business Manager

The new business operation is so crucial that the head of the shop usually takes over. *Wrong!* Because he/she can't be held accountable. If there hasn't been any activity, how are you going to say, "F'Chrissake, Alex, we haven't had any new business action in six months." He'll say, "I'll give you action. You're fired."

Further, your C.E.O.'s experience and ability is not used most productively when he/she is burdened with the nagging nitty-gritty that could be performed by someone more affordable. Being relieved of the time-intensive administration, your C.E.O. can then concentrate his/her talents on the contact and strategy functions where it can do the most good.

Instead, assign a hunt/kill type person to manage the new business program—who must answer to the C.E.O. This will assure the necessary accountability.

Notice, I said "manage" this function. I was semantically careful in not describing it as being "in charge." Because when the latter phrase is used, this person assumes that their responsibility includes making the initial contacts, developing the presentation, plus spearheading the pitch. And in trying to perform this job, it dies of its weight.

By contrast, at Agencies where this system works so successfully the manager:

- may not make a call—but can find out for whomever the prospect which person in the Agency would be most effective in contact
- probably doesn't develop any plans or materials—but will persevere to get it done by those most qualified. (Of course, it helps if he or she is Sicilian.)
- might not even participate in a presentation—but can recommend the team of personnel likeliest to appeal to and impress that particular prospect

Since this function is the hub of the program, let's examine the attributes required of this person. He or she should:

- have the **executive** characteristic and willingness to delegate responsibility among the broadest group of personnel
- be a good **talent scout**, familiar with the ability and experience of all appropriate staff members, and taking advantage of their capacities whenever warranted
- be **traffic-oriented**—a buttoned-down type willing to get their hands dirty in following through

- be **assertive** enough to get whatever cooperation is needed from anyone in the Agency

- above all, have the **desire** for this assignment—realizing how critical growth is to the Agency and the individual opportunity it offers to become a hero

From where in the Agency might this person come? Anywhere. Here is the evidence.

Upon making this point in my New Business seminar at Smith & Yehle (Kansas City), their President, Karl Yehle, interrupted with, "Hold it." Being the kind of guy who makes things happen, he said, "Since this person would quarterback our new business effort, let's select this individual now."

The Account Executives, as one, gazed at the ceiling. After what seemed like endless dead air time, the Comptroller raised her hand and volunteered, "I'll accept this responsibility." I don't recall her name, but I remember her as "Marian the Librarian." Because she was so prim and proper. Genteel and Refined. At this, the A.E.s came to life and popped questions at her, like, "You? How d'ya figger?"

She softly and demurely replied, "Well, for three reasons. First of all, I'm not directly involved in any tangible Agency function. Second, who could realize the importance of additional income any more than I? And third, I won't take any bullshit from the rest of you." Needless to say, although an unorthodox choice, she got the job.

I've spoken to Karl several times since. He told me, "This is the best thing that has ever happened to us in the new business area. She is after us constantly. And we're getting things done like never before." He concluded with, "Because not only has responsibility been assigned—but also accountability required."

I would urge you to select this key person now. Because nothing consequential will happen—soon enough and to a significant extent—until someone with a winner syndrome can be held accountable. Not a committee. A statue has never been erected to a committee. Rather, a gung-ho individual who would set the pace—and whose feet could be held to the fire.

As an incentive for action, and to generate interest in your new business program, survey all your people to find out who they believe would do the most effective job. Upon selection, this delegation of responsibility and ensuing organization will provide an operation based on deliberate action—rather than just hopefully lucking out. The crux of the matter is that your new business thrust should be as well orchestrated and disciplined as the servicing of your most important client.

D.   Composition of New Business Team

Who should be on your new business team? Members are usually selected arbitrarily—including some dead wood because of rank. And others are overlooked whose contribution could be vital.

Actually, for the most effective new business team, it should consist of *every employee* in the Agency. This provides the maximum source of talent and experience, which can be applied as appropriate. Further, this action will make all staff members more new business conscious—thereby increasing your potential for scoring.

It is worth stirring up this reservoir because your next major account may come from the unlikeliest source. Like the Agency secretary who had a blind-date. During this fertility rite, each identified their present job function. He then carried this mating dance a step further by revealing he was switching to the Supermega Company to become its Ad Director.

Since this potential romance didn't take precedence over her paycheck, our Mata Hari reported this development to her boss. The new Ad Director was promptly contacted, congratulated and offered his own Agency team.

The blind-date was so amazed by this discovery (never associating the source) that he agreed to a meeting prior to his actual move. Then, being predisposed toward the soliciting Agency because of their heads-up follow-through, he steered his new affiliation to them.

So make it known to your enlisted personnel that they can be a hero as much as any officer. This strategy registers that your objective is growth—which could enable each of them to fulfill their personal ambitions.

To attract interest, bulletin all of your people to inform them of:

- your Agency's intention to become very aggressive in the new business area

- their appointment to the new business team

- the appointment of the New Business Manager who will coordinate all activity

- the opportunity for them to contribute to the success of the program

Since they are now officially members of your new business team, and to maintain momentum, send them activity reports on a regular basis. These would include:

- progress made in solicitation efforts (i.e., "Our persistence has paid off in lining up a full-scale presentation to the Acme Company on November 12")
- news of wins or losses—with reasons why, if possible
- notable contributions by anyone in respect to contact, ideas, information, planning, preparation and presentation

A valuable by-product of this total Agency involvement is the impression conveyed that each employee, regardless of function, is vital to the Agency's success. This acknowledgment is also a great morale-builder because it implies that each is as important as anyone else on the staff.

E. Develop Marketing Plan

The next step involves doing for yourself what you have done for so long for your clients. Develop your own Marketing plan to provide organized direction for your new business activity. This plan, with all the makework distilled from it, involves defining these four matters—by taking the action indicated.

1. Where your Agency stands—
Analyze:

- image
- financial status
- client stability
- employee attitude
- strengths/weaknesses

2. What you want to become—
Decide on:

- services to be offered
- account type/size desired
- growth rate
- profit expected

3. How this is to be accomplished—

- Identify problems/opportunities.
- Formulate objectives/strategy/tactics.
- Determine future needs.

4. Who will be held accountable for results—

- Assign responsibilities to specific individuals.
- Set completion dates.
- Provide for periodic assessment and fine-tuning of progress made.
- Evaluate payout.

Obviously, all four stages are necessary—in the order indicated. Of these, though, it is the second that is your catalyst for action: *What you want to become*.

As evidence of this, are you familiar with Hesselbart & Mitten? It's not a vaudeville team. They are a very successful Advertising Agency.

For many years, they were an art studio. Then one day, Bob Mitten decided to convert this operation into a full-service Agency. However, Bob further concluded that he only wanted to work on accounts in the Fortune 500. That was quite ambitious for yesterday's art studio.

But Bob was a shrewd head. He started out by going after the smallest Division of each of these prestigious Companies. Those too modest for the heavy-hitter Agencies to be bothered with. Then after knocking off these $100,000—$300,000 accounts, he would move his foot farther into the door, and solicit the next larger divisions.

You may call this scavenging. Bob calls it highly profitable strategy. Because in 1989, H & M billed about $60,000,000—headquartered in the megamarket of Fairlawn, Ohio.

Bob Mitten gave much credit for this achievement to having established *who* they want to work with. This goal provided direction and incentive. And in answering, "Where do we start?"—this served as a springboard for action.

Thus, you too can determine the results desired. This takes the Management leadership necessary to apply a bold plan such as this. That's how the winners get "lucky."

Yet, too often, an Agency will shoot its wad in developing a New Business Marketing Plan—and then not have enough ambition left to implement it. However, this blueprint is just the means, not the end.

Agencies slough off due to an unlimited number of reasons. As a result, they flounder through their solicitation activity in a manner considered inexcusable for their clients.

Whatever the excuses, the overriding incentive to apply the plan developed is that it will provide you with a *competitive edge*. Specifically: the organization, accountability and timing required will enable you to better sell your Agency. Therefore, it is the Agency who best applies this direction and discipline that is likeliest to win.

So get off the dime. Cash in on your Marketing Plan. There are dollars to be made.

F.   Set Goal for Growth

Next, institute the payout phase of your Marketing Plan: the action necessary to produce profitable growth. This begins with a commitment to a specific goal—including provision to make it happen. (Most Agencies use billing as a guide, but income is more meaningful.)

What amount of growth is necessary—and realistic?   There is a top 10 Agency which, for many years, promulgated the theory that 50% of Agency growth comes from existing accounts. Thus, it was assumed that their new business activity would have to produce only the other half.

However, they discovered in the last recession that clients can also account for 50% of an Agency's *loss*.   Therefore, this theory has been dumped.   And although they are still as diligently attempting to grow clients, their new business program has since become a 100% effort—receiving the *full* attention it deserves.

In order to go the full nine yards, here is the best route to take. It is estimated that account attrition amounts to 15% annually. Thus, shooting for this increase would mean no more than statistically breaking even. Not until you exceed this percent will you achieve real growth. So tack on an additional modest 10%—thereby going for 25%.

Granted, a dollar amount might be idealistic—and could frustrate you into giving up. But you can give your goals substance by scheduling a specific number of full-scale "missionary" presentations. (Those accounts you want to go after, even though not knowing of their inclination to change Agencies.)

Recapping, your best strategy consists of establishing a combined goal: for dollar growth—and a commitment to consistent "missionary" presentations to enable realizing this growth.

In connection with this, I'm frequently asked, "How many new business presentations should we be making?" And I'll reply, "Whether competitive or 'missionary,' one full-scale pitch per month."

The usual reaction is, "Geez, Jack, we got clients too, y'know." It is assumed this is an unrealistic effort—and too tough a goal to shoot for. However, the new business water is cold only until you get into it.

Upon following through with these Agencies six to nine months later, I'm informed that the roughest part was getting underway. They are then pleasantly surprised to discover that after hitting a rhythm of one presentation per month, conducting three in two months isn't that much more effort. Then it becomes an integral part of the Agency operation. And as it starts to pay off, it is readily accepted as such.

This consistent and increasing activity leads us to the secret for getting more new business—faster. Not some revelation. Rather, the most overlooked, underrated basic.

It was proved by what is acknowledged to be the most authoritative study ever made on this subject. In a desire to discover the secret for landing accounts, a top-10 Agency compiled every conceivable factor involved in the new business operation. Then all these were fed into a computer. This extensive input was then tabulated and analyzed.

I can now reveal to you the conclusion produced by this scientific project: "The more presentations you make, the more new business you get." A lot of money was spent—but this Agency felt it was worth it to confirm this truism.

Be willing to become more successful. Don't base your new business program on assuming how little can be done. Rather, on how much you want to accomplish. An Agency can't take the plunge and then just tread water. The competitive undertow will drag you under.

G.   Stature of New Business Program

This planning, however, won't be worth a damn unless you allocate definite time and funds to implement it. Without a tangible commitment, you'll just be firing blanks.

In order to succeed, consider the new business function as being a "client." And the person assigned to manage this program would act as the Account Executive on this account.

Then estimate the amount of time it would take to service it—and the budget necessary to do so. Specifically, upon establishing your goal for growth, you can figure from your time records the amount that need be applied to achieve this.

Summing up, if your new business program were a *contractual* client, somehow you would find the time for it. Therefore, according it this stature means there is no excuse for not giving it your best shot.

Based on this concept: congratulations! Because you just landed your Agency as an account. As with any other, though, its longevity will depend on your dedication in servicing it.

To accomplish this, and generate the devotion necessary, break out the champagne for your staff. You would sure celebrate if you landed an account the size of your Agency. Well, you did: your Agency. Get them thinking in terms of your Agency being the sum of its clients—so your new business operation will receive the attention it deserves.

H.   Use Weekly Traffic Report

The only way you can have a new business program that will produce results is by bringing this function into the mainstream of the Agency operation. This means beginning with the lifeline of your Agency: the **Weekly Traffic Report**.

On most, there is a glaring omission: *The Agency*. Even where included, it is generally relegated to the bottom of the client list as an afterthought. However, your Agency is *your most important client*; move it right to the top of the listing. This prominence will constantly remind one and all where their primary loyalty belongs. And again, while doing the most dedicated job of serving clients, it will continuously register that an Agency is a grow-or-die business.

Therefore, the Weekly Traffic Report should also itemize new business assignments, the personnel responsible for each, and by what dates. If not included, then you're treating the new business function in a cavalier manner—and wondering why you don't get lucky. You won't. Not unless you are willing to begin with the discipline necessary to win.

I.   Create Unique Selling Proposition

Advertisers planning to change are issuing fewer Agency cattle calls. They no longer have the time to sweat out an unlimited number of presentations. Rather, now many internally select approximately six for consideration—and confidentially invite them to present.

What are you doing to rate being included in this esteemed group? You're so good at selling for others; what are you doing on your own behalf?

This involves more than getting the word out to the Reps. It must start at square one: *with yourself*.

This means creating your own Unique Selling Proposition. One that is distinctive, compelling and memorable. Further, to be meaningful, it should contain a promise of benefit.

Agencies procrastinate in developing their U.S.P. because of assuming it is expected this consists of some awesome combination of words never before assembled. Since this improbable bolt from the blue doesn't occur, nothing happens. And the Agency is at a disadvantage because of inadequate identity.

Instead of tacitly accepting drawing a blank, try this for inspiration. If a prospect asks, "Why should we hire you?" and then walks away, what would you shout as he escapes? (Preferably it should be something ingratiating rather than an expletive.)

However, don't mistake a catchy phrase for appeal. For instance, there is an Agency in the Southeast who has expended considerable money and effort promoting the concept that, "Our clients are better known than we are." And they said, "Dynamite, huh, Jack!" My answer was, "That sounds like an excuse!"

Instead, compare this approach with that taken by MacLaren/Toronto. They simply state in all their promotional material, "MacLaren advertising works." And then do an excellent job in relating this claim to the prospect and their message. As a prospect, which appeal would be likeliest to turn you on?

To whatever extent your U.S.P. can be made newsworthy will compound its effect. Ideas for this purpose can emanate from any area of achievement. There are the obvious ones: a captivating Creative approach, a breakthrough in Research technique or Production process, or an especially shrewd Media buy.

In addition, however, don't overlook capitalizing on your development of an exciting client sales meeting, trade incentive plan or consumer promotion. These are significantly likelier to receive ink and attract attention.

To obtain a steady stream of ideas from which to select, periodically query all your people as to what Agency characteristics and achievements are newsworthy enough to warrant an announcement.

Then a regular routine should be established for notifying the Press, clients and prospects. The Press is always eager for worthwhile material. (In fact, if your news is so important, place it as an ad—to assure it will be announced exactly as desired.) As to the others, clients want to be associated with a winner. And regarding prospects, this provides reason for regular contact.

J.   Treatment of Agency Philosophy

Must you have an Agency philosophy? That depends on whether it is used as a working objective or an ego-trip.

For perspective, its purpose is to officially set forth what you stand for—plus distinguish your shop from the others. And above all, to show why this claim will benefit your clients.

Unfortunately, this usually consists of a lengthy sermon in which triteness is exceeded only by dullness. Even worse, advertisers consider this just blah-blah puffery.

An Agency should have a positioning statement. However, not as a device for competing against other Agencies with the usual string of clichés. That is only defensive, anyway.

Instead, consider this strategy. Deny having any *generic* philosophy. Rather, state that you develop a new objective for each individual client based on the action required to fulfill their specific needs. In contrast to an all-purpose panacea, you customize your contribution per client.

On this basis, your philosophy becomes a tangible commitment as opposed to a hollow gesture. Taking this approach, the prospect will be more inclined to relate to and accept it.

K.   Document Advantages

All else notwithstanding, an advertiser's objective is to have the Agency that can best contribute to increasing their sales profitably.

If you don't register why you have achieved this for yourself, then what can they expect? Take the time to document your personnel and operational advantages. And keep this current as improvements occur.

L.   Generate Employee Involvement

Most Agency new business activity operates in fits and spurts. After getting lucky for a while, they will declare a moratorium. Supposedly, to absorb the new clients landed. More likely it is to justify a breather until circumstances require that the Agency become aggressive again.

Then, because of this sporadic type of effort, your people's interest and ambition varies accordingly. This combined Agency/personnel lethargy after being on a roll is analogous to the client who advertises only when it is assumed they have to.

By contrast, soliciting accounts needs to be an on-going function. Granted, sometimes there will be greater emphasis. Nevertheless, a *consistent* program need always be underway. Because the winning athlete is the one who always stays in shape—not just training on a crash basis.

To stimulate employee involvement, institute a *"What have you done for us lately?"* challenge. Promote this concept on a regular basis (i.e., signs, memos, flyers attached to paychecks, buttons—plus whatever offbeat approaches you can conceive). This would include providing direction on *how* they can contribute (i.e., furnishing leads, originating promotional ideas, developing solicitation tactics, etc.).

Then, by all means, acknowledge the efforts of each, its value—and what will be done about it. Beyond this recognition, you may want to consider tangible reward to hypo participation. One angle could be to offer days off—the number being contingent on the value of the contribution.

This plan can establish a corporate and individual frame of mind that will compound each other. The result will be an up-front consciousness of the new business function being an ongoing part of the Agency operation. Not just a responsibility restricted to a select few—to be undertaken when an account is lost.

And above all, this "What have you done for us lately?" tactic offers the entire staff the opportunity to be a vital part of—and benefit from—the success achieved.

M. Institute Employee Incentive Plan

Recently, in serving as a facilitator at a retreat for an Agency's Management, the matter was raised regarding instituting an employee incentive plan for attracting new business. Its intent would be to encourage greater staff initiative and cooperation in this activity.

It was acknowledged that the usual practice is unacceptable. This is the device sometimes used by under-capitalized Agencies when getting started. As a means to generate cash flow as quickly as possible, the following inducement is offered. Any employee who submits a bona fide prospect lead that Management converts into a client, is awarded 10% of the gross income received from this new account during the first six months.

Thus, if you were to land a $1,000,000 account on this basis, the individual who furnished the information could earn as much as $7,500.

(Some Agencies get carried away in their eagerness to score and also make this deal available to outsiders. Then the word gets out on the street that this shop must be desperate because of having to resort to mercenaries. And no Agency lasts long using hired guns to solicit new business).

The concept of this expedient has built-in seeds of discontent within the Agency. In particular:

- Who is excluded from this opportunity due to their management position or new business responsibility?

- It is assumed that some staff members have a better opportunity than others. (Media and Production personnel because of their contact with reps and suppliers respectively.)

- Then, after the Agency gets rolling, it's tough to discontinue this offer. You promised them candy—and now you're taking it away.

Having rejected this approach for the above reasons, it was decided that an inducement plan is still worthwhile—but it must be uniformly fair and appropriate for an indefinite number of years.

Prior to formulating any plan though, it is necessary to establish a goal for dollar growth. This was based on the 25% rationale previously furnished. Thus, for an Agency such as the one involved billing $10,000,000—obviously this requires landing $2,500,000 in new business during the coming 12 months. (Exclusive of increases received from existing clients. Otherwise, you won't start out, and continue to be, hungry enough.)

Having established this money-oriented goal, it inspired an exceptionally appealing plan. This consists of giving *every* employee a packet of 12 checks made out for $100 each—unsigned. When the Agency reaches 1/12 of its goal for *new* billing, the entire staff can bring their first check in for signature. Upon achieving the second plateau, they do likewise. And so on.

Therefore, the more each employee contributes to the new business effort, and the more successful this program becomes, *every* employee benefits proportionately and uniformly.

Upon attaining their objective of $2,500,000, the Agency will have paid out a total of $32,400 to its 27 employees. This amounts to an 8.6% bonus to employees from gross income received.

Pretty cheap price to pay for a 25% growth. And correspondingly, the Agency also received a wonderful bonus along with it. Specifically: a staff with better morale than ever before—willing to go that extra mile as a team.

Wonder what happened to that Agency after implementing this plan? You can bet the Media and Production people exploited their contacts. Those in a Contact capacity, who had always been too busy with clients for solicitation activity, suddenly found the time for this initiative. Creative and Research types served as a catalyst by generating ideas for action. And no secretary complained about staying late to type what was needed for a presentation the next morning. Because the entire staff has a constant tangible reminder of what's in it for them: found money.

The payoff is that the Agency blissfully signed the checks—well ahead of the timing hoped for. (How's four months!)

> NOTE: In case any of you ruled out this opportunity because of being five or ten times the size of this Agency, merely divide your staff into five or ten teams. Don't deny your Agency the benefits offered by this proved success. A little imagination can enable you to easily adapt this concept to your operation.

N.   Finding Additional Time

Probably the most common excuse for not giving the new business function the amount of effort required is "lack of time." Actually, there is as much time as needed—free. Here is how to get it.

Of course, no *individual* has enough time; however, the total Agency does.

The solution to this problem was inspired by a common frustration at most Agencies. It was brought into focus by this experience.

The Exec V.P., in charge of new business at his shop, complained, "I should be devoting half my time to new business. But I just can't spare 30 hours a week."

I asked him, "How many employees do you have?" He said, "Thirty." I replied, "Great. There are the 30 hours you need."

Then I explained, "Have each employee *donate* one hour per week." This would be beyond, and not interfere with, their regular work. For this cooperation to materialize, every person would be given specific assignments—commensurate with their ability and experience. It might be prospect contact, creative or marketing ideas for prospects, execution of portions of the new business marketing plan, research, typing, etc. To preclude any employee resentment of this modest donation, remind them that they can only succeed to the extent the Agency does.

Obviously, there can be a variety of applications of this plan depending on your goals and size. If you have just ten employees, you may want to ask for two hours from each. The more people you have, though, the greater their impact.

The strategy is to have *everyone* contribute. However, the key to the success of this plan is accountability. The New Business Manager needs to track the contribution of every employee on a regular weekly basis.

This simple, easy-to-execute plan can overcome the largest obstacle to adequate new business activity: "Not enough time."

Chapter 7

Criteria for Evaluating Prospects

A. Perspective
B. Opportunity
C. Quantity
D. Type
E. Fifteen Standards
F. Worth Time and Effort?
G. Transom Business

A. Perspective

The new business operation, conducted as diligently as necessary to win, is a laborious procedure. There aren't any fast miracles. Or quick magic. Just the thorough, all-out effort to prevent coming in second again.

One of the most critical functions in the sequence of events consists of evaluating prospects for solicitation. The purpose is to explore, before hardly any time or money has been spent, whether they would be a viable client. Thus, this chapter contains all the significant means for qualifying prospects. It will be well worth applying as many of these standards as possible. Because even though you can't pick your relatives, you *can* pick your prospects.

B. Opportunity

Your new business list can consist of whatever prospects desired—for which you are reasonably qualified. Then, rumors to the contrary, go after them. (These were probably started and perpetuated by the incumbent Agency anyway.)

Is this plausible? Well, Agencies are inclined to believe their own gossip—making it a self-fulfilling prophecy.

It is assumed that certain accounts are locked in—and thereby unapproachable. But as with any marriage, you never know what goes on behind closed doors.

I'm not being Pollyannaish. The most indelible impression made upon me in working with advertisers is that no Agency owns any client.

Thus, the matter of *least* concern to you is an account's vulnerability. Because a supposedly satisfied client may be surreptitiously planning an Agency "review."

C. Quantity

Don't minimize *any* new business factor due to its being "so basic." Even if it is as basic as "How many prospects should an Agency have?" Because this operation is only as good as the sum of its parts.

For perspective, let's first define **prospect**. It is an account you plan to actively pursue.

It could be *competitive*; (one that has announced its intention to switch Agencies). Or *missionary* (an advertiser you want to go after—even though not knowing of their receptivity to change.)

Soliciting in these categories is in sharp contrast to conducting impersonal mass mailings just to create awareness. Because these addressees aren't prospects. Without direct follow through, they are only suspects.

With this understanding, now let's answer the question: *"How many prospects?"* It should be as many as those for whom you will go the full route in soliciting—ranging from introductory letter to post-presentation activity. And they should be worth taking whatever ethical action is necessary to score.

Obviously, the specific number of prospects would vary according to Agency size. To determine the appropriate quantity for your shop, don't base it on what time you might have left after all other matters are squared away. Rather, challenge yourselves. Establish an amount that can produce significant growth—not just replace that lost by attrition.

D. Type

Is your new business success causing you to lose by winning?

There are Agencies who become smugly satisfied with their new business performance because they are scoring so well. And blithely equate conquest with success.

They are only right if the criterion for achievement is based solely on the number of accounts and billing landed. But are these the accounts they really *want*?

Be as self-serving in selecting clients as they are in choosing Agencies.

If aggressive enough, you can always pick up transient and slow-pay dogs. Or dull, stagnant accounts. Or those that are production-oriented— who consider advertising a necessary evil.

Instead of being a collector for the sake of numbers, convert your operation into one you can *enjoy*—both financially and professionally. It doesn't cost any more to go after desirable business than to pursue drudgery.

Advertisers don't want a blah Agency. Then why should you settle for that type of account?

As a result, advertisers with any degree of sophistication establish specific criteria for Agency selection. Correspondingly, it is just as appropriate for Agencies to develop standards for qualifying prospects. To save you the time and effort, here are the fifteen required. (If you can think of any more legitimate ones, I would appreciate hearing about it.)

E. Fifteen Standards

1. Although the list of client attributes desired could be endless, it needs to be headed by *profitability*. If the dollars aren't satisfactory, nothing else can make up for it. Therefore, don't be lulled by intermediate words such as billing or income. All that matters is the amount of profit you come away with.

2. Having passed this hurdle, the second most important consideration is whether you could get *excited* over working with this advertiser.

   If so, it will justify coping with all the aggravation and frustration inherent in any account. Otherwise, if there isn't the ecstasy to offset the agony, this will be a brief encounter of the worst kind.

3. If the prospect's product or service is sufficiently appealing, then the potential for a *compatible relationship* need be determined.

Are they *your* kind of people? Could you live with them? Would they make your Agency look good?

If the prospect doesn't bring these traits to the altar, you are not going to change them after the wedding. Yet, if they seem sexy, but you have reservations regarding a commitment, have an affair: *solicit a project*. If it proves to be a bummer, you didn't get stung by staffing up for them. But if you find this trial marriage worked, you can then propose for keeps.

Even if the dollars seems right, though, if the chemistry isn't there, you can't afford what would soon become an ex-client. Thus, without being paranoid, be sensitive to a prospects's conduct. It is the clue to the type of client they would be. Do they treat you like a potential partner or supplier? Are they cooperative or combative? And remember: at this stage they are on their good behavior.

After getting underway, Agencies are reluctant to admit that whoever they have solicited would be too miserable to get along with. And that they couldn't cope with it. For that matter, pride will rationalize that we can convert them into a pussycat client. (Do I have ocean-front property for this Agency in Kansas!)

Therefore, regardless of how far you've progressed with a prospect—and how much has been invested in time, effort and money—if necessary, bite the bullet while you can still spit it out. Where do you draw the line? *An Agency should never take abuse from a prospect.*

For example, here are two recent Agency experiences in presentation. In one case, the head prospect person kept moving his forefinger in a circular motion—giving them the speed-up signal. In the other, the prospect honcho repeatedly interrupted with the dare, "C'mon, tell me something I don't know." In both instances, this rudeness had a devastating effect on the presentations.

I was asked by each Agency what they should have done under the circumstances. There is only one answer. At the onset of this adversarial behavior, pack up your tent and leave. Because an obnoxious prospect becomes an obnoxious client. If you persist, you're a masochist. Besides, this type doesn't deserve you. Scroom!

Despite the critical nature of compatibility, there are Agencies, for economic or competitive reasons, who have a "new business at any price" attitude.

The purpose of solicitation is to satisfy more than the "hunt/ kill" challenge.   Its ultimate intent is to acquire profitable clients—with whom there can be a harmonious relationship.

4. How do their *expectations* of an Agency compare with what you believe to be reasonable? Actually, whatever their expectations may be, if willing to compensate you accordingly, they qualify. (Of course, this presumes the prospect measures up based on the previous three requisites.)

5. If the prospect is planning to change Agencies, flush out *why*. Then objectively consider whether you buy their reason. Or do you have the gut feeling of becoming their next screwee? Better satisfy yourself with their integrity now—rather than ending up as another one of their capricious changes.

6. You will also want to be sure that the advertiser is conducting a *legitimate Agency search*. As opposed to using this event as a device to get a batch of ideas—cheap. Or as a means to scare the hell out of their present Agency. It's bad enough being had by clients. You shouldn't have to be taken by prospects, too.

7. What about the prospect's *marketing problems and opportunities*? Would you be associated with a winner? Or one you could help become so? An Agency is considered only as good as the successes achieved for its clients. If for whatever reason you can't become a hero, back off.

8. In addition, how about the *dynamics of this prospect*? Are they aggressively introducing new products? Or stagnating with those at the tail end of their life cycle? Instead, go with the company that thrives on the same stimulation you do.

9–12. Basic as it may seem don't overlook appraising the prospect's *Advertising/Sales Ratio, attitude toward marketing and potential for growth*. And if appropriate, pull a *credit check*. Any of these factors could strongly influence whether this would be a go or no-go proposition.

13. If the prospect requests *spec Creative*, this introduces a new element. Is what is specified reasonable? Are they worth the expense? Although a price tag can't be put on an idea, there are circumstances under which you shouldn't have to eat the entire cost either. (Unless you want to retain ownership.) If their intentions are honorable, your contribution should be an investment

with sufficient possibility for payout. Not dues required to play the game.

14. Unfortunately, there will always be a hard core of advertisers who will impetuously fire their Agency as soon as any difficulty occurs. Or this tactic is used as a panacea to cover for whatever is wrong with themselves.

Little can be done about this breed, but for new business purposes, you should know who they are. (Who are the Ernst & Julio Gallos in your area?) Thus, prior to spending any time or money on a prospect, check the duration of their previous Agency affiliations. And if you find it to be unstable, recognize that being associated with this type of client would be a crapshoot—with whom it wouldn't be worth gambling on the outcome.

If, despite this, though, one comes along that seems irresistible, only become involved if they can be profitable from the first day.

15. Finally, *think bigger and bolder*. For three critical reasons:

First, it can cost just as much in time to go after a used car dealer as in trying to get your foot in the door at General Motors. Then why not invest the same effort in greater, surer potential.

Second, the larger account is likely to be more profitable. Since their people are usually more knowledgeable, there is less need to educate them prior to presenting your plans and materials. Thus, meeting time can be reduced to a minimum—which translates into being able to service the account more economically.

And third, Agencies have found that, in general, the larger the account, the greater the longevity. By contrast, they have learned that the smaller the account, the likelier it is to overreact when any difficulty occurs. And naively assume that changing Agencies will provide the solution.

There you have it. The fifteen means for judging a prospect. If they don't measure up by as many of these as applicable, why start out with one or more strikes against you? Instead, concentrate on those with as much as possible going for you.

So be discriminating. Because it costs much less to lose a prospect than it does after they become a client. Further, they will stay longer. And you will have a happier, more profitable operation.

F.   Worth Time and Effort?

When an Agency gets the opportunity to pitch an account of acceptable size that is loose, they will jump at the chance—without first determining whether it is the best use of their time and effort.

If the presentation requires going all out, this total immersion usually precludes doing so for another prospect during this one/two month period. And the latter may be substantially bigger—yet entail only the same amount of activity.

So don't take yourself out of contention for a much more valuable account by settling for a bird in the hand—unless you flushed out the rest of the bush first.

G.   Transom Business

Sometimes, though, this system gets thrown out of whack. That's when an advertiser contacts *you* offering their account.

This is such a wonderfully flattering experience that your objectivity vanishes. There is much to be said for being wanted. And in this warm glow, little thought is given to their desirability—and you succumb to their initiative.

But they might be unprofitable, dull, incompatible, unreasonable, fickle, a loser, lethargic, cheap, anti-advertising, stagnant, unrealistic, slow-pay, adversarial and/or too small. Even worse, you had to staff up for this dog. And now you're faced with the heartache of having to cut back.

Here is how to be spared this possible trauma. When approached by an advertiser, representing an effortless conquest, apply this sobering judgment: **Would we have contacted them?**

If not, don't get carried away by having your ego massaged. However, if they do measure up according to this criterion, it is likelier to be a successful relationship.

Chapter 8

Insight to Developing Prospects

A. Perspective
B. Strategy
C. Market
D. Potential
E. Account Conflict?
F. Rifle Shot
G. Buckshot Approach
H. Advertiser Vulnerability
I. Overlooked Business
J. In-House Advertisers
K. Parlaying Accounts
L. Sponsor Seminar
M. Other Agencies
N. Acquisition/Merger
O. Hip-Pocket Accounts
P. Clients

A. Perspective

A key failing in prospecting is the appalling waste of time spent chasing rainbows. A procedure for efficiently developing leads likeliest to be productive is essential. This can be achieved by applying the method of organization furnished in this chapter. Also, included is the strategy for expanding this opportunity.

In connection with this, I'm often asked, "Do you have any magic for going after new accounts?" In solicitation activity the only magic is what *you make happen*. This takes commitment to an aggressive plan, consistently applied. I'm going to give you the rabbit. However, you'll still have to pull it out of the hat.

But first, let's get this straight. An individual tactic such as a house ad campaign, direct mail program, using old-boy contacts, getting the word out to the reps, a country club membership, civic involvement or an occasional speech is *not* a new business program. Each is worthwhile and contributes to a cumulative effect. However, the results depend on the possibility of action by others. Instead, *you* take control—and make things happen. Because you—rather than fate—should determine your new business results. This chapter will concentrate on the direction necessary for this purpose.

B. Strategy

I keep hearing this good news/bad news scenario. "We have an unusually high rate of scoring—however, we don't get up to bat often enough."

It's assumed there must be a single secret for solving this problem: one that Agencies landing accounts more frequently have discovered.

Upon delving into the matter, I found the reason why these underachievers are unable to present more often. I'm told, "It's because we don't *hear* about enough advertisers planning to switch Agencies."

This passive approach abdicates your new business responsibility to fate. This program should not be restricted to advertiser vulnerability. Rather, it is those accounts *you want* to go after—at the rate and quantity desired. A valuable by-product of being pro-active is that this will cause information on available prospects to materialize.

Next comes opening doors. There isn't any arcane angle for getting in. The proved means consists of establishing and applying a planned series of efforts ranging from initial contact (letter/phone call) to follow-through.

Your Agency—rather than events—should determine growth. This requires your taking the initiative—not waiting for the advertiser to do so.

By the time they hang out the welcome sign, it is for those Agencies for whom they have already developed a preference.

Summing up, you can pitch as often as you like—if you're willing to commit yourselves to making it happen. Your more successful competitors have dedicated themselves to controlling their destiny—and are achieving what you are hoping for.

C. Market

The geographic area in which an Agency can prospect for new business is influenced by economic feasibility. And the smaller the Agency, the more restricted its activity.

As a result, Agencies will carve out a region consisting of a few counties or states. And assume this to be the extent of their market. But this severely restricts their opportunity to the confines of the boundaries arbitrarily established. Also, this strategy obscures *who* their market actually is.

For perspective your market is *not* geographic. Rather, it is those accounts to whom your expertise is especially appealing.

There are countless cases of Agencies serving accounts 1,000—even 2,000—miles away. Because they convinced these advertisers that they couldn't get better performance or dedication anywhere else.

Yet, Agencies will limit their potential due to assuming that servicing a distant client would be unaffordable. Not necessarily. Granted, the standard procedure is for the Agency to pay its own expenses when traveling to and from a client. But the client picks up the tab if they request that you conduct field work.

However, if a prospect is that sold on your preferability, they will negotiate a compensation arrangement that will enable your realizing a satisfactory profit. Therefore, your value is exportable.

So don't hamper your new business growth by mistaking geography for market. You're not going after land. Your objective is getting clients.

D. Potential

When attempting to determine the feasibility of going after a desirable prospect, don't assume that *any* advertiser can't be had. Regardless of how good a job their present Agency may seem to be doing, as a client they will always have a nagging concern as to whether they are getting the best advertising possible.

So exploit this uncertainty—which exists in the mind of every advertiser. Because they can never be *really* sure.

E.   Account Conflict?

Agencies sometimes arbitrarily assume that a prospect they are interested in would be competitive with some client. And thus write them off. Don't.

Rather than second guessing, check the client in question. First, it is impressive to them that a somewhat related advertiser could also want you. Second, contrary to your assumption, they may not perceive your opportunity as being a direct conflict. Even if they do, though, the worst that can happen is that this client will object to your accepting that account.

Then, while you graciously acquiesce, the point is made: that a firm they consider too dangerous to be in the same shop is hot for your body. So, capitalize on being wanted. It makes you more appreciated by those who have you.

F.   Rifle Shot

Your opening round is a rifle-shot approach. This consists of bringing to bear a double-barreled blast. First, start out with your best shot: the category of account in which you are a proved authority. (Is it Food, Finance, Business-to-Business, Healthcare, Agrimarketing, etc.?)

Having earned a reputation for producing results in that field, you're a natural for any non-conflicting account—wherever it is located. These are your *likeliest* prospects. The ones you *should* get. And you surely haven't exhausted this source of your greatest potential.

Next, your follow-through shot should be aimed at the void that exists in your client roster: the type of account particularly wanted. (Other than Frederick's of Hollywood, what do you really want to work on?)

For both the established and new category, select the five most desirable, viable accounts. (Using as many of the criteria I provided you.)

Then go all out—taking whatever action is necessary to score. This would be based on that flushed out in your pre-presentation meeting with the prospect.

This dual objective becomes the spearhead of your new business program. In this way, *you* are deciding on Agency direction. And results are based on your initiative—not some external surprise.

To multiply the potency of your targeted plan, the individual devices previously mentioned (house ads, direct mail, old-boy contacts, reps, country club, civic work, speeches, etc.) would then be used to specifically support it.

Agency after Agency has told me that this concentrated, full-court press is the most successful strategy for landing new accounts. (Because among other things, your efforts will be better organized and you'll be more persistent.) And they are the accounts you especially want.

G.   Buckshot Approach

To broaden your opportunity, here is the back-up buckshot phase. These are the advertisers with whom you might get lucky. In this case, you are playing the law of averages. The first law of which is: The more presentations you make, the more new business you get.

But first, let's dispel the misconception that exists at some Agencies that the source of new business is essentially loose business. With all due respect to the value of ferreting out accounts planning to change, this is only the tip of the new business iceberg. The mass of your potential lies submerged.

Yet, advantage can be taken of this opportunity through systematic missionary work (i.e., those accounts you want to go after, even though not knowing of their willingness to switch Agencies). Here is how this can be done most productively:

1. Identify all feasible prospects.

2. Qualify them according to as many of the 15 criteria furnished.

3. Upon selecting your hit list, itemize them according to their short- and long-range potential—short-range being those prospects you can offer a reason so compelling as to induce them to change soon, and the others ones so desirable that they are worth cultivating over an extended period.

4. Organize both lists according to priority of action. Of course keep your ear to the ground. But while doing so, get your hands dirty. In this way, you can control your Agency's destiny by making things happen.

H.   Advertiser Vulnerability

Beyond the combined effect of this rifle-buckshot strategy, there are a variety of other opportunities just waiting to be exploited.

Because one Agency's poison can be another's meat. Due to circumstances, it is always open season on *some* accounts. They are susceptible to change when any of the following situations occur:

- **Change in Top Management**
  Whenever a key executive change is made, it is a foregone conclusion that their Agency is placed at risk. Instead of being considered a source of stability during this transition, the Agency comes under scrutiny as another means for shaping up operations.

  Thus, when a new Marketing VP or Ad Director is announced by an advertiser, contact him and offer to complete the fresh start sought by your providing him with his own team. This assurance of loyalty when coming into a new position can be a very appealing inducement.

- **Significant Drop in Sales or Profits**
  This causes the type of advertiser uneasiness that another Agency can capitalize on. Whatever measures for improvement you can provide will at least earn an audience—and maybe enough gratitude to be named their new Agency.

- **Radical Change in the Economy or Their Market**
  This condition often causes an advertiser to reexamine their entire marketing operation. And if the concern is deep enough, this could also include the status of their Agency. Be alert to these circumstances because your timing, and fresh approach, could be very propitious.

  Being aware of these opportunities, there is no excuse for not taking advantage of them. Particularly, since the news of such is published. It's just a matter of being a little more alert—and doing something about it. The reason is already there. You should be, too.

  Therefore, institute a system for keeping informed of these advertiser developments which cause them to become susceptible to changing Agencies. Don't be deterred by the phrase, "institute a system." This can be as easy as that being effectively used by some smaller Agencies.

  This simply involves having your receptionist start her day at the office with the business pages of the newspapers in your area. She uses a red magic marker to circle news of advertiser losses in sales or profits and management changes.

  These tear sheets are then placed on the desk of the New Business Manager. This procedure puts the onus on him/her to take action now.

I. Overlooked Business

The whole world may be your oyster. But you still have to find out where the pearls are. And decide on which ones you want and can get.

Here is a bed where some of you can really make out.

Agencies, like people, have preferences in the work they will do. And the larger they are, the more discerning they become—particularly in respect to concentrating on the most prestigious accounts and creaming off the more appealing work.

However, this still leaves a lot of essential nuts-and-bolts work. Maybe not as glamorous—but possibly, more profitable. Further, these maintenance jobs can provide an entree to lure the balance of the account.

This opportunity occurred to Ed Nowak of Spencer Bennett Nowak. They had been plodding along for years with only incidental growth. Being success-oriented, Nowak concluded that there are many valuable assignments being individually jobbed out by larger advertisers. Work that the heavy-hitter Agencies consider too menial; nitty-gritty.

To exploit this potential, they compiled a list of accounts having seven-figure or more media budgets—and only one Agency. Then they developed a presentation as to why the prospect should have a second Agency. In particular, a back-up Agency. How well have they done? It was found, as did Ed McMahon and Art Carney, that being second banana can still be very nourishing. After the Agency's first nine years of existence, they plateaued at $5,000,000 in billing. In the next two and a half years, after instituting this plan, they grew to $16,300,000.

You can probably think of a number of prospects to whom this strategy can be applied. Those you didn't contact because some other Agency has already scored with them. Yet, an end-run could make you a high-paid player in their game, too.

Now that you have the idea, how are you going to apply it? You're limited only by the extent of your ambition—and the desirability of the business that exists.

For this purpose, in what shape is *your* Unique Selling Proposition? Hopefully, it is more appealing than the commonly used claim: "Our Agency is different." If legitimately so, then how?

With the profusion of new business activity, distinguish yours from all the other "different" Agencies. Then apply it—making it easier for the prospect to select you.

J.   In-House Advertisers

Here is an opportunity worth exploring that is too often ruled out.

Agencies assume that when all or part of an account goes in-house, this eliminates the advertiser from being a prospect. Not at all. They are every bit as viable as accounts at independent shops. Often even more vulnerable.

Many advertisers eventually discover that an in-house operation is incestuous. No fresh blood. Ergo, no fresh ideas. And no improvement; just the same experience, repetitively applied.

As a result, research has found that advertisers stay in-house for an average of three years—and then return to the real world. Therefore, many of these accounts could be accorded front-burner status. And lured from their monastic environment by creating envy and regret for what they are missing.

K.   Parlaying Accounts

Here's how to parlay one account into many new ones. It is based on a worthwhile lesson learned by an Agency who got stuck with a lemon—and made lemonade. There are hardly any of you who can't benefit from this experience.

This involves two Agency types who left their employer to set up their own shop—accompanied by that Agency's largest account. On the strength of this client's commitment, these budding entrepreneurs entered into a long-term rental lease—plus the purchase of office furniture and equipment.

Although the client's word was solid, what wasn't anticipated was the fury of the incumbent Agency's president. Upon finding out about this fast shuffle, he threatened to sue for piracy.

Attorneys for the two defectors advised them not to get into the ring because the fight was fixed. First, they were outclassed since they couldn't begin to match the existing Agency in funds for legal expenses. Second, the laws in their State tend to favor the injured party in this type circumstance.

Since there was obviously no sense in trying to take on Goliath without a slingshot, the new operation decided to forgo the disputed client. And it now looked like they were going belly-up before issuing their first insertion order.

Fortunately, they weren't in the usual under-capitalized position—having some financial staying power. This provided them with a grace period. Yet, not enough time to chase rainbows. Their new business funds had to be productive reasonably soon—skipping as many stages in the prospecting process as possible.

This would require getting directly to the decision-makers—in an ingratiating environment. One in which they would be exposed to the Agency's great work—and could be receptive to it.

Coincidentally, the boards and committees of the various civic and charitable organizations are populated by many prominent executives in the production and service industries. These movers and shakers are very dedicated to their pet projects—and have an affinity toward those who contribute well to these causes.

It occurred to this fledgling Agency that these institutions would offer an excellent means for showcasing their talents—among those with whom their efforts would realize the fastest payout. So they attempted to become the volunteer Agency for as many of them as possible.

They went after every operation ranging from the Zoo to the Symphony to the United Fund. And for good measure, their hit list also included the Museum, local Lung Association, S.P.C.A., etc. The city fathers bought this altruism. And this Agency began to knock off one after another of these organizations. As planned, this strategy served a wonderful dual purpose. It enabled them to rub shoulders with the heavy hitter influentials—and provided high visibility for the Agency's work.

Yes, Sharp Hartwig in Seattle succeeded. In fact, new accounts began materializing much faster than they had hoped for. And you can bet the ranch that this Agency hasn't forgotten the source of these valuable prospects—and aren't letting go.

How many of these trigger accounts does your Agency have?

L. Sponsor Seminar

Here is the most productive idea for attracting your likeliest prospects.

How would you like to have a room full of captive prospects—grateful to you? All drawn there because you can offer them a valuable insight on how to compete more successfully. What an opportunity to crowd the hero bench—and when they would be especially receptive.

Here's how: *Sponsor a one-day seminar for the Marketing Executives of the Suppliers to the industry in which you are a proved authority.*

This is actually fairly easy. Because your function in the program would be primarily to M.C. those you invite to speak. They would be the pros acknowledged as expert in the areas of sales, marketing, promotion, distribution, trade relations, pricing, packaging, etc. in dealing with this industry. For that matter, if one or more of the speakers could come from clients of yours, that is tantamount to endorsement.

And you could cover the Agency's role in the total mix—without seeming self-serving. Because in providing this forum, of itself, this builds stature for your Agency—and serves as evidence of your leadership.

Since this environment furnishes the potential for creating such a favorable impression of the Agency, each attendee becomes a very good prospect. Thus, your follow-through activity is likelier to be successful in converting them into clients.

As with all other recommendations supplied you, this isn't a hunch. Rather, it too was inspired by an actual case history.

Noble and Associates in Springfield, MO, has a fast food account: Tyson Foods. As a result, they have become highly experienced in this field.

When first hosting this event, they invited the marketing executives of the suppliers to this type of operation: poultry purveyors, paper producers, flavoring suppliers, furniture manufacturers, etc. All relevant—but none competitive with their client.

After three of these annual events, Bob Noble told me, "If we never do anything else in the new business area, this device is sacrosanct." Because, as he expressed it, "It's like fishing in a well-stocked barrel." Of course, there is ample activity planned for during and after this seminar to take advantage of this great exposure.

The beauty of this strategy is that it can be implemented by any Agency—regardless of size or type—with the opportunity to benefit limited only by the effort they are willing to expend.

M. Other Agencies

Here is an intriguing opportunity. Its premise is based on Agencies being like shoemaker's children. This is evidenced by how they typically operate. Sequentially:

1. Client work dominates.

2. The new business function is a spare-time activity.

3. There is hardly ever the time for efforts on the Agency's behalf.

That's why some shops, in frustration, are retaining other Agencies or P.R. firms to promote them. They stress that it is not that any other operation could do a better job. It's just that this is the only way it will get done.

This action is not an admission of failure on the part of Agencies turning to outside help. Rather, it is an acknowledgement that they are their most important client—thereby deserving priority service. And if this is what it takes, so be it.

Since a number of Agencies are resorting to this strategy, apparently there are many others who would be receptive if solicited. Seemingly, there could be worthwhile potential for an Agency to aggressively go after this business.

All the signs are favorable.

- There is the market for this service.

- There is certainly the need.

- You are more qualified to handle this type of account than any other.

- No other Agency is actively exploiting this opportunity.

Then what are you waiting for? (Besides, you could learn a lot from this involvement.)

N. Acquisition/Merger

One means of achieving substantial growth quickly is by acquiring or merging with another Agency.

When this new business route is taken, the candidate's obvious characteristics are analyzed: financial status, desirability of accounts, client conflicts and caliber of personnel. Assumedly, this is the essence of what needs to be explored.

These criteria are the basics necessary for consideration. But not the deciding factor.

Agencies who have used this strategy have learned—painfully—there is one more qualification. There are too many horror stories about Agencies who have joined forces only to discover that their Management—particularly the C.E.O.s—couldn't stomach each other.

This animosity wasn't apparent during the good behavior conduct of the courtship. However, after they moved in together, the warts and offensive idiosyncrasies surfaced. And it is found that for instance, both C.E.O.s are such prima donnas that any kind of duet is impossible.

In the case of a buyout, compatibility is much less of a concern. Although preferable, authority is clear-cut. Yet, the viability of this arrangement still needs to begin with the chemistry factor—and how it will be dealt with.

As to merger, the situation is more complex. There is the jockeying for power. And determining which of the two factions will emerge as the dominant force. Actually, as Harry Paster, Exec. VP of the American Association of Advertising Agencies puts it, "There is really no such thing as a merger. One Agency acquires; the other is acquired." It's called a merger as a sop to the clients of the absorbed shop so they won't feel like second-class citizens.

Since the matter of relationship is so crucial, here is how to ascertain in advance whether it would be satisfactory—before any commitment is made. Namely, would you be better off with or without each other?

Volunteer to work together on a civic project that takes several months (i.e., street people, abused children, etc.). This will reveal whether the principals of both can hit it off together under actual working conditions. If so, it minimizes risks when a formal agreement gets underway.

If this experience proves otherwise, you can prevent getting involved in a union that will suffer from friction at the top.

O.   Hip-Pocket Accounts

There are four basic means by which Agencies land accounts:

- conducting a planned, consistent new business program

- acquiring another Agency with desirable clients

- lucking out on transom business

- hiring someone supposedly wired into an account

The first three matters have been dealt with as necessary thus far. The latter needs to be treated head-on in its entirety before we go any further. Because it can be an expensive trap. One sorely regretted afterwards.

The woods have always been full of promoters claiming they "control" a large, appealing account. And there have been instances in which this was true.

Then they will use this claimed clout as bait for employment. You've probably heard it. "I'd be willing to join you—and bring Monumental Conglomerate with me." Of course, involving a handsome financial arrangement for this individual.

The temptation is terrific. What an *effortless, free* way to get a major new client! Further, this heavy hitter seems honest. And in some cases they have been.

However, more often than not, they are long on promise and short on delivery.   And somehow, that fabulous hip-pocket account didn't materialize.

Giving this person the benefit of the doubt, there may not be any intent to deceive.   Instead, he/she may not have the inside track assumed. Especially now with the advertiser having more committees and layers of authority.

This is not a skull-and-crossbones warning against considering any such proposition. Sure, hear them out. This hustler just may be on the level. But protect yourself in advance.

Here's how you can go along with *any* deal—without getting burned. Hire any such person on the basis that their salary will begin when the Agency starts receiving income from the account promised.

If bringing in this business is just a formality, there shouldn't be any objection. But if he/she balks at these terms, it is indicative of the soundness of their offer.

Therefore, this 4th source of new business can be exploited—without gambling on the outcome. By applying the procedure suggested, you can *afford* to be interested—and profit from legitimate overtures.

P.   Clients

I saved your likeliest opportunity for getting more business until the end for emphasis. *It is growing clients.* Sure, you'll fully agree. But what specific action are you taking?

Agencies usually have a written marketing plan for soliciting prospects. And a person or team responsible for this function. Yet, there isn't any organized effort to generate further business from *all* clients—with this overall project assigned to anyone.

However, existing accounts are your most probable source for growth. Here's why. You know their needs, what will appeal to them, who the decision-maker is—and have already proved your worth.   Not having to start from scratch, clients are also your most economical targets for prospecting.

With all this going for you, there should be a documented plan of action for upping client budgets and getting additional assignments from them. Here's how to make it happen:

- Establish objectives for what you want to achieve.
- Develop a detailed course of action necessary to succeed.
- Appoint a new business team for going after clients.

• Set dates by which results should be produced.

Then head up this operation with the individual who operates in the capacity of Director of Client Services. The one with the most account familiarity and who has the authority to pull together and execute this plan.

Now, implement this program for growing clients as aggressively as if it were a full-fledged new business campaign. Because at the very least, even if this activity doesn't produce immediate results, it could serve as a deterrent to clients cutting or cancelling budgets.

Chapter 9

Exploit Seventeen Sources of Leads

A. Perspective

There are a variety of sources of leads—usually unused or misused. This is due to misconceptions regarding their worth—and how to benefit from them.

Such being the case, here are 17 opportunities—brought into perspective. How many of these are you taking advantage of?

B. Employees

Start with your most logical source of leads, those having the greatest stake in your Agency: your employees. They offer two mutually valuable opportunities. Here is how to benefit from them.

First, bulletin all employees informing them that their potential for raises and promotions depends on Agency growth. Then ask them to furnish the names of anyone they know at advertisers who would be worth contacting. This could be a friend, relative or neighbor who might influence Agency selection.

To encourage employee cooperation, inform them that other than supplying these names, they don't have to do anything else in this respect. In fact, could remain anonymous if desired. And then they should be surveyed on a regular semi-annual basis for this purpose.

Some of you may assume this idea isn't applicable due to your shop being too large for it. Yet, Lintas/New York has been conducting this survey for years—and they have 751 employees in that office! I am told they get more leads than they can possibly follow up. Because what more compelling appeal could there be than raises and promotions?

Apparently, this is one of the many things they are doing right which has contributed to such a successful new business record.

Second, have every one of your people submit the name of a single advertiser, (appropriate to your operation), that they want your Agency to get more than any other. These should then be placed at the top of your new business list.

These advertisers are particularly wanted. And there must be a feeling of what can be achieved for them. So why not channel your efforts towards those who turn your Agency on—rather than grinding away at uninspiring but assumedly more vulnerable accounts. And in doing so, you will encourage employees to volunteer additional leads.

Considering the number of nights and weekends you work, if you aren't enjoying yourself in this business, you might just as well go back to mud wrestling.

C.   Agency C.E.O.

The most valuable antenna for new business leads is often the least used: the head of the shop. Human nature being what it is, those having such news prefer to divulge it to him/her—assuming this could do them more good.

However, having reached the top spot, there is no longer the time for this person to be as available. Yet, if the C.E.O. isn't exploiting his/her position to attract leads, the Agency is being done an injustice. By contrast, maintaining a high profile for receptivity will encourage both employees and outsiders to volunteer such information.

This can be accomplished by making it known that anyone with a legitimate new business tip has automatic entree to the C.E.O.s office. To most people, this is a powerful incentive because it enables ingratiating themselves with the most important person in the Agency.

D.   Clients

Of course, evidence of client satisfaction is the most impressive tactic for attracting leads.

But you can't ask clients to take any initiative on your behalf. If so, they consider themselves being used. You can only request their *endorsement*—not their efforts. In doing so, though, it is implied you would welcome any new business information—and appreciate their recommendations.

E.   Retail Accounts

There is a virtual cornucopia of leads if you have or land a retail account. Then every brand name stocked in their stores becomes fair game for you.

This point-of-sale experience is highly merchandisable to such prospects. Because while other Agencies can only assume their proposals will produce as promised, you *know* due to working where the action is. Understandably, this hands-on expertise is especially impressive to an advertiser—and enhances your credibility.

For example, in a recent major account change in the Northeast, the advertiser gave as their reason for selection: "Retail understanding." What's meant by this? They believed that the new Agency had the insight as to *why and how a sale is made or lost*. According to this definition, it could apply to any account—in any category. And you certainly have this capability in the fields in which you have become expert. Exploit it!

F.   Client Board Members

The best new business lead is a matchmaker, like this one.

Unless any of your clients are one-man bands, they probably have some sort of board of directors. And it is possible that some of their members sit on additional boards.

They should have a favorable attitude toward your Agency and they could be quite influential on your behalf.

Therefore, identify your client board members—along with the other advertisers with whom they are involved. Then decide which of these accounts would be appropriate and desirable for your Agency.

Ideally, your client relationships should be such whereby they would be willing to set up a meeting for you with whatever board members you desire. Its purpose is to arrange for entree to the decision-maker in Agency selection at their other contacts. If they will pave the way, it enables going in with the blessings of a person very important to this company.

Capitalize on this pre-conditioned source of clout. Because entering on a red carpet sure beats the usual bed of hot coals.

G.   Clients' Suppliers

Apropos of your clients being a springboard for additional business, find out who all of their suppliers are (i.e., parts, ingredients, services, etc.). Since these are kissin' cousins, they are prime prospects.

Inasmuch as a mutual interest exists, there is a bona fide reason to see your Agency. And you are going in with the implied endorsement of a shared client. (Being its Agency, evidently you're considered preferable to any other.)

Obviously, your thrust is based on the logic of serving both. And why this arrangement would strengthen this supplier's relationship with the client.

This action should then be taken for each new account landed—thereby compounding your new business opportunities.

H.   Questionnaires

When a questionnaire is received from an advertiser, it receives priority attention. How you handle this challenge will be a door-opener or door-closer.

As you know, this is their screening process to choose candidates for presentation. Besides obtaining the information needed, this tactic saves them from many time-consuming pitches.

For this tool to be worthwhile for them, though, it must be professionally conceived—consisting of sound, relevant inquiries. And then the Agency responses have to be evaluated by qualified personnel.

From the Agency standpoint, the caliber and pertinence of the questions provides a valuable insight into the character of the prospect. And whether they would be desirable as a client.

Nevertheless, some of these exploratory surveys are mailed because it is assumed this is a procedure that must be observed. As a result, a generic form is sent to a ridiculously long list of Agencies. Or this procedure might be used by the person conducting the search to impress associates and play C.Y.A. Or even worse, it may be a device to legitimatize a hidden agenda.

Because a questionnaire can range from a considerable amount of work to a cover-up, critically appraise each. Then take off the rose-colored glasses and decide whether you can justify the effort and risk.

If you conclude that the odds are acceptable—and this advertiser is on the level—here is how to win in the questionnaire game.

For openers, if it is deemed worth participating in this charade, you need to begin by distinguishing your Agency from the multitude of competitors. This applies equally to the following factors.

Concept
Your reply is the first impression received of your Agency. It must be business-like—but not come across as a legal document. Rather, your straight-forward answers should be packaged with a flair. Be visually as well as verbally intriguing.

Appearance
This is the first indication of your creativity. I'm not advocating popout inserts or die-cut pages. However, your visual treatment should be highly conducive to being read. Specifically, lay out that typed as if these are ads you want to be proud of.

Then, as evidence of its importance, insert these pages in an impressive binder. And this, too, should serve as a vehicle to demonstrate your creativity.

Content
At this stage of the project, the prospect will have neither the time nor inclination to sweat out a thesis. So don't try to impress them by the pound.

To encourage your reply being read, and receiving a favorable reaction, the clue is brevity. Take the time to write a short book.

It is important to comply precisely with their directions. In particular, answer *every* question. And your replies should deal directly and fully with what they want to know—not what you prefer to promote.

For instance, if they inquire as to what extent your Agency is involved with Direct Response advertising, don't come back with, "We are a full-service Agency." It seems like you are ducking this issue. And it is a smoke screen for inadequacy or lacking this function.

Remember: if any license is taken, or if there is any omission or evasion, the Agency becomes suspect. And it provides the prospect with an out for eliminating you.

However, while playing the game, there is still a selling opportunity available. Here it is. After having completed this exercise, strictly adhering to the ground rules set, add a brief statement at the end on why your Agency should be selected. Being the final shot, if compelling enough, the prospect will be likelier to retain what you most want them to recall.

Yet, even with this disciplined approach going for you, you're still one of too many Agencies who have responded. Now go the payout step further. When returning their questionnaire, include one of your own—seeking the input needed to customize your presentation for them. (If they cooperate, you have a live one.)

This action will separate your Agency from the others in the cattle call, conveys professionalism and initiative—and registers that your presentation will be based on their needs, not your desires. This strategy can provide the competitive edge that will enable your shop to make the cut at this stage.

Summing up, the advertiser questionnaire is a means for weeding out Agencies so they can concentrate on a manageable size group for consideration. Granted, you can't *win* them all. But you sure ought to at least *qualify*. This can be accomplished by taking advantage of the tested direction and ideas provided.

I.   Agency House Advertising

There is the matter of whether Agency house advertising will produce leads. Of itself, don't hold your breath.

Getting back to the basics, regardless of how brilliant, it can only create a favorable environment for subsequent *direct* selling effort. It doesn't have any tangible value—unless merchandised. Sound familiar?

Sure it does. But when it comes to *your* operation, you can't be objective. Pride gets in the way.

Here's where I'm coming from. On occasion, an Agency C.E.O. will inform me that they have finally instituted a new business program. I will congratulate him and ask what it consists of. And he enthusiastically announces that they are going to run a series of ads in the *Wall Street Journal, Ad Age* and *Adweek*.

So I'll ask, "And then what?" And he counters with, "What do you mean, 'Then what'?"

I'll elaborate with, *"Then what are you going to do?"* His response is, "I'm going to open the transom and watch the inquiries flood in!"

My next question is, "How do you figure?" At that he pulls a yellow pad out of his desk, points proudly at the scribbling, and exclaims, "I wrote this sucker!"

Not being on his payroll, I can come back with, "But isn't that 180 degrees opposite from what you preach to clients? That their responsibility doesn't end once an ad or commercial appears. Rather, that's when their opportunity begins."

Of course I am in favor of advertising by Agencies. However, *only* if it is the springboard for an action-oriented plan to capitalize on it.

Another caveat. For whatever message developed, again take the advice you give clients: Research it. Ego is a lousy basis for justifying its worth.

A prime example is that experienced by the Swink Agency. Prior to teaming up with Fahlgren & Ferris, they were one of the most ambitious Agency advertisers. Many of you probably still remember their headline: "What is an agency like Swink doing in Marion, Ohio?"

Their competitors loved it. They came back with, "Because that's where they belong!"

So don't be smitten by your handiwork and rely solely on your own judgment. *Research it.* Otherwise, it could backfire to your detriment.

J.   Direct Mail

And then there is your direct mail activity. It is time this lazy program goes to work for you.

Agencies seem resigned to a very low response rate. This is rationalized as due to its purpose being just to create awareness.

Well, if you ever told a client that your efforts for them were intended to accomplish anything short of contributing to generating sales, you'd have an ex-client in a helluva hurry.

Even worse, provision is seldom made for following up on mailings with phone calls to set up appointments for initial meetings with them. This is excused because "We have a list of 315 prospects and couldn't possibly contact all of them." If they aren't worth phoning, why have them on your new business list?

This is not meant to imply that there is no room for mass promotional mailings. However, this is a luxury compared to the necessity of having a targeted group that you can actively solicit. Only after providing for this direct activity can an impersonal approach be taken.

Therefore, it's not only *what* you have to say. It is also to *whom*. So decide on the purpose of your mailer. Are you looking for business? Or a nice warm feeling?

Since it's action you are after, pare your list to a manageable quantity. Otherwise recognize a mass mailing for what it is: just getting the word out—with the remote possibility of getting lucky.

If you promoted for clients like you do for your Agency, they would fire you. Thus, instead of being like shoemaker's children, the objective of your Agency's direct mail program should be to produce inquiries—and diligently follow through. Otherwise, this expense should be donated to a worthier cause.

K.   Media Reps

When an Agency's growth flattens—or worse, it loses a major account—a quick-fix solution is often sought to rebound. A tactic that will produce immediate new business. Yet, when these circumstances occur, Agencies seem to forget that overnight success in this area can take years of dogged, systematic work.

However, the situation is emotional. Sometimes desperate. Thus, the need to recoup as quickly as possible will transcend logic. And Agency Management will confuse a new business *influence* with a program. Following is an example of the most frequent delusion that exists.

Agency heads will reveal to me, "We are going to become aggressive in the new business area." Figuring I may learn something, I'll ask, "What are you going to do?" And the C.E.O. will disclose their secret weapon: "We are going to get the word out to the Media Reps."

When I question the originality and dynamism of this concept, they will defensively justify it with, "Well, we have a damn good relationship with the Reps!" Congratulations. But you can't entrust the future of your Agency to the possible initiative by outsiders. Neither can you exaggerate their clout with advertisers nor loyalty to you.

Therefore, because of misconceptions, let's bring into focus the value of Reps as a source of new business leads—and the extent to which they affect Agency reputations.

Ego notwithstanding, any reliable Rep will admit that their worth as a means of leads is highly overrated. And after a few belts, will confess that what information they do get is used as a selling device to ingratiate themselves at Agencies with whom they have schedules pending. And the confidential information provided you was probably confided a dozen times before.

So be realistic regarding the Reps potential for you in the New Business area. They are a dicey source of tips—from which your efforts might result in getting an appointment. But as far as providing an inside track, it is highly improbable.

Of course, make use of the Reps. But don't count on their being your salvation.

Actually, here is how to make the most productive use of Reps.

Forgo the standard practice of supposedly doing something for them by throwing a bi-annual cocktail party. They can afford their own booze. Besides, they prefer fresh hors d'oeuvres.

Then, for their assumed influence, those invited are usually the heads of offices of national media. But they don't get their hands dirty at accounts.

Instead, schedule a *Breakfast Press Conference* for the Reps of Trade Publications that concentrate on the category of account you intend to target on. These are the ones most knowledgeable regarding this industry and the advertisers within it.

The purpose is to announce your new business thrust—and give this specific group an eight-minute presentation on why your Agency is especially qualified to serve clients in their field. You're not asking them for anything. Or giving them anything.

Rather, they are being taken into your confidence and informed of your forthcoming activity in their area. And the possibility of your calling on their expertise.

Implicit in this tactic, though, is that any information furnished or efforts on your behalf that contributes to your landing an account in their field, could benefit them via space placed in their book.

Reps can also be of value to you in another respect. Advertisers encourage them to furnish news and impressions of various Agencies. Advertisers consider it part of their responsibility to keep current on Agency developments. (And it makes for pretty good gossip.) The Reps are delighted to oblige. Regardless of whether they have ever been at the Agency. Assuming it will improve their position.

Such being the case, does your Agency command the respect of Reps—or is their attitude one of contempt? Their good will can be vital to you. Nurture it.

This doesn't require costly cocktail parties. Rather, their opinion is based essentially on treatment received. And you can be a hero so easily. Simply by accepting or returning their phone calls. And don't keep them waiting too long when they have an appointment. Thus, it really only takes the Golden Rule.

An excellent example is the action taken by Bill Biggs for his Agency in Kalamazoo. They realize that Kalamazoo isn't exactly the crossroads of America. In fact, when a Rep does show up, they get so excited!

So for openers, they offer him or her coffee, tea or wine. (They have a wine account.) Further, there is a phone for their purposes. And as a final touch, being in the boondocks, a typing service is made available to them. It's a sure bet that Biggs shop is getting good press from Reps to advertisers.

L.   Banks

A highly authoritative source of leads is the Corporate Loan Officer of your bank. His intimate working arrangement with firms gives him an inside track on their forthcoming developments and needs which could be very meaningful to you. Further, he knows the pecking order at each.

Cozy up to this Corporate Loan Officer; (Or his title may be Commercial Loan Officer). Probe discreetly and he might reveal just enough for you to be at the right place, at the right time, with the right people.

To increase the likelihood of this occurring, put on a credentials presentation for this person and his/her staff. Sometimes they are in a position to suggest Agencies for consideration by their clients. This will create top-of-mind awareness of your shop—and justify why it would be in their best interest to prefer yours.

M.   Business Services

Although not as directly involved, there are other sources with whom you do business that could be influential on your behalf. Namely, your legal, auditing and insurance services. Inform them that you would appreciate whatever clout they could apply at advertisers with whom they have contact. And periodically, (after paying one of their invoices), check them as to what advertisers you were recommended to. Because people do what you *inspect*—not what you expect.

N.   Other Agencies

Here's a twist. How about your competitors: other Agencies. On occasion, they are approached by, or tipped off to susceptible advertisers with whom there would be a client conflict. Or the account may be undesirable to them for whatever their reasons.

Therefore, develop a reciprocal arrangement with a key group of Agencies, so that when such situations arise, they could suggest you as an alternate. Or at least inform you of the availability of the prospect. Obviously, the incentive for them to cooperate is your willingness to do likewise.

For this plan to be meaningful, take it beyond the hollow gesture state. To get underway, select Agencies in your area who, by virtue of their specialty or size, would not be head-to-head competitors. Then arrange to put on your credentials/capabilities presentation for them—and they would reciprocate. Now each can knowledgeably and confidently recommend the other when appropriate.

Then multiply this source by going beyond it. Also make this handshake offer to Agencies not as remote, where you have a close personal contact in top Management. Since there may be instances in which you might come up against them, obviously you will have to be more circumspect in what is revealed. However, it is worth negotiating this agreement for the insider advantage it can provide.

In fact, to cover all bases, the person who heads up the new business operation for a major New York Agency has a concerted plan for having lunch with his counterparts at other shops. And these back-scratching sessions are scheduled with maximum frequency. While no one is giving the store away, he has found he can thrive on the free samples collected.

This strategy of one hand washing another could clue you on techniques and accounts planning to change that you might not hear about otherwise.

O.   "Hot Shops"

Agencies get rutted in thinking of new business leads in terms of the obvious sources: employees, clients, reps, etc. And all wind up tilling the same worked-out fields.

Go beyond the routine into a relatively untapped area. In particular, explore this fresh opportunity—for which there is hardly any competition.

On the surface, it is so seemingly improbable, few Agencies exploit it. *It's the "hot shop."*

Having achieved this reputation, it is assumed their accounts are untouchable. However, sometimes a closer perusal of the Trade press reveals that while they receive front page coverage on accounts landed, the parade of those lost get only incidental mention toward the back of the issue. There are several reasons for this revolving door effect.

- Success can beget complacency. The Agency is lulled into figuring its reputation will make their accounts safe from assault. Then they become careless. And their clients, vulnerable.

- A hot new business streak can also cause arrogance. This results in illusions of omnipotence. And the Agency lapses into sloppy account handling—whereby their clients can be had.

- Then there are the Agencies experiencing explosive rather than controlled growth. And they begin to unravel before knowing what hit them.

- Finally, there are the cases in which the "hunt/kill" factor becomes more fulfilling than the original objective of servicing the new clients. Upon discovering this, the latter quickly become live prospects.

    (Conversely, this list of circumstances could also serve as caveats for those Agencies on a roll.)

So just because some Agency has been scoring heavily on landing new business does not mean they are correspondingly "hot" in holding on to accounts. Actually some effort may have been diverted from the follow-through service function—with their client roster becoming more susceptible to change.

Thus, regardless of how formidable these showboat Agencies with the headlines may seem, their preoccupation with conquest could enable you to lure their disenchanted clients before their susceptibility becomes evident.

P. Trade Shows

You've targeted on a specific industry to be cultivated. (One in which you are a proved authority; another for diversification.) Now comes the laborious task of contacting each prospect individually.

But what if one or more key executives from most of these companies regularly congregate in the same building for the same several days? They do—at their industry's annual Trade show.

Sure, you know that. Because when you have a client exhibiting at this type event, you try to get over there and roam around for a while. And of course, dutifully put in an appearance at your client's space.

In addition, if you should happen to run into a prospect, that would be a welcome bonus. For solicitation purposes though, instead of this being a casual occasion from which something might accidentally occur, exploit this opportunity via a planned course of action.

Compared to the usual time-consuming series of letters and follow-up phone calls attempting to make contact, prospects attending these events are like ducks in a shooting gallery.

With them being available all at once, set up a procedure for intentional contact. This would establish:

- what individuals you want to reach

- how this would be conducted in this environment

- what you want to accomplish at this time

By contrast with your previous leisurely stroll down the aisles, capitalize on this massive source of leads all under one roof. The ducks are all lined up. And there is no limit to how many you can bag.

Granted, those you want to contact are there for another purpose. One very important to them. And your interfering would be resented. *Unless you are perceived as being worth meeting.*

Here is how this stature can be gained. Offer to deliver a report to this event on a matter currently critical to this industry. This could consist of vital research or case histories that would result in solutions of value to them.

If your offer is accepted, then you achieve somewhat of a celebrity status. Further, it amounts to endorsement by the sponsoring organization—and makes you an authority in their field.

When approaching your prospect, you aren't just another hustler. But rather, a personality with pre-conditioned acceptance to whom they will be receptive.

Q.   Help Wanted Ads

Advertisers actually publish clues to impending change. These appear in the help wanted section of your newspaper. Check the display ads for a Marketing VP or Advertising Director. Obviously, there has to be some state of flux at this company.

This opening could be due to a variety of reasons. Any of which could justify hiring a new Agency, too.

When a Company announces through this medium that they are looking for a new marketing or advertising heavyweight, it is an admission that they need help. And it's quite possible this could extend to their Agency affiliation.

Why hope to find out about it? You know something is happening now. Be there! Entering on the ground floor is a lot easier than trying to crash the party after the prospect has sent out their list of invitations.

R. Job Applicants

Here is an opportunity that is seldom capitalized on—but can result in landing your next major account. *Exploit job applicants*. In the interview, they can reveal advertiser vulnerability—and possibly clue you on what's necessary to win.

Flush out why this person left their Agency—or wants to do so. Is an account shaky? Or the Agency? The latter would indicate the receptivity of existing clients to change.

Of course you will have to take whatever they say with a grain of salt. Is this person bitter? How privy is he/she to what is really going on? Interpretation is required. But it is worth the effort. Because even if it is a matter of finding the rare pearl in an oyster, the reward can justify the dive.

The value of this tactic was confirmed by Jim Stein. He was Executive Creative Director at Campbell Mithun in Minneapolis when I was conducting a New Business seminar there. Jim mentioned that he manages to spend some time with whoever comes in to apply for a job in Copy or Art. (This is no minor feat considering there are 410 people employed in this office.) "Admittedly," he said, "Nine out of ten are a pain in the ass. But from that *tenth* one, I get something! And it pays off."

So make a practice of probing those looking for a job. Sure, there may be time wasted on gossip. But among the clinkers there might be the gem that could give you a crack at a live one before anyone else.

S. Summary

We have now dealt with planning your new business program, developing prospects and exploiting leads. Critical to the success of these functions is setting timing for each. Because goals without due dates are just wishes.

Chapter 10

Procedure for Getting Appointments

A.   Perspective

Some Agencies will keep a low profile in the new business arena for fear of antagonizing clients. Others claim they don't have to bother because their outstanding performance will produce so much transom business. And the parade passes both of them by.

Because there is a direct correlation between Agency new business activity and prospect interest. Since they equate such effort with success.

Agencies are discovering that when it becomes known they are aggressive in this area, prospects begin to contact them. If you slack off, though, they will do likewise.

Beyond this, becoming more active offers a valuable by-product: this makes it likelier that you'll find out about accounts planning to change.

B.   Advertising Medium

Once an Agency decides to become aggressive in the new business area, they then want immediate results.

Next, lengthy meetings are held to determine what medium will generate the most leads—fastest (i.e., Trade pubs, Newspapers, Radio, Outdoor, etc.?).

After running whatever was scheduled, though, comes the rude awakening: *Nothing happened*. Such brilliant copy—yet no response. Why should there be? As far as advertisers are concerned, if you want their business, *come after it*. But you can't feasibly find out who saw your ad or heard your commercial. Thus, you're stymied.

Sure, you created favorable awareness. However, your objective is to get appointments at advertisers with persons who can take action on your behalf. And the only way this can be accomplished is via one-to-one contact. Namely: **Direct Mail**.

This is the most effective approach. Because you are reaching targeted individuals—whom you have qualified as prospects.

Bearing repetition, then your follow-through activity can be gotten underway. Specifically, phone calls to set up meetings. Persistent in practice—and with compelling reason why it would be to their advantage to clear time for you.

Therefore, while impersonal media can develop a positive image for your Agency, they don't actually *sell* for you. In the final analysis, only you can do that through *direct contact*.

C.   Level of Contact

Since everything begins with your first contact—in particular, *who?*—I'm often asked, "At what level should you start in initial prospect contact?"

Agencies will usually begin by targeting on the Ad Manager/Director. Understandably, you can better relate to the person in this function—and are more comfortable with him/her.

Wrong. Because if this person is feeling sorry for himself that day, and refuses to set up an appointment, you're ruled out for that prospect. Then your only alternative is pulling an end run. And he will cut you up if you try it.

Instead, *start with who your research indicates would be the decision-maker*. Maybe it is their Executive Vice President. If you luck out and he'll hold still—great. You've landed on Boardwalk.

However, it's likelier that he won't see you. It is quite possible though that he will buck you to the Ad Manager.

Now you have acceptance. Next, send the Exec. V.P. a thank you note, with a copy to the Ad Manager—confirming that you will follow through *per his request*.

Of course his subordinate will see you. And then you will at least get your day in court. Now it is a matter of convincing the Ad Manager of why it would be to *his advantage* to explore your value further.

Your initial contact should be where the power lies—rather than with whom you feel more confident. So go for the gold. It's your likeliest way to get into the games.

Actually, your approach is limited only by its appeal. Fallon McElligott in Minneapolis attributes a significant amount of its new business success to their level of prospect contact: the C.E.O.

They *start* with the decision-maker—and invariably get in. Here's how. The Agency selects a short list of desired blue-chip accounts. Then, under the guise of being a major investor, they contact approximately ten financial firms (Merrill Lynch, Shearson Lehman, etc.) regarding the advisability of buying this prospect's stock. This survey also includes inquiries as to growth potential, R.O.I., etc.

Upon completion, a letter is sent to the prospect's C.E.O. informing him of the confidential financial study just conducted on his Company. This lists the prestigious Security Analysts contacted—and the series of critical questions asked. The letter concludes by mentioning they will phone two weeks hence for an appointment to reveal these vital findings.

Obviously this insight is irresistible. So you can bet the C.E.O.'s first act is to get on the phone to the Agency and insist, "How about today at 2:00 PM?"

This strategy enables Fallon McElligott to cut through all the bureaucratic layers of management and get directly to the yes-or-no man. Then, if sufficiently impressed, the C.E.O. has the authority to at least institute an Agency review.

Thus, you can start as high as you wish at a prospect—if your reason for contact is intriguing enough. And get action sooner, too—because of leading from strength.

D. Letter: Content and Appearance

Every attempt to get an appointment should be initiated by letter. This implies importance to your contacting them and makes you a known quantity. If you don't identify yourself in advance, in your follow-through phone call you will be, "Charlie who?"

Bear in mind, your initial letter to a prospect is an introductory ad for your Agency. Both visually and in content. So apply the same standards.

The following analogy will provide you with the direction needed. Considerable thought and effort is given to oral skills for new business purposes. And there are a variety of training firms specializing in this field who are retained to improve speaker delivery.

Yet, there is nowhere near as much concern for your *written* communication. However, this is even more important because it is your *first* contact with the prospect. And your continuing inducement until they agree to a direct meeting.

Such being the case, are your solicitation and follow-through letters as appealing as your presenters have been programmed to be? Are these mailings as personable and disciplined? From what I have seen in my cross-pollinating, probably not.

Vocally, you want to be so appealing as to attract and hold attention. And be effective enough to persuade. These accomplishments depend on your appearance, interest-level created and command of the language.

Well then, shouldn't these same objectives and requirements be applied to your written approach? You're just using a different medium for the same purpose: to convince the prospect of why your Agency is best for them.

To accomplish this, here are the ground rules for your letter:

- To encourage its being read, the clue is brevity. Write it telegraphical-ly—as if you were paying for it by the word. For that matter, according to a study by the Direct Marketing Association, no paragraph should be more than four lines long.

- For the reaction desired, the opening statement should contain a promise of benefit.

- Then, pay it off with your plans for follow-through contact.

- And finally, from no less an authority than Bob Stone (who is probably the ultimate maven on direct response activity): "If there is anything said in the letter that would require any thought, either simplify it or omit it."

To apply these ground rules most effectively, considering what is at stake, forgo any false pride. Get your Copywriters' reaction to how the content of your new business letters are expressed—and any suggestions they may have for its improvement. And get your Art Director's thoughts for enhancing their visual effect.

This action does not cast doubt on your ability. Rather, it is evidence of your good sense to take advantage of whatever Agency sources that will increase the potency of your new business activity.

Summing up, any prospect letter should be the best ad that can be produced for your Agency. The contact person should draft the letter to establish direction—and the Creatives apply the specialized expertise for which they were hired.

Finally, there are conclusive reasons why you should pave the way with a letter. First, cold-turkey phone calls smack of canvassing. And second, without creating interest, it's too easy to brush you off. So use the letter/phone sequence of contact. It makes the difference between being a professional and being a peddler.

E.   Getting Through

Supposedly, your phone call is intended for your contact. Usually, however, that isn't who receives it. Rather, it is routed through his/her secretary or assistant. To get through, this person then becomes your *primary* contact.

Only after her screening will you be cleared for conversation. Getting through this filter doesn't require several dozen long-stem American Beauty roses. Here is how to emotionally, and safely, ingratiate yourself.

A secretary, like anyone else, thrives on recognition. Therefore, your *first* phone call should be to the receptionist, or the Personnel Department if necessary, to find out her name. Then call back so you can address her accordingly.

This gives the impression that you have so much respect for the importance of her function that it was worth the effort to learn her name in advance. As a result of this deference, she will be a conduit rather than an obstacle to communication with the contact desired.

F. Telephone Techniques

Since the telephone can be your new business friend or foe, here is what you need know regarding the content and conduct of your phone conversation. (And if you are afflicted with phoneaphobia, this will help you pick up the 10,000 lb. phone.) Because regardless of how intriguing the written contact, if the personal approach isn't correspondingly appealing, you will have run out your string with that prospect.

To begin with, your phone call should start *before* you dial. Come up with a reason why your contact should listen to you. In particular, identify what's in it for him in advance. Rather than hoping that something occurs to you after he answers.

Now for your opener. Is there some grabber that is irresistible? Don't strain yourself. The prospect has probably heard most of the hackneyed nifties before.

How about starting with something as logical as *why* you are calling him. Then you're obviously not wasting his time (which is inviolable), and this makes you acceptable up front because of not playing games.

Then, having opened by leveling with the prospect, skip the weather forecast and Polish jokes. Your reason for contact should be intriguing enough so that you don't have to resort to small talk. Instead, stay on target with why they would benefit from meeting with you—and set a date for this.

Granted, they may have reservations about seeing you and he might offer some resistance. Sure, you will want to overcome these objections convincingly and unemotionally. However, for whatever your rebuttal, apply this criterion: "Would I put this in writing?" Could you afford to have it on record?

Then, be easy to talk to. Certainly not confrontational. Above all, though, hear him out.

Yet, don't let the conversation drag. End it on a high note. And especially leave the impression that it was worth his time. If ever the prospect's reaction is to the contrary, that was your last phone contact.

Before getting into what may actually happen, be prepared for this possibility. Don't be shook by the coldness of your contact. He/she may be a delightful person but have a lousy phone personality. Listen to *what* is said—not how. Don't let your impression influence your judgment. Because your concern should be with the message. Not its delivery.

In this initial phone conversation, you will probably be asked one of the two following questions. How you field these will determine whether or not there will be any further contact.

- First, don't get caught off base by the most common question they ask. That is, "Why do you want to see us?" Well, why *do* you want to see them? And your answer should certainly be more imaginative than, "Cause we want your business."
- Or if they snap, "Why the hell should we see you?" Most often, Agencies will counter with, "Because you owe it to yourself to know more about us." They don't owe themselves anything of the sort.

In both instances, tell them what they most want to hear: "Our Agency can better contribute to increasing your sales profitably." If asked, "How?"—their inquiry provides the reason for the appointment: "This would be accomplished based on the ten questions we need to ask you."

Or putting it more bluntly, there was the reason given by J. Walter Thompson to Schlitz as to why they should be selected: "Because our Agency can help you sell more goddamn beer than any other."

That clinched it. With that response, they cut through all the competitive clutter—and reached the prospect's jugular. (Significantly, they also knew their audience.)

G. Inducements

As Red Motley said, "Nothing happens until a sale is made." In your case, nothing can take place unless you set up an introductory meeting.

However, a prospect will hardly ever see you just because you desire it. Running leaner and meaner, they now need to be given a compelling reason to justify clearing the time.

Here are your eight tickets for admission. Any of these can get you in:

- research on their Company, Industry, Market and/or product hitherto unavailable (If you just conducted the research, of course it's been unavailable.)
- a new marketing insight that would be of particular value to your contact
- an unusual industry development that he/she might not be aware of
- an idea for a new product—or the repositioning of an existing one
- If the advertiser is planning to change, offer the input and direction for conducting an Agency search and selection procedure. Even if they presume they have all the information needed, they will be curious enough about what you may have to set a date.
- an exceptional occurrence at your Agency that would be relevant to their interests and needs

- or a choice bit of information about their competition (That's irresistible!)

Yet, despite the appeal of any of these inducements, there will be some prospects who will flat-out refuse to see you. However, you hate to accept defeat because this would be a marvelous account to have.

In that case, play your trump card. Reveal that "We have an idea for your industry that is so great, some Company in it is going to use this. And because of our respect for your operation, we would like to give you first crack at it." (If your Agency is good enough to solicit this account, it should be able to come up with this great idea.) It is inconceivable that a prospect could turn down this offer. But if they are still obstinate, take it to any of their competitors who will want to see a good thing when they know it.

Whatever the approach, though, it had better be amply intriguing.

H. Persistence

A prospect has only as much potential as the extent to which they are pursued. The importance of perseverance in follow-through activity can't be stressed strongly enough.

Get this. Advertisers frequently express surprise at how easily Agencies give up in soliciting them. Apparently, there is a substantial amount of new business going begging by default. There are several causes for blowing these opportunities:

- **Lack of Stomach for Following Through to the Jugular**
  It takes a killer instinct to go after new business. The successful thrust requires attack—not just scouting. Any approach less than this amounts to only motion—not action.

- **False Pride**
  Here is a typical example. An Agency had a very encouraging reaction to its pitch. So much so they thought they had scored. But was later informed they were rejected because of being considered too small. The Agency President was devastated by this seeming injustice. I asked if he countered with the fact that they aren't buying numbers— but rather, people. And his team convincingly demonstrated their talent and experience. His reply was, "I'm not going to kiss their ass."

  He lost perspective. There aren't any principles compromised by offering a logical rebuttal to a sales objection. The only shame is allowing temperament to overrule judgment—thereby succumbing to an obstacle instead of conquering it.

So don't get in the new business pool unless you intend to swim the entire length. Because the deep end is a helluva place to quit.

• Lack of Confidence

You'll get underway so enthusiastically on a very desirable prospect. But if they don't respond accordingly, and soon enough, you assume you are out of their league.

That's not the problem. Rather, you became discouraged too easily.

Regardless of how awesome they may seem, a concerted effort might ultimately pay off. This was proved in a novel manner by Cosmopolitan magazine.

It occurred to them that many exceptionally beautiful women are married to extremely homely men. Because of its editorial value, a survey was taken to find out *why*. The usual answer was startlingly simple: "He kept on asking me." Sure makes the point, doesn't it?

Anticipating you, the question is often raised as to what is the right amount of contact? What frequency, and for how long, before you antagonize the prospect?

You can follow-through to whatever extent desired—as long as it is of value to them.

There must be a worthwhile reason for every letter, phone call and meeting. And any such communication should provide useful information. In doing so, you won't wear out your welcome.

Don't be like the person who created 6-Up. Nothing happened, so he developed 8-Up. Again, nothing. So he quit on it. Establish a system for *follow-up*: based on frequency and appeal—with accountability assigned.

I. Extent of Follow-Through

When attempting to make contact, and unable to do so, there is a point beyond which you're beating your head against the wall. And these efforts could be used more productively elsewhere.

To what extent should you persevere before it comes useless? Experience has proved the following series of attempts to be the optimum amount:

1. Send introductory letter: applying the direction provided.

2. Follow up with a phone call one week later.

3. If not accepted or returned, phone again after one more week.

4. If you draw another blank, write this person an empathetic letter acknowledging their burden of being on a fast track—and set forth why they would benefit from responding to you.

5. A week hence, if still no response, give it one last shot by phone.

Then if this action is also futile, move on to another prospect who will have either more courtesy or curiosity. If these five attempts in five weeks don't stir this person, you're not going to get lucky. Instead, redirect your energies to a more deserving prospect.

> NOTE: Whenever leaving a message, in addition to your name and phone number, include an intriguing one-liner as an inducement to return your call.

J. Rejection

Sometimes though, despite these irresistible inducements and your dazzling charm, a prospect will still refuse to see you. Although his/her behavior is totally irrational, nevertheless it hurts.

You're in good company. For most people involved in the new business operation, the toughest aspect is dealing with rejection when contact is made. Yet, you can cope with this downer by realizing these two facts.

1. In solicitation activity, rejection is the norm. It will usually happen— and is not necessarily a reflection on your performance. Rather, it is a routine part of the prospect mating game. Thus, your efforts— and attitude—need be comparable to the horny guy standing on the street corner propositioning women. Sure, he got his face slapped a lot. But he scored now and then, too.

2. When turned down by a prospect, there is hardly ever anything *personal* in this. It is the concept of change that is being rejected—not you as an individual.

You needn't suffer a wounded psyche. Instead, recognize that a certain amount of failure comes with the territory. However, when acceptance does occur, how sweet it is!

K. Use of A.E.s

Knocking on doors is usually thought of as the responsibility of a few charmers in top Management. However, to whatever extent you restrict this function limits your potential. Instead, expand your contact activity by using your contact people: the Account Executives.

Here's how. Assign two appropriate prospects to each A.E. Based on the direction provided them, these would be "serviced." Then, a monthly report is required on action taken and progress made in setting up an appointment for a full-scale presentation. All that is being asked of the A.E. is to get the Agency in. Then you can bring up your heavy artillery.

This does not put an A.E. on the spot—or risk his/her status. If after a reasonable period of time a prospect is judged hopeless, this experience of itself is worthwhile since it precludes wasting time. Rather, the prospect is reclassified as a suspect, moved to the back burner—and the A.E. is assigned another without any loss of face.

At an Agency Network session, a President interrupted and stated, "That's not a good idea. I asked my account people to do just about the same thing—and they never followed through." So I mentioned, "Why didn't you *tell* them?" And he said, "Now *that's* a good idea!"

Beyond the broader opportunity this strategy offers, this targeted effort provides the efficiency usually lacking in new business activity.

L.   Unexpected Contact

A new business presentation is usually thought of in terms of being a structured event conducted in a conference room.

But how about when unexpected contact is made with a prospect? It might be on an airplane, at a cocktail party or on a golf course. You know: the ambush presentation. You don't have your flip chart, slides or reel—just opportunity. However, there may be only a few moments to take advantage of it.

Are you prepared with a succinct statement, compelling enough, for the prospect to be willing to explore this matter further? This could be only several sentences summarizing why your Agency is especially desirable. Therefore, don't rely on being able to react well when the opportunity arises. Rather, literally develop your "impromptu" statement for whatever the circumstance.

To assist in accomplishing this, poll your people on why they believe your Agency is preferable—in 25 words or less. This will provide a fresh interpretation of your strengths—and can inspire how to best capitalize on them. Then, a composite of their claims can be developed that will afford the most potent appeal you want to convey.

This will also furnish a valuable insight as to how your people perceive the Agency—and reveal any upgrading in their impressions found necessary.

By applying the above disciplines, you will all be speaking out of the same mouth—saying what you want said.

M. Gimmicks

Yet, a few words of caution regarding solicitation activity. Don't let your eagerness to score obscure good sense. Like mistaking desperate devices for aggressiveness.

Here is a pertinent example. Not long ago, a Chicago Agency President phoned me and asked, "How about lunch with me and my Exec. V.P.? We have a great idea for a new business program and want to bounce it off you." I said, "Sure"—figuring I'd learn something.

He opened by mentioning being quite bitter with his Account people because of their lack of initiative in the new business area. He went on to say, "Then I got introspective and it occurred that maybe it's because I didn't give them the necessary inspiration and direction. Well, now I'm going to do exactly that."

He then described his plan: Have each Account Executive conduct a blitz telephone campaign. Specifically, call five prospects a day, 25 per week, for four weeks—a total of 100 prospects.

I told him, "I've heard that before." And he countered with, "But these will be *structured* calls." He explained that they will all use the same tactic in opening with, "Hey, we just got the confidential news that you're going to change Agencies!" His rationale was that even if 99 out of 100 deny it, this is worth the coincidence of the 100th saying, "How did you find out? This was just decided yesterday at 4:00 PM."

But is it worth it? I told him, "Look, to 99 out of 100 prospects, you come across as the Agency that doesn't know what it's talking about. And the next time you contact them, they will suspect you of trying to trick them again."

This President hasn't asked me back. Actually, he couldn't. He isn't there anymore.

N. How Innovative?

Summing up, there are probably as many devices used for door-openers as there are Agencies.

Thus, the question comes up as to how creative can you get in solicitation activity? You can get as innovative as you wish—as long as it never demeans the Agency. If it does, that's not creative. That's dumb.

Like promising them a real dog-and-pony show. And coming in with a real dog and pony. A Boston Agency tried this tactic. The prospect had just installed new carpeting. They never got past the reception room.

Chapter 11

How and What to Flush Out of a Pre-Presentation Meeting

A. Perspective
B. Function/Purpose
C. Attendees' Report on Appeal
D. Strategy for Conduct
E. Prospect Expectations
F. Advertiser Changing Agency
G. Prospect's Marketing Needs/Objectives
H. Agency Function(s) Desired
I. Request for Spec
J. Compensation: Amount/Attitude
K. Prospect Audience at Presentation
L. Decision-Maker
M. Three Forms of Protection
N. Deciding Factor in Selection
O. Why Desirable Client?
P. Introductory "Leaver"
Q. Confirming Conference Report
R. Refusal to Furnish Information

A. Perspective

What is the *most* important requirement for landing a new account? Without a doubt, it is holding a pre-presentation meeting with the prospect. Whether the pitch is competitive or missionary, this action is essential to winning.

Since this may be begging the obvious, I won't belabor its necessity. Suffice it to say, though, it is incomprehensible to an advertiser as to how an Agency can put on a presentation without getting any reading from them first. If attempted, you're thought of as being a one-shot canvasser.

B. Function/Purpose

The *function* of the pre-presentation meeting is to obtain the information necessary to determine if and how to develop a presentation for this prospect. If you conclude they would be a desirable client, then the *purpose* of this meeting is to convince the prospect of why it would be worth their receiving a full-scale presentation from you—and schedule a date.

You aren't trying to land the account at this point. Only the opportunity for doing so. You want the circumstances in which you can give them your best shot—consisting of the combination of your people, program and place likeliest to succeed.

C. Attendees' Report on Appeal

Who would attend this pre-presentation meeting?
  From the Agency, these two people:

1. The executive at the management level who would be ultimately responsible for their account. (With all due respect to your President and Creative Director, this is the one person they want to meet more than any other in the Agency.) Specifically, the one who can take action on their behalf without having to get approval from anyone else.

2. Someone with a research orientation who is especially adept at conducting a probing interview—and can get into their heads.

From the prospect: Try to get as many as possible from their Selection Team to attend.

This experience should be followed by a brief report from your team on the appeal of this advertiser. All else notwithstanding, this should net down to their assessment of the following four key matters:

- prospect profitability

- expectations of Agency

- human equation

- presentation strategy necessary to win

It would then be summed up by a recommendation as to whether this is a go or no-go situation—with the reasons why.

This approach enables kissing or killing it while spending hardly any time or money on the prospect.

If they are sufficiently desirable, the information and impressions received will provide the direction on how to pursue them further—and by whom. If your reaction is negative, though, keep moving until you hit a prospect for whom you believe *it is worth going all out*—both in effort and expense.

D.   Strategy for Conduct

Advertisers claim that Agencies waste this meeting. It is used as a general warmup session, instead of obtaining the information necessary to develop the most appropriate presentation.

This is not a selling opportunity in the usual sense. Rather, you will impress them with the soundness of your questions. So don't ask for published information. Only that unobtainable elsewhere. Namely, their expectations of an Agency—not statistics. Otherwise, they will resent doing what is considered as your job.

I'm going to give you the ten factors plus one that you need to know regarding the prospect's policies and attitudes in order to put on a presentation. You needn't be reluctant to ask any of these questions because they all pertain to Agency performance and relationship.

It is evident to them that you aren't seeking any proprietary information. Only that necessary to determine whether this could be a mutually satisfactory arrangement.

Work from these factors at the meeting—thereby leaving nothing to chance. Their answers then become the basis for your prospect situation analysis.

In fact, send the prospect a list of these 10 factors prior to the meeting. It will enable them to provide better prepared, more reliable answers. And this will protect your contact from being embarrassed by any inquiry for which they don't have an immediate reply.

Next, at this meeting, *you* initiate the questioning. Even if prospects refuse to supply all the information desired, they will still respect your professionalism.

However, it is unlikely they won't cooperate. Get this. Advertisers often express surprise and disappointment at how few questions Agencies ask of them.

They *want* to talk about their business—and the Agency's involvement. And they are particularly impressed by those with the smarts to seek their input in both respects.

Also, throughout, be alert to their use of any inside buzz words or expressions in their responses. This can be subsequently played back to them in the presentation—enabling you to come across as being their kind of people.

E. Prospect Expectations

Here is where to start. To develop a new business presentation likeliest to penetrate, it must be based on what the *prospect* perceives as their needs—not what *you* assume these should be. Remember: It is not a matter of what you have to sell. Rather, it is what they want to buy.

Therefore, your first question to the prospect has to be, "Have you defined what you *need* from an Agency; the involvement expected of them? And the reasons *why*."

Their answers will clue you on whether you want the account. And if so, it provides the insight to what approach will most appeal to them.

Granted, it is improbable that they will have formally set forth the attributes desired of their new Agency. However, they aren't about to admit it. But they will be grateful to your Agency for providing this professional direction. And you will be recalled as the one who has already been of value to them.

This initial meeting also offers an excellent opportunity to find out what the prospect *really* wants from an Agency. So since this is a get-acquainted session, you can informally inquire as to what they consider their present Agency's three greatest strengths. Those most admired and respected. Then *wait* for a reply. No matter how long it takes.

In all likelihood, their answer will consist of what they *hope* to receive from an Agency—but aren't necessarily getting. This desire can then be exploited in your presentation; capitalizing on the incumbent's inadequacies—and featuring your dedication to fully satisfy their expectations of an Agency.

NOTE: When soliciting an account, any reference to the incumbent should always be as their "present" Agency. This registers the transient nature of this relationship. If the prospect picks up on this tactic, you can justify its use because of being aware that "No Agency owns any client." They can only be wonderfully impressed by this attitude.

In fact, while you have them thinking, assist them by confiding the six strengths that should be sought in an Agency. Coincidentally, these also happen to be *your* six strengths (or five or seven). Then, of course, these are referred to in presentation—capitalizing on the knowledge you instilled in them.

F. Advertiser Changing Agency

In the case of an advertiser who is planning to change Agencies, find out *why*.

Don't settle for rumor or gossip. What actually happened can be learned directly from the prospect if you convey your intent is constructive and will enable developing a more appropriate presentation. In turn, they will be inclined to cooperate in revealing this background because of wanting to reduce the risk of this problem recurring.

As proof of this, an advertiser recently told me of their experience with Agencies before settling upon their present one.

When their budget became big enough to warrant retaining an Agency, it was decided they needed the most creative shop obtainable. After an extensive Agency search, they were satisfied that the one selected best met this qualification. However, several months later, they discovered that the billing was terribly fouled up. As this advertiser put it, "It looked like the Agency operated out of a cigar box." A few months later, having had enough of this casual bookkeeping, they fired them.

Then this advertiser decided maybe it would be better to settle for one not quite as creative—but more business-like. This compromise didn't work either.

The third time around, they notified the candidates that the primary requisite for Agency selection was: The one with the most efficient Billing Department." Then they parenthetically mentioned, "And if we get some good Creative with it, this would be a welcome bonus."

This drives home that the advertiser's *reason* for changing Agencies becomes the thrust of your presentation. And there is another moral to this story: While Creative can be instrumental in landing an account, it is too much to expect this function alone to keep it for you.

G.   Prospect's Marketing Needs/Objectives

Next, ask the prospect to provide any general indication of their short and long-range objectives. Then, as evidence of your desire to get to the guts of their needs, inquire as to what they consider to be their most critical marketing problem. Whatever information they furnish will clue you on which of your successes to present. Those most relevant and meaningful to them.

In particular, case histories that could be related directly to the prospect's interests. And how they would specifically benefit from your experience and ability.

The most obvious use of this strategy occurs when an Agency loses a client. Then every previously conflicting account immediately becomes fair game. And the Agency details chapter and verse the value of their hands-on experience and proved performance.

H.   Agency Function(s) Desired

Usually there is a certain Agency function that the selection team is especially impressed by or for which they feel a particular need. (Creative? Media? Research? Collateral?)

Determine this interest in advance so it can be emphasized accordingly in presentation. How do you find out? *Ask them.* Because that is what they want to hear about. And then treat their reply as gospel!

Here is tangible proof of why this action is essential. Not long ago a major beer account conducted an Agency review. (To their credit, they were decent enough to level with the incumbent on not having a prayer— thereby saving them the considerable expense of competing in a no-win situation.)

Upon narrowing down to two finalists, the Senior V.P. at the brewery in charge of the search mentioned to me, "It's going to be interesting to see how literally both of them take the pre-presentation input I furnished." He went on to explain, "I told each that what I want of my new Agency is *Creative leadership.* I want to be taken by the hand through the Creative process." Then he came down heavily with the admonition, "Don't tell me how well you buy Media. I'll tell *you* what Media to buy. And if I need Research, I know where to get it."

Being curious as to how the finalists would deal with this autocratic direction, I followed through after the presentations were made.

The Senior V.P. told me, "Agency 'A' who pride themselves on their Marketing capacity did an outstanding job. They featured how shrewdly they select and buy Media. The profundity of their Research service. Outstanding." He then capped off his reaction with, "But I couldn't care less."

By contrast, Agency "B" came in and told the brewery team what they wanted to hear about: Creative. And they won the account. This does not mean that is all they presented. The ground rules, though, did set forth the amount of emphasis and sequence for this subject.

Thus Agency "B" opened with Creative—and gave it the attention expected. Next, they followed with how capably their Research operation will serve Creative. Then they continued with how their Media function will provide the best environment for the Creative message. And the same related technique was used for the other services worth covering.

This approach enabled Agency "B" to present whatever they desired. Because the total presentation was *Creative-oriented*. By playing with the stacked deck dealt them, Agency "B" won.

I. Request for Spec

If a prospect requests speculative creative material, find out precisely what they mean by this. There can be a substantial variation between your interpretation of extent and that actually desired. From their clarification, you can then decide on the appropriate effort and expense, avoiding extravagance and unnecessary work.

Your on-premise activity, however, would be influenced by two factors: time and staff availability. These matters will govern the extent to which you would farm out your ideas for execution.

Sometimes, upon sharp-penciling their request, you will conclude that the expense required cannot be justified. Agencies are discovering, though, that they can return with a typed list of what their out-of-pocket expenses would be—*and offer to split it with them*. And on occasion, the prospect will say, "Okay, that's fair enough." Thus, sometimes spec creative can be affordable. Further, this prospect involvement can set the stage for their investing in your services thereafter.

If, however, they refuse, that tells you how sincere they are—and what kind of client they would be.

Incidentally, if the prospect throws up to you that the other Agencies are willing to do this for nothing, you can matter-of-factly observe, "Well, they ought to know what their work is worth."

J. Compensation: Amount/Attitude

The most critical development in the new business area is that you can expect much more negotiation on compensation. The line has been broken on 15% uniformity. What had previously been a standoff in now no longer sacred. Thus, the financial factor has become an important criterion in Agency selection.

Understandably, advertisers are strongly opinioned regarding Agency compensation. So espousing a contrary method can be a deadly blunder.

This especially applies to Agencies who use some concession as a selling device, offering bait like, "Have we got a deal for you"—without first having checked out how the prospect would feel about it. This tactic gives the impression that your work isn't worth what you charge for it. Most advertisers realize there is no such thing as a free lunch.

It comes down to this. It is bad enough to be conned into an arrangement in which some of your income is taken from you. It is even worse giving it away.

Therefore, it is essential that you find out the prospect's present method of Agency payment—and, as important, their attitude toward it. (They may harbor some unexpressed resentment which can be brought to the surface.) This is the *first* thing you should learn about a prospect. It will also prepare you for whatever bargaining occurs.

This is the time—*in advance*—to find out whether a satisfactory profit can be made. If so, they are *your* kind of people. However, if it is concluded that their terms are unacceptable, you can save the time, effort and expense of developing a presentation which could cause you to lose by winning.

A tactic currently being used by one of the nation's largest retail chains in a Midwestern state illustrates the importance of this advance knowledge.

They have been contacting local Agencies and informing them that, "We have been watching your progress and are quite impressed with your performance. In fact, we would even welcome a presentation from you."

Being romanced by this mammoth retailer, the Agencies approached would salivate. And then, because of seeming to have an inside track, they spent a bundle on the pitch. (Comped-up layouts, videotaped commercials—the full nine yards.)

Afterwards, the scenario would conclude with the Agency being told, "You have confirmed the soundness of our judgment. Thus, we hereby award you our account for this State." Then comes the catch. "Now, because of the vast prestige of being associated with us, and the tremendous potential it offers, undoubtedly you will be amenable to working for 5%."

Thus far, none of the Agencies have touched it. But they were out a substantial amount of time and money. Why didn't they check out the financial arrangement beforehand? This is inexcusable—unless you can afford to run your Agency as a hobby.

Sometimes the question is raised, "But what if they won't tell you?" Then pack up and move on. You wouldn't take a job without knowing the salary.

Have I belabored this matter of profit? No way. An Agency would make such a poor hooker because it gives so much away.

K.   Prospect Audience at Presentation

Although Agencies are diligent in defining client markets, they seldom bother to adequately explore their prospect audiences. A little digging here could unearth the secret for winning the account.

To begin with, basic as it may seem, find out how many the prospect will have in attendance—who they are, along with the function performed by each. And if possible, learn their pecking order.

Then obtain one usable fact about each member of the selection team. (With the proliferation of "Who's Who" books, you can probably find one or more of them in this source.) Having this additional familiarity will provide another means for involving them. *Without involvement, a presentation is just a recitation.*

By contrast, as one Agency head observed, "The more the prospect talks, the more appealing we become." This background will also enable you to relate to the selection team and present to them as acquaintances rather than strangers.

L.   Decision-Maker

Among those on the selection team, obviously, one has more authority than the others. (The Ad Manager may be responsible for *recommending* the Agency to be chosen. But who *approves*?) Find out who the decision-maker is—and how to appeal to him accordingly.

Here's how. It's likely that the individual at the prospect who would provide the pre-presentation input would be the Ad Manager—or somebody at that peer level in the pecking order. You can't brazenly ask him *who* the decision-maker will be in Agency selection. It probably won't be he. And being reluctant to admit this, it is possible he will give you misleading information.

Therefore, instead of confronting him head on, ask *how* the decision will be made. If asked what you mean, you can guide him toward the desired answer by elaborating, " . . . by committee or an individual?" If the Ad Manager hedges with, "Committee," you can target tighter by inquiring as to who would exert the most influence among them. By this process of elimination, you should be able to deduce where the power lies.

If you have any doubt regarding the validity of the prospect person identified, and want confirmation, here is an informal—but effective—means for doing so. At the presentation, note the prospect individual to whom they direct most conversation. And correspondingly, the one who is doing the most listening. If this is the same person, that's the yes-or-no man.

Next, flush out his career background so you can *speak* his language.

- If he came up through Production, compare the disciplines applied to your work with their Product Quality Control.

- A Financial person will spark to any reference to Return on Investment.

- And if his career began in Sales, use the phrase "sales support" synonymously with advertising.

Here is an example of an Agency whose homework really paid off. They found out that the decision-maker at the prospect was the Exec. V.P. and he came up through sales. But he had a total aversion to advertising—even though they had a media budget of over $2,000,000.

The Agency opened their spec Creative presentation by featuring the "sales support" proposed for Newspaper. When their presenter moved on to the next layout, the Exec. V.P. interrupted by asking, "What's that supposed to be: advertising for Magazines?" And he was told, "No, we recommend that you concentrate with 'sales support' only for this medium. Now if we can dim the lights . . ." And the Exec. V.P. said, "Here come the ads for Television, right?" This time the presenter replied, "On the contrary. We suggest the exclusive use of 'sales support' here."

Sounds hokey? This Agency landed the account. Because they came across as being *his kind of people*. No principles were compromised. They just spoke his language.

Yet, even with having done this important bird-dogging, don't overlook the possible power behind the power. Because sometimes the source of approval in Agency selection isn't the decision-maker.

A $9,000,000 Agency just learned of this possibility the hard way. They spent $50,000 on a new business pitch for a loose $5,000,000 account because the Agency President had such a close personal relationship with his counterpart at the advertiser.

Further encouraging an Agency of this size to dig so deep into the till was that the prospect's president confided to them what he expected of his new Agency: in regard to personnel, operations and creative approach. Having this confidential insight, they assumed they had it made.

Then the prospect's president delegated responsibility for the agency search to his V.P.-Advertising—with instructions that his friend's shop be included. However, this responsibility also included establishing judging criteria—which turned out to be significantly different from the specifications of his president. According to the revised ground rules, a different Agency proved preferable. The Ad V.P.'s documented justification of his choice prevailed—and the favorite son candidate was defeated.

The explanation given by the ex-prospect's president to his Agency buddy provided a retrospective reminder of corporate life. Namely, if the president were to overrule his subordinate's decision, it would strip this person of his authority and stature internally—and seriously weaken his hand in dealing with the new Agency. And the head man wasn't about to cause these problems. Thus, when it came down to deciding between backing his Ad Director versus accommodating an Agency friend, the wired-in Agency was short-circuited.

The upshot is that the Agency with the supposed clout was lulled into a false sense of security because of having mistaken authority for action. So, of course, cultivate whoever will "officially" okay the Agency picked. But never at the expense of convincing those who will supply the reasons for the recommendation made.

M.   Three Forms of Protection

It would be wise to smoke out whether any members of the selection team have ever served time at an Agency. If so, prepare for closer than usual scrutiny. In particular, guard against being cut up by someone who may try to look good at your expense. Brace yourself. It happens.

And speaking of smoking, find out if there is any objection to it. If it offends anyone, this is a handicap you don't need. To play it safe, there are Agencies with heavy smokers who have a policy of total abstinence while at the presentation.

There is one more matter that is seldom considered—and well should be. It can directly influence the thrust of your pitch. What is the selection team's experience in conducting Agency searches? If they have participated in this event previously, they will be more performance-oriented. If this is their initial exposure to new business presentations, their reaction to your people will dominate.

Determine how long the prospect has been with their present and previous Agencies. And their members past amount of involvement in the search process. Then adapt your appeal accordingly.

Remember: your presentation has to be customized not only for the prospect corporately, but also for any individual's degree of sophistication. With the content and conduct of your presentation geared to be most appropriate, the prospect will better relate and be more receptive to your Agency's message.

N. Deciding Factor in Selection

Thus far, I have furnished nine of the ten factors required. Finally, here is the one you need know the most.

Wind up by asking, "What will be the deciding factor in Agency selection?" Then offer direction. Ask them, "Beyond all the judging criteria established, if allowed only one ultimate consideration, what would it be?" Do they feel strongest about:

- agency top Management involvement?
- extensive Agency contribution to their Marketing function?
- cutting-edge Creativity?

This will help them jell their thinking. And their answer will become the key thrust for your presentation.

Another couple of pluses. Your assistance will be a catalyst for a prompt decision being made. And since they probably didn't think of this factor either, your Agency will further benefit from tipping them off to its worth.

O. Why Desirable Client?

And now for that *plus one* that I referred to. The ten factors detailed will provide you with the necessary input on the prospect's needs and selection strategy. This will help you prove why your Agency is best for them. *But are they right for you?*

Sure, you want to land the account. But is it worth the price? For instance, would the income be commensurate with the demands on you? Finding out afterwards that they are unaffordable can be brutally expensive.

Thus, ask them, "What makes you a desirable client?" Besides the unique insight this will furnish, it will also clue you on what kind of people they are. If you get good vibes, you can get under way positively—without reservations.

P. Introductory "Leaver"

Leave the prospect with a brief description of your Agency, clients and personnel who would be assigned if awarded the account. And include the six strengths (yours) that should be sought in an Agency. However, this written description shouldn't steal any of your forthcoming thunder. Finally, even though the cover of this "leave behind" may be a stock item, the package must give the impression of having been developed especially for them.

This wrap-up gets the relationship underway and enables devoting more time to the prospect in the presentation.

Q. Confirming Conference Report

Upon returning to your office, promptly send the prospect a Conference Report confirming the input they furnished. This will reduce the risk of any misunderstandings.

It will also provide advance indication of your thoroughness. This tactic can be quite impressive because advertisers accuse Agencies of doing a lousy job on Conference Reports. By contrast, you fired one off to them before even having the Account.

R. Refusal to Furnish Information

Granted, sometimes a prospect planning to change Agencies will refuse to meet to supply this necessary background information. Ostensibly this is because of not wanting to bias or give any candidate an advantage.

If this occurs, counter with the fact that your objective is to develop the most appropriate presentation. That most meaningful and pertinent to them—thereby making the most productive use of their time. You won't offend them by registering your awareness of the importance of being relevant—and respect for their time. On this basis, they might relent.

If, however, this rationale doesn't work, ask for 15 minutes on the phone for him to answer the questions that will enable customizing a presentation for them. If he won't cooperate in this respect either, ask if you can *send* him your list of ten questions. His response could be furnished by mail or in a subsequent phone call, whichever means is most convenient for him.

Then if he still refuses, the hell with him. Shooting from the hip is tough enough. And without ammunition, you would die there. Instead, move on to another prospect—with whom you would at least have a fighting chance.

It nets down to this. *If you can't get any pre-presentation input, you can't put on a presentation.* Because you can't sell a service without knowing what the buyer wants.

Chapter 12

Assessment of Agency Required Prior to Getting Under Way

A. Perspective
B. Agency Name
C. Agency Image
D. Vitality

A. Perspective

To enable planning from strength, analyze your Agency as calculatingly as if it were a client's product or service. Then implement the findings for a more successful new business program.

B. Agency Name

Let's start with the first factor by which advertisers are influenced: *Your name*.

How well is it known? Are you one Agency, invisible, with anonymity for all? And as important, what impression does it convey? As reported in the Ad Agency Quarterly Survey of Agency Reputations, there is a direct correlation between the awareness of an Agency and the respect for them. Therefore, your Agency name should be a salesman—not a secret.

Be they right or wrong, advertisers have pre-conceived notions about many Agencies. And if the attitude toward yours ranges from apathy to contempt, it is unlikely you'll get a day in court regardless of how fascinating your approach.

This was driven home—painfully—to a supposedly dynamic new business man. The Agency was scoring so well that he actually believed he was solely responsible for the success achieved. As a result, he confronted the Agency president with the ultimatum that he be made President—and have his name put on the door.

I'll spare you the details, but his desk was cleaned out for him. He did relocate—a number of times. However, he couldn't catch fire again anywhere.

I ran into him after several subsequent tours of duty. Always curious regarding how a rainmaker fares afterwards, I inquired as to how he was getting along. In a burst of frustration (and rare humility), he said, "I never realized how his name opened doors for me."

What is your Agency name doing on behalf of your new business effort? And how well are you capitalizing on it? Your goal should be to create enough favorable awareness among prospects desired, so when the time comes for change, your Agency will be included among those invited to present.

C. Agency Image

What's the word on the street about *your* Agency?

Advertisers planning to change Agencies usually base their invitation list on some vague impressions received. Often, no more authentic than rumors or gossip.

And they have developed definite opinions. Of particular significance is the basis for the advertisers' assumptions. These are formed according to not only *what* you do—but *how* you do it.

What's your Agency's image? Acquiescent; an implementer? Or are you regarded as having the courage and charisma that will appeal to the new accounts desired?

For that matter, how do you improve your image? Land two new big accounts. This makes you a hot Agency—and it is assumed you must be doing an outstanding job. This success, then, is highly merchandisable to prospects.

In the interim, though, level with yourself on your character of operation. So that before trying to tell someone else how to run their business, "Physician, heal thyself."

The importance of this warrants more than acknowledgement. Internal action should be taken. Specifically, have all employees cite one single area requiring Agency improvement—and why.

To assure compliance, this assignment is to be in writing. However, for the candor desired, they are not to identify themselves.

This will provide uninhibited, constructive criticism. Then, the combination of these replies will set forth your needs—and priority of action to better gear your Agency to attract new business.

D.   Vitality

For the vitality sought by prospects, it is necessary to realize that this must be a constantly regenerating process. Fresh ideas don't come from a stale Agency.

As impetus to reach and maintain this level, periodically survey your people to determine what they assume the Agency doesn't have that they would like to boast about. Further, in what respects do they believe the Agency is at a disadvantage in soliciting new business. This amounts to probing for whatever areas in which the Agency is considered lacking from a personnel and operational standpoint.

The sum of their responses should then form your list of objectives of what needs to be accomplished to enhance your appeal to prospects.

Chapter 13

Planning Required to Prepare a Winning Presentation

A. Perspective

It takes more than the will to win new business. It also takes the will to *prepare* to win. Because the same quality of effort required to keep accounts is what it takes to land new ones.

Despite this, development of the new business presentation is the most disorganized activity in the shop. This is because circumstances require it being sandwiched in between client work—and it is usually conducted on a crash basis.

Although somehow the various aspects seem to fall into line, this is despite conditions. In retrospect, it is often discovered there were oversights which lessened its effectiveness.

For optimum impact, it is necessary to begin with the basics by applying the following controls. You know what these are—but seldom literally use them. Put these disciplines to work for you—and minimize the frantic factor.

B. Three Controls

Traffic

Although a key executive is in charge of the overall presentation project, he or she cannot ride herd on every detail with certainty. Therefore, until your new business manager is selected, it is essential that a person performing this function for client's work also be assigned to keep tabs on and coordinate every phase—assuring that the strategy is implemented and material prepared.

Checklist

All responsibilities, materials and devices involved should be itemized with logistics established for compliance.

Importantly, note that in addition to the items, it should also set forth the personnel accountable for each. This will also serve as an inventory for use prior to leaving for the presentation—thereby precluding any sins of omission.

Timetable

Priorities for all components should be set at inception—rather than competing for time when the work is being performed. And because of the interdependence of the variety of factors, completion dates must be strictly observed. This will prevent any "Oh my God" oversights and useless fault-finding.

Granted, the above procedure isn't a shocker. Only your laxness in implementing it. Therefore, in the crunch of developing the presentation, don't succumb to the expedient of skipping any of these necessary routines.

There are enough ways for fouling up without depending on a presentation that was somehow pulled together. Remember: Victory doesn't begin at the podium. It starts with all the activity it took to get there.

C. Fact Book/Source

The development of new business presentations is becoming too sophisticated to start with a hunch. You need to begin by assembling a prospect data base.

Specifically, prepare a Fact Book containing all data of consequence on the prospect's Company, Industry and Market. This will provide you with the insight necessary—and serve as evidence at the presentation of the professionalism that can be expected if you are awarded the account. (Bring this with you and use it as a prop.)

The following sources can furnish you with practically any information needed:

- Logically, begin with the advertiser. (Check on whether they have a P.R. Department.) Get a copy of their Annual Report and any promotional material published. Obviously, this is what they want you to know.

- Your next most valuable source is their Trade Association—a key function of which is compiling all possible market data.

- If your company subscribes to a computerized information service, fully mine this mother lode.

- If they are listed, get a spec sheet on them from your Stock Broker. This will supply you with worthwhile financial information.

- Also, if appropriate, pull a D&B. (But take it with a grain of salt.)

- Make use of your Public Library—which has developed an extensive information retrieval system.

- Take advantage of the library at Ad Age. If they haven't got what you are looking for, or can't find it, it probably doesn't exist.

- Cultivate the Financial Editors of newspapers in the prospect's headquarters city. They can provide you with another perspective that could be capitalized upon.

- Check the Media reps—however, recognizing that their attitude toward the prospect will be influenced by whether or not they are getting a schedule from them.

- Finally, if you belong to the A.A.A.A. or an Agency Network, by all means take advantage of your membership to receive whatever information, help and support they can supply.

Remember, when soliciting new business, it's not only *who* you know, it's also *what* you know.

D. Research

Although it is a routine consideration for clients, not too many Agencies conduct focus interviews or group dynamics sessions with people representative of the prospect's market. The revelations produced by those taking this initiative, and the plans it inspired, have resulted in a much higher rate of closing. Because more ideas come from information than inspiration.

For example, advertisers have informed me of instances in which they had no intention of changing Agencies. But the information furnished in presentation was so valuable, and the action proposed so worthwhile, they couldn't resist switching to take advantage of it.

Besides the necessary familiarity this research technique provides, it offers a valuable inducement for them to move—now. This potency warrants considering its appropriateness for any new business activity. Because at the very least, it is a great door-opener.

This research will identify the prospect's *needs*. Your pre-presentation efforts will flush out their *wants*. Now go the final payout step: In addition to whatever field research you perform, arrange to spend some time traveling with their field personnel. Then, in presentation, your name-dropping of their people on the front line can be very impressive. (For elaboration and results, see Chapter 15.)

Having this combination of insight, while your competitors may come across as having done their homework, you will give the impression of having written the book.

Finally, after conducting all the orthodox methods for researching the prospect, there is also some cloak and dagger work that can pay off. All the information accumulated notwithstanding, this approach might reveal how they *actually* operate and the kind of people they *really* are.

It's dicey. But if reliable, the value of that exposed can transcend all the prospect's pronouncements and numbers.

Here it is. If the advertiser has decided to switch, get a reading on them from their previous Agency. Understandably, the worth of their horse's-mouth input will depend on the conditions under which the severance occurred.

If the Agency resigned the account because of having landed a larger conflicting one, or had to divest it due to merger, they will probably be objective in their reporting to you. But if the Agency was fired for any reason, they are bound to be bitter to some extent. And that confided will be biased accordingly.

Yet, it is worth exploring this source. Being sensitive to the circumstances, you can interpret their response and determine its degree of validity. And then cautiously decide how to apply this information to your selling activity.

E.   Presentation: Visuals

Having done your homework, your next objective is to develop a presentation that will prove why your Agency is best for them. And you have such a great opportunity to distinguish your Agency from the others.

Advertisers claim most Agency pitches are stereotyped—characterized by a dull sameness. Or as it is also described: a same dullness. This could be due to the incestuous nature of this business—or the misconception that it takes a particular type of presenter.

Break the pattern of what has become regulation format for the treatment of subject matter and its appearance.

This especially applies to the graphics of your presentation. The prospect's first reaction is: "Would we want this work to represent us?" They feel its visual effect is the first and possibly most important clue to your creativity. In effect, your slides, poster cards and flip charts are considered ads for your Agency. How well do they compare to those to be shown which were created for clients? If less appealing, it is a letdown—and your creativity level is considered inconsistent.

Therefore, for the impression desired, involve your creative people at inception in the development of your presentation. Their responsibility would range from its design to the visual communication of your message.

And then, have a senior Art Director critically appraise the results as if these were actual ads requiring his/her signature prior to being released for publication. That's the kind of discipline that should be applied for your presentation to pass its physical.

Typically, presentation materials (slides, poster boards, etc.) are produced at the last moment. If this crash effort prevents preparing what you could be most proud of, don't go through with it. Otherwise, you'll be representing your Agency with inferior work. Then, regardless of how dynamic your message, it will suffer from a weak depiction of it.

As a result of being placed at this disadvantage, you'll seriously lessen your chance of winning. And adding insult to injury, the prospect will trash your Agency to their peers at other advertisers as the one who came in with sloppy visuals.

F. Presentation: Content

As to the content of your presentation, advertisers are expecting it to be more profound.

You can't count on last year's approach anymore. Namely, basing it on your ability to create outstanding advertising ideas—and trying to overwhelm them with examples by the pound. This is no longer enough.

From here on you need to demonstrate your capacity to develop a great Marketing Plan—supported by an outstanding advertising application. As such, this furnishes the evidence of the *totality* of your Agency's involvement that prospects are looking for.

Here's the situation. The advertiser is no longer mesmerized by any of the glamorous definitions of advertising. They have now become coldly realistic regarding its role: *to fulfill a marketing objective*.

Under these circumstances, how compatible is your thinking with theirs? If otherwise, then they will conclude you are out-of-date—and out of contention.

G. Presentation: Value

You're a finalist for a very desirable account. The prospect assumes that any of those qualifying from this esteemed group would be acceptable. Now, who would be preferable?

Thus, a key objective in presentation is to distinguish your Agency from the others. In particular, that you are more memorable—favorably so. However, although they may have loved you, this might not be enough for them to agree to marriage.

Thus, a prime requisite for presentation is its *value* to the prospect. Sure, you will concentrate on communicating "Why our Agency is best for you." Yet, was there anything in its content that they could benefit from—now? Did they *learn* anything? This contribution provides a very meaningful recollection of your shop.

Therefore, build some gems of information into your pitch that the prospect can use. Then, when applied, they will recall—and be grateful to your Agency—for having made them look good. And their appreciation is bound to provide you with a competitive edge. So while promising a better future, deliver now.

H.   Creative Strategy

There is a constant dilemma when an advertiser changing Agencies requires a Creative shootout from the finalists.

If this account is that desirable as to warrant the expense, what's your strategy?

• Develop the approach believed to be in their best interest?

• Or what you assume is likeliest to land the account?

Bet on your convictions. Give them your best shot. Because spec Creative should lead, not follow.

If you try to second-guess their desires, you could wind up shooting yourself in the foot. Further, there is the risk of the prospect being able to sense that your work was created to sell them—rather than their market.

Therefore, go with the concept on which you would spend your own money. You'll be more convincing in presentation. And be able to field questions with greater authority.

So lead from your strength—rather than pandering to what might be their weakness. Your odds on scoring are much better. And even if you lose, what you created will be so dynamic it could be highly appealing to another prospect in the same field. Particularly, one more perceptive.

I.   Three Forms of Protection

Better find out about these three land mines when planning your new business presentation.

Conveying a knowledge of the prospect's Company, Industry or Market can be a valuable tactic. Because your experience in these areas forms the basis for their confidence in your Agency. Such being the case, be sure you know what you're talking about. Particularly, in these three respects:

Statistics

Obviously, the prospect is intimately familiar with their numbers. Thus, any error causes whatever you say to be suspect. And be especially careful when referring to those they live with.

For example, when you started developing your presentation for them two months ago, you found that their Share of Market was 18.6%. And to show your familiarity with their operation, you mention such in presentation. But actually, this figure has since dropped to 12.4%. And it's inconceivable to them how you can be wrong on so critical a matter.

Therefore, if you are going to quote any numbers, verify them just leaving for the presentation. And mention the source—to provide authority and attribute responsibility.

Vernacular

Be adequately familiar with their trade talk. Any mistaken use indicates you don't know their business.

A prime example is the case of the Agency that learned that the President of a very large advertiser had become disenchanted with their Agency—but not yet enough to let the word out on the street. Fortunately, the Agency had a 3rd party contact who was able to arrange for a presentation to the President—and figured they had it made. Because he would be very receptive—and there wasn't any competition. Thus, they figuratively went all out with a full-blown dog and pony show.

Since the Agency's approach was based on unusual prospect circumstances, here is a brief description of their operation.

First, it's a wine company. For that matter, they make very cheap wine. In fact, research has found that the primary location of consumption is on curbs.

As a result, the Agency came up with an intriguing Creative concept. This consisted of depicting the wine being imbibed in the most posh surroundings. And it featured uncharacteristically beautiful people—always in formal attire.

However, one-third of the way through the presentation, the president of the wine company interrupted and said, "Pack up. All you've demonstrated is an ignorance of our business."

What I didn't tell you was the headline for the ads—which was very appropriate to the graphics: "The rich wine!" If anyone at the Agency had taken a few moments and checked with editorial at their local beverage journal, they would have learned that in this industry, the word "rich" means "fattening." And no advertiser is going to switch to an Agency that couldn't bother to do such basic homework.

Marketing

Finally, if you're going to tout strategy, then first find out how they operate.

For instance, a couple of summers ago, the Michigan Apple Commission was up for grabs. They had a cattle call. One of the Agencies based their presentation on having developed an approach for investing the prospect's budget in the shrewdest, most economical manner.

Expectedly, the Commissions's antenna vibrated to this opportunity. And after having piqued their interest, the Agency revealed that this would be accomplished by concentrating the total expenditure in the State of Michigan.

The Commission Chairman said, "My God, how can you recommend that when 80% of our crop is shipped out of State?" Well, before anyone from the Agency could throw themselves on the grenade, the Chairman announced, "Next."

Therefore, any error—be it statistical, or in respect to trade talk, or regarding marketing—can blow the credibility of your entire presentation. So make judicious use of this tactic—because you can't be too careful when venturing into their area of expertise.

J.   Rehearsal

The largest single cause of presentation failure is a lack of adequate rehearsal. No argument there.

Yet, agencies use a variety of excuses to avoid rehearsing. The list is usually headed by: "No time." As a result, the rehearsal consists of whatever is conducted in the elevator on the way down.

However, the time factor isn't the *real* reason for sloughing off on a complete run-through. It is often more deep-rooted than that. Rather, it's awfully tough performing in front of your co-workers. Your palms will never be sweatier than in this environment.

However, after having survived this ordeal, you can go into the actual presentation with the confidence this baptism of fire will provide. And the knowledge that the worst is behind you. This preparation will then enable you to do yourself proud.

If the conduct of this dry-run is just a recitation, though, it fails to take into account the make-or-break factor in presentation; prospect participation. Regardless of how polished your delivery, they can devastate you with a zinger.

A key function of the rehearsal is throwing these zingers at your presenters. Cutting them up in rehearsal can be merciful compared to the prospect's version of the Spanish Inquisition.

To cope with this, I know of an Agency who compiles an ongoing list of bizarre prospect questions and comments that have occurred in previous presentations. It is then used to prepare their team for actual combat. (This procedure will also prevent your rehearsal from degenerating into a free-for-all vendetta. And preclude any of your participants from taking this grilling personally.)

I'm told that after these maneuvers, even green troops behave like seasoned veterans in battle.

Under these circumstances, you can't afford any presenters who are thin-skinned. Granted, this simulated combat can be a traumatic experience. But being forearmed, it will protect them against any low blows by members of the selection team. And better your people should learn to deal with getting shot at in your office rather than at the prospect's.

Be sensitive to the prospect being quick to discover and lose respect for fouled-up timing, repetition among speakers, missing props, etc. Therefore, this full dry-run to protect against unprofessionalism need be provided for as much as any component of your presentation. This would include individual speaker participation, operation of A-V equipment, use of props and display of material. In doing so, this will furnish a synergistic team effect—which is certainly more impressive than a series of individual efforts.

Bear in mind that the purpose of a rehearsal is to plan and evaluate the content and delivery of a presentation. However, it can be only as productive as the rehearsal technique employed.

Here is what it takes to achieve the results desired. It is based on my being contacted recently by a very frustrated head of new business at a hungry Agency. Seems as if they are doing everything necessary. As a result, no difficulty in getting up to bat. But they usually strike out.

He had concluded the problem must be with the presentation. Yet, this is baffling too, because they are so diligent about rehearsing.

Since the planning of the presentation was so thorough, the content that relevant and the materials very impressive, it occurred to me that the culprit might be the *conduct* of their rehearsal. This Director of New Business Development took strong exception to my assumption by stating, "That can't be it. I personally rehearse each presenter. Individually and privately."

I then asked if all the components are pulled together for a complete dry run—*simulating the actual presentation*? He replied that it wasn't necessary because each knows his/her part so well. And then summed up with, "Besides, it precludes anyone being embarrassed by criticism."

This confirmed my hunch. The Agency didn't lose in presentation. They had already blown it by their *method* of rehearsal. For these reasons:

- Their practicing isn't how the presentation will be conducted. Thus, they will be winging it in a situation in which there isn't any room for error.

- The Agency's approach consists of a series of individual efforts. This forfeits the synergism produced by a team effect.

- This technique precludes any team interaction. Its absence sacrifices compounding your activity.

- The upshot is the impression of a canned pitch. And this is one of the worst indictments by a prospect.

For perspective, this Agency lost sight of the purpose of rehearsal. *Its function is to stage a winning presentation.* Not parade a series of reciters.

Therefore, your preparation needs to literally be a *dress rehearsal.* Anything short of this thoroughness is the extent to which you handicap yourself. And *no* Agency can afford to concede *any* advantage to another.

Here is still another key function that needs to be performed in rehearsal.

Beginning with your entrance for the presentation, it is imperative that every Agency person stay strictly relevant to your message. Particularly if the prospect stipulates duration.

Those at Leo Burnett diligently apply this discipline because of a costly experience. Some years ago, after considerable pursuit, they succeeded in lining up a presentation with a very desirable advertiser. And were granted 45 minutes for this purpose.

Coincidentally, just prior to this event, they hired a new Senior V.P. It seemed like a good idea to bring him along as it would provide an instant Agency indoctrination. And he was duly instructed that his purpose in being there was solely to learn—*not participate.*

One end of the prospect's meeting room was dominated by a massive moose head. As the Burnett team entered the room, despite his vow of silence, the new Sr. V.P. blurted out, "Who shot the moose?" At that, the prospect spent the next 45 minutes confessing to the murder. And then informed the Agency that their time was up.

Burnett Management doesn't make too many mistakes. And never more than once. They incorporated this lesson into their rehearsals thereafter. Since then, when any presenter strays, one of the others will interrupt with, "Who shot the moose?" This immediately makes the point—without offending any sensitivities.

Also use this opportunity to anticipate any ridiculous situations. Such as this scenario. Take the idiot prospect who slates five presentations in one day. You're third. Upon entering the room they "request" that you cut your presentation in half because they are running far behind schedule.

This can be shattering unless you have an alternate plan whereby you can rebound with a condensed version. So it is in your best interest to expect the worst—beginning with the prospect being totally unreasonable.

Then there is the matter of how long you should rehearse. Try this for size: Just short of being confident. You need *some* anxiety to guard against complacency. And there must be the juices flowing going in. Therefore, go into the pitch ready to kill. But no overkill in rehearsal for it.

Finally, remember: there are three requisites for a successful presentation. The first is rehearse, the second is rehearse, and the third is rehearse. The importance of this is such that if you haven't time for rehearsal, you haven't time for the presentation.

K.   Agency Team No-Shows

Regarding your presentation team, provision need be made for any no-shows. Failing to anticipate this possibility can be disastrous.

This isn't an academic principle. Let's learn the hard way. However, at someone else's expense.

We can take what happened to D'arcy Masius Benton & Bowles—and what they now do about it. They have a smoothly honed opener. Diamond polishers could gain from their performance.

The DMB&B list of clients is very impressive. But so is that of their peers. Yet, not many had a spellbinder like their C.E.O., Jack Bowen. Therefore, they led from strength by using his ingratiating charm to recount their achievements for these blue-chip clients.

Although this is basically a new business tactic, circumstances can require other applications. Like this one.

One of their largest clients had a total top Management change. To DMB&B's credit, they decided to treat this venerable client as a prospect that had to be pitched all over again. They decided they would start with the device which has always proved so effective. The format consisted of a draped table—underneath which was located a representative group of the actual products of their prestigious clients.

Then, upon removing the cloth with a flourish, Jack Bowen would casually reminisce on his Agency's remarkable contribution to their success. Seemingly, this opening shot would be every bit as appropriate for indoctrinating this client's new brass.

Among Jack Bowen's attributes are his reliability and punctuality. Yet, on this occasion, for whatever reason, he never even showed up. The Agency team did a soft shoe number until they couldn't fake it any longer. With the situation becoming tense, it was decided that the Management Supervisor on the account had better fill the breech and do Jack Bowen's shtick.

Afterwards, the M/S told me, "I heard Jack do this countless times; I was reasonably familiar with the case histories—but I had never done this before. Thus, I was uncomfortable, lacked confidence—and stunk."

The experience drove home to DMB&B the necessity of having an understudy for each star in the cast. The assumption that every scheduled participant will always be available is an unaffordable luxury. Therefore, in your preparation for the unexpected, also provide for adequate back-up support.

At best, a presentation is an uptight experience. Vital to its success is minimizing speaker tension. So spare them the further worry of having to deliver more than they are prepared for. And you will have presenters who can control rather than react to an opportunity.

L.   Presentation Agenda

There is an opportunity available to you at presentations that is seldom exploited. It is the one-page ad for your Agency and presentation distributed prior to the meeting: **The Agenda.**

Since this is considered to be a routine device, it is given short shrift. However, the Agenda is your introduction to the prospect at this event.

Is this initial impression exciting? Does it generate interest in your Agency and presentation? Further, to the prospect, this is the first clue to your creativity.

Therefore, this Agency house ad is much more important—and valuable to you—than may be realized. Accordingly, the standard for development is its being good enough to be published. Here's how it can serve to enhance your appeal:

- Create the **graphics** that will represent the Agency in the most desirable manner—and provide a visual incentive for the Agenda to be read.

- Write the **subjects** outlined in so intriguing a fashion as to put the prospect in an anticipatory frame of mind.

- List the names of your **participants**, their present Agency functions—and proposed involvement if awarded the account. This could also contain a small photo of each so members of the selection team will know to whom they should direct their questions and comments.

- Feature the prospect's **logo** on this sheet. This implies that your presentation was developed especially for them.

- Cite the **reason** for your presentation. This should establish in advance why this event will be very worthwhile for them.

- Include your Agency's **Unique Selling Proposition.** This keeps before the prospect why your Agency is best for them.

- Prominently note that you welcome their **participation** throughout the presentation—so you can talk with them—rather than at them.

Summing up, while the function of your agenda is to inform, it can also be a worthwhile sales tool. As with every other component of your new business activity, it should be used to compound the potency of your total effort—beyond the basic purpose for which it is intended.

So also use this prelude to whet the prospect's appetite, build acceptance, encourage involvement and create preference for your Agency.

M.   Prospect Objections

Finally, here are four forms of insurance you can take out to overcome prospect objections to your Agency or presentation:

1. Throughout the development of your presentation, continuously apply this acid test: Is this worth a portion of someone's life? Not yours; theirs. In effect, that is what you're asking for. Thus, the first criterion your pitch must satisfy is that it's worth their while. If so, you are on your way. Because advertisers rate most Agency presentations as "a waste of time."

2. Take advantage of the smarts in basic salesmanship as applied in other fields. Specifically, forgo any false pride and anticipate whatever objections might occur. Then prepare your rebuttals—to be held

in reserve in the event needed. (But for God's sake, don't bring any up unless they do!)

3. The only way you can go into a new business pitch is as a winner. Otherwise, your negative attitude will be reflected in the material developed and your presentation of it. And the prospect is sufficiently experienced to sense it. Thus, your only approach is gung-ho—since this is the prerequisite for winning.

4. Don't ever forget your status in this buyer-seller relationship. Your objective is to convince the prospect—not compete with them. Never try to look good by comparison with them. No one-upmanship, being patronizing or putdowns. Even if you should win a battle, it's for sure you won't win the war.

N.   Extent of Preparation

Summing up, I'm often asked. "How far should you go in preparing a presentation?" There is only one answer: whatever it will take to win. If they aren't worth this total effort, then don't present at all. Because the most expensive presentation is a half-ass one.

In fact, *over-prepare* so you can under-present. If your material is so thorough—and incisively applied—you won't have to include a soft-shoe number.

Chapter 14

The Use of Logistics as a Selling Opportunity

A. Perspective
B. Prospect Ground Rules
C. Timing
D. Duration
E. Location

A. Perspective

If there were a single commandment for New Business presentations, it would be this.

Regardless of how dynamic your concept:

> THOU SHALT NOT LOCK IN ON A SPECIFIC SWAT TEAM, FORMAT, CONTENT OR SEQUENCE.

Agencies have a tendency to try to develop a generic winner—and then stick with it thereafter. However, what may be very impressive to one prospect could antagonize another.

Therefore, *dynamism exists only if it is pertinent.*

B.   Prospect Ground Rules

To prevent being finished before you get started, let's clear the air on this matter.

If the prospect stipulates duration, format, content or sequence of presentation, don't fight them. Comply with what they set forth. It fulfills what they determined to be their needs, enables a basis for comparison—and indicates your willingness to cooperate and work with them.

When ground rules are set, Agencies that don't adhere to them are usually eliminated. Despite a highly appealing presentation, if the prospect can't match it against their judging criteria, or compare it with that of the others, the contrary Agency is dropped from consideration.

The direction furnished need not be restrictive. There can be ample opportunity for innovation within the parameters prescribed. At this stage, they want evidence of your imagination—not your independence. Thus, satisfy their wants at inception in order to remain in contention.

Playing the game can pay off. Here is an example that can also be useful for you.

Prior to my critiquing a new business presentation recently, I was shown the sheet of instructions given each candidate by the prospect. This set forth the subjects they wanted dealt with—in numerical sequence.

The Agency president then informed me, "Of course, we'll cover most of these—and work them into our pitch as is appropriate to the format." I interrupted and asked, "Why are you fighting them? The prospect specified what they want to hear about—and in what order." And he fired back, "Well, what the hell do you want us to do: blow up this sheet to poster size and prominently display it throughout the presentation?" I said, "Damn right. Then have each presenter check off their topic upon completion with a red magic marker."

Continuing, I proposed, "And as further evidence of your compatibility: reproduce this instruction sheet, imprint *AGENDA* on it, and distribute it before the meeting.

The Agency apparently figured they might as well amortize their investment in me, so they applied my recommendation—and landed the account. Granted, this device of itself wasn't totally responsible for the Agency winning. But the new client confided it was the tie-breaker among otherwise rough competition. Because this strategy graphically demonstrated, more than any claims or promises made, that this Agency is client-oriented.

Yet, how about when a prospect says, "All right, come on in and we'll just talk. Don't bother preparing anything." (Translation: they don't want to pay for it.)

And then some other Agency comes in with comped-up layouts and videotaped commercials and blows you out of the water. How do you reconcile not fighting them versus giving it your best shot?

If you want to go beyond what has been stipulated, here is your alternative. After having followed their instructions to the letter, acknowledge this and then mention, "There are some further matters worthy of your attention. Shall we cover them?"

Having proved your willingness to cooperate, they will probably acquiesce—if you can be reasonably brief. You can then dip into your black carrying case and come up with the plus desired—without having violated the prospect's requirements.

C.   Timing

The prospect views Agency solicitations as a competitive event. Do you? If it is a missionary presentation, they are comparing you with their present Agency. And if they are planning to change, they are thinking in terms of you versus the others.

Therefore, in addition to communicating what's in it for them, it must be convincingly registered why your Agency is preferable to any other. And the way the new business game is being played now, your velvet glove better have an iron fist in it. Because in this league, the meek shall not inherit the earth. Only the dirt.

So, for instance, don't lead from weakness by requesting a specific positioning when a series of presentations are to be made. Some Agencies swear by going first because they coincidentally lucked out then. Others shoot for going last—assuming that this final exposure will increase their memorability. However, there is the risk that after the first couple of Agencies, the prospect may have already made up their minds—with the remaining presentations being just a formality.

Of further significance, this superstition is demeaning to Agencies— and is interpreted by advertisers as a lack of confidence. All that matters is the effectiveness of your presentation—not its sequence vis-á-vis the others.

If you have any druthers, though, avoid being slated right after lunch. That's too tough an act to follow.

Actually, the best timing for presentation is first thing in the morning— before the prospect has become fatigued, bored or concerned about other matters.

D. Duration

When an advertiser is planning to move, and interviews a quantity of Agencies, a length of time for presentation is usually specified. Generally, for screening purposes, one hour is granted. As a finalist, usually it's whatever amount of time is necessary to put on the most appropriate presentation—and do it justice. (If so, show the prospect the courtesy of informing them of the amount of time desired—so they can plan accordingly.)

As to prospect interest, a presentation is never too long if totally pertinent to their wants and needs. It only drags if it becomes irrelevant.

Thus, there are two matters governing duration: prospect ground rules and appropriateness.

For whatever amount of time is needed, use it entirely for selling. To whatever extent you digress is the amount of advantage given to your competitors. So skip the extraneous warmup patter and be strictly pertinent throughout.

Because the duration is usually exceeded, much to the prospect's annoyance, here is an ingratiating device that will increase your memorability—favorably. Open by announcing that your presentation will take no longer than 57 minutes.

This rare cooperation will pull them forward in their chairs. (Of course, this makes adequate rehearsal all the more necessary.)

Because this matter of timing is so important, let's clarify what the prospect means by 60 minutes. It's simply that you are not to go beyond this. By contrast, it is not expected that your presentation run up to 60 minutes.

If it is determined that for a certain prospect you can be most effective in 35 minutes, do so—and get out. Don't be like the Agency who had everything going for them—except they couldn't take yes for an answer. Namely, don't sell for so long that you end up buying it back.

Because there is such deep concern about not wearing out your welcome, I was asked at a Los Angeles Agency, "Then how do you know when to stop?" I couldn't do any better than the profound reply given by their Research Director: "When the prospect starts to puke."

Finally, here is the most important reason for complying with timing set forth. Prospects interpret violating this requirement as fighting them—and indicative of the relationship that would exist if such Agency were awarded their account. As a result, ignored timing is sometimes the first and easiest means used to eliminate Agencies.

E. Location

Whenever possible, arrange to hold new business presentations at your office. This affords more effective planning, better staging—plus the confidence from familiarity with your own turf.

Also, it will minimize the risk of Murphy's Law: "Whatever can go wrong, will go wrong." Actually, you're better off applying O'Toole's Law: "Murphy is an optimist."

However, if the prospect requires that it be conducted on their premises, it is essential that the room be checked out in advance. (Because wherever held, the Agency is considered responsible for the logistics.) And that doesn't mean a cursory walk-through. Beyond this, draw a diagram of the room's configuration.

* Indicate windows and doors for their effect on your speakers and materials.
* Locate electrical outlets and light switches. (Do they have dimmers?)
* Decide on positioning for audio-visual equipment.
* Determine facilities for display (ceilings, walls).

Further, if the prospect stipulates that the presentation be put on at their place, ask if you can hold your rehearsal in their meeting room. This will provide your team with the knowledge and confidence of a familiar environment. Being able to go in comfortable rather than cold is bound to improve their performance.

If this request is refused because the room will be in use at the time desired or whatever, here is what DDB Needham Chicago does. They ask if a photographer can come when the room is available. This is invariably granted—and he takes 360 degrees shots of the room.

Based on this information, the Agency rearranges its conference room (adding or removing furniture as appropriate) to simulate the prospect's room. Then after rehearsing under these conditions, when their presentation team arrives at the prospect, they have a feeling of déjà vu.

The importance of being adequately familiar with the prospect's meeting room was proved in an exceptionally dramatic manner. This experience was played back to me at dinner by Kelly O'Neill who headed up Gardner in St. Louis. Their flagship account was the Grocery Products Division of Ralston-Purina—a significant part being the Pet Foods Business.

One day, Kelly got a call from his contact at Ralston-Purina informing him they had to hold still for a pitch on the dog food portion from another

Agency that afternoon. And he didn't want anyone from Gardner to hear about it on the street. The client went on to stress there was nothing to worry about because this is just a political accommodation—"and we'll get rid of them fast." He further promised to phone Kelly the next day to confirm this brushoff.

Sure there is nothing to worry about! Then why the hell is the client seeing them? Instant panic sets in. Imagination runs amuck—winding up by fearing the worst possible scenario.

To Kelly's amazement—and relief—his client contact phoned that same afternoon to notify that the soliciting Agency had left. Kelly said, "You sure *did* get rid of them fast." And the client replied, "Nope. They got rid of themselves."

He went on to explain that the Agency C.E.O. opened the purported extravaganza by exclaiming, "Not only are you going to love the advertising we are proposing, the dogs will love it, too!" At that, (as rehearsed in their *own* conference room), one of the Agency staffers, dressed in a dog costume, bounded into the room barking gleefully.

The dog head part of the costume apparently obscured his vision and he slammed into a low glass-top coffee table. And his barking quickly changed to howling. Having lacerated his shins, he bled profusely and they had to call the paramedics.

Time elapsed: 1 minute, 27 seconds. And that was it. This act was too tough to follow. Thus, their dog idea turned out to be a bitch. Adding insult to injury, the Agency was out a bundle because nobody presents pencil roughs to Ralston-Purina.

So be intimately knowledgeable regarding every aspect of the prospect's meeting room. As much as your own. Because the location should work for you—not be a trap.

Beyond this "your-place-or-mine" consideration, increasing use is being made of a third location: *a neutral spot*. Usually this is a room at a hotel or club. There are two reasons:

1. The prospect may have some interest, but doesn't want to risk having their present Agency find out about their infidelity. Thus, they would rather not chance being seen at a soliciting Agency by a third party who might play it back. Nor do they want this held on their premises—and be discovered by someone from the incumbent.

2. They have decided to switch and schedule a series of consecutive presentations. However, they want to get away from their office distractions. Further, the prospect wants the common denominator of the same environment for all contenders. Instead of being unduly

influenced (favorably or otherwise) by each Agency's quarters.

When a neutral spot is used, it makes for a difficult situation. First, the prospect may have stupidly slated too many Agencies. Then, they are harried all day about the time factor. In addition, you are up against their growing fatigue.

Complicating circumstances is the matter of logistics. When a string of Agencies are being run through the grinder, the set up of your A-V equipment and display of material becomes a serious problem. Especially if this needs to be done while the prospect is present. And invariably, you are rushed, clumsy—and uptight. Any of these feelings can negatively affect your performance.

Here is how a Cleveland Agency took this lemon of a situation and made lemonade. *They rented the room next door to the advertiser.* And arranged the room to their advantage in advance—plus held their rehearsals in it. Then when their turn came, they invited the prospect to simply step in—with the Agency being relaxed and confident.

After having set up the prospect for the kill, they applied the coup de grace—to the other Agencies. Get this for gamesmanship.

The night before, they had their Agency name posted on the hotel Directory of Events—right underneath that of the advertiser. The next day, when their competitors arrived and saw this, it was assumed there was collusion—and the listed Agency was wired-in. I was told the effect of this device was awfully demoralizing to the other shops.

Of course, the Agency having this foresight won.

Summing up, comply with the prospect's ground rules. But this shouldn't inhibit you from enhancing them—in your favor.

Chapter 15

Selling Tactics That Work

A. Perspective

Here is the most critical matter you need to know regarding the advertisers' attitude toward new business solicitation: Switching Agencies is deadly serious to them.

In effect, you're touting divorce. And regardless of how justified, there isn't any room for being flippant. By whatever means an impression is

made: appearance or dress, conduct or language, claims or promises—
treat this matter with the same respect as the prospect does in order to
make the cut.

The depth of their feelings was exemplified by this experience. An Ad
Director once asked me, "Jack, have you ever spent any time on this side
of the desk?" And I told him, "No, my entire tour of duty has been on the
other side." So he said, "Then you have never known what it means to lie
awake at night, knowing you are forced to fire your Agency—and trying
to figure how to cope with the three personal factors involved."

"First, how many jobs will be lost? Second, how many lives will be
affected? And finally, how much of a sonofabitch can I be?"

I always assumed clients had ice water running through their veins.
Apparently the majority have warm blood. And this is a truly traumatic
event.

You must be sensitive to the emotionalism involved. Because if any
behavior smacks of being cute, you are bound to antagonize them.

It nets down to this. When an advertiser decides to change Agencies, it
is an admission of failure on their part. Either in the selection made—or
in their inability to work with the Agency.

So be aware of this tender nerve. And don't rub it the wrong way.

B. Promotional Activity

Agencies are inclined to equate aggressiveness in the new business area
with *exposure*. I'm frequently asked, "We're active in the following
respects. Have we missed any . . . ?"

- scheduling house advertising campaign?
- conducting direct mail program?
- getting the word out to the reps?
- capitalizing on a country club membership?
- exploiting civic involvement?
- delivering an occasional speech?

I'll ask, "Why?" And they will say, "To create awareness."

This presumes that familiarity with an Agency's existence, of itself,
will generate advertiser response. That's like telling a client that if you
advertise, you can get rid of your sales force.

Of course, these various promotional devices are of value—if there are
coinciding plans to exploit them. In whatever the activity, develop the
reasons for this—and what you will do to gain from it. Specifically:

• Sure, advertise—but only if you intend to merchandise it.

• By all means use direct mail—however, provision need be made to follow through with phone calls seeking an appointment.

• Certainly take advantage of the reps—setting forth how . . . with expectations established.

• Don't rationalize club dues unless their membership includes an adequate number of prospects—and you have a discreet angle to romance them.

• Civic involvement on behalf of the Agency is meaningless—except if there is the opportunity to rub shoulders with desirable prospects.

• Accepting an invitation to speak is an ego-trip—unless there is a means to work the audience for the Agency.

Consequently, creating awareness doesn't produce results—just a warm feeling. It's only of value if used as a vehicle to eventually stimulate advertiser response. Promotional tools for their own sake are luxuries. Rather, they should be planned as the first in a series of events geared toward landing new business.

C.   Extent of Effort

A new business presentation is the culmination of all the activity it took to get the prospect to this event. However, it won't reach this stage unless each contact along the way is sufficiently intriguing.

Agencies don't take a prospect seriously enough until they are selected for the finals. Because ostensibly, it is from this shootout that the winner is selected.

Not necessarily. During all the preliminary activity (initial contact, pre-presentation meeting, screening pitch, Agency tour, etc.) the prospect forms impressions of the various Agencies. As a result, when they get to the short list, often this serves as a confirmation of preference developed—and those who will come in 2nd.

Therefore, *every* prospect contact should be considered as a form of presentation. Whether this is a letter, phone call or meeting, treat this as if it were your last chance. Accorded as much importance as your final pitch. Contrary to the old show biz adage, *never* leave 'em wanting more. Leave 'em wanting your Agency.

There should be no such thing as *just* a letter. Or *only* a phone call. If shown less dedication than the formal presentation sought, there probably won't be any. Because if these inducements aren't appealing enough, there won't be further contact.

So don't hold back until it's too late to win. If a prospect is worth the presentation effort and expense necessary, *all* types of communication to lure them into your tent should be irresistible. *Gear up for each prospect contact as if this were the deciding factor in Agency selection.* Not only will this discipline increase the likelihood of your show going on, but it will prime the audience and make them more receptive to your performance.

D. Honesty

I would be remiss in not revealing this raw insight regarding advertiser reaction to new business solicitation. This will also answer the question "When is it okay to lie in presentation?"

At best, you're suspect. Often they just don't believe you. It is assumed you will promise them anything to get the business. Therefore, the only answer is: *Never*!

Instead, to receive objective consideration, you must persuasively communicate having a very unusual attribute: *honesty*.

This is the first criterion used for judging Agencies. After you've left, the very first question the members of the selection team ask each other is, "Did you believe them?" If you're unable to satisfy this initial requirement, the finest performance will be down the drain.

Further, honesty will furnish the discipline to prevent offending the prospect by the tendency to exaggerate. And they have become very adroit at smoking this out.

Honesty can also provide a competitive edge. Depending on whom you are competing against, it could supply you with an exclusive.

In the advertiser's vernacular, the first compliment you need receive from them after your pitch is, "They're straight." If you don't get this one, there won't be any others.

All right, how can you register that they could even buy a used car from you? By not making any claims about your operation, or promises to them, which could be in any way suspect. If there is the remotest doubt that a statement will wash, omit it. Or it can blow the entire pitch.

What is honesty? Just this. *Whatever you say should be able to stand up to their checking on it.* That's your best test for truthfulness. And the best reason for telling the truth is that you will never have to wonder afterwards what you said.

There are a variety of tactics used by Agencies to convey honesty—with varying degrees of success. For instance, there is the device used by an Agency in St. Louis. They make provision for stating in their presentation, just once, "I don't know." It's assumed this candor will make all else said believable.

The most impressive expression of your commitment to honesty is the offer to make your books on their account available for inspection at any time. (Even though they are entitled to this, your initiative sets well.)

In the final analysis for whatever angle you may come up with to communicate honesty, first try it out in the mirror. And then ask yourself, "Would I buy it?"

E. Contact by Prospect

Ask an advertiser what they are looking for in an Ad Agency, and they will say: "Great Creative ideas and shrewd Marketing strategy."

However, these don't occur by immaculate conception or spontaneous combustion. Rather, ideas and strategy emanate from *people*.

Therefore, since it is people whom the prospect is actually buying, encourage them to contact any of your staff who would be assigned to their account. (Furnish list.) Invite them to get to know the proposed members of their team and find out directly why their talents and experience would be of particular benefit.

It takes courage to risk this offer. It indicates that apparently *your* people must be especially right for them.

Finally, this tactic provides you with the most valuable form of contact: personal, under relaxed circumstances. And gives the impression of your Agency being a completely above-board operation.

F. Advertisers Changing Agencies

In soliciting an advertiser planning to change Agencies, your objective is to convince them of: "Why our Agency is best for you." Seemingly, they could only benefit *after* you have been awarded the account.

Yet, whatever you could do for them *before* selection would be appreciated. And provide you with competitive advantage.

In particular, their immediate concern is the procedure for conducting an Agency search. Plus establishing the criteria for evaluating the contenders. Therefore, in addition to being a great door-opener, any insight you can furnish to make the prospect's job easier and faster will be highly valued. And is bound to influence them to some extent in your favor.

This service would consist of providing input and direction for the following components:

- Performance and relationship expected.
- Agency search/Investigation.
- Use and content of questionnaire.
- Analysis of responses.
- Screening Agencies for presentation.
- Criteria for evaluating presentations.
- Appraisal of results.
- Decision-making process.

Needless to say, the insight supplied will be subtly geared to your interest. Why not? If some other Agency had thought of this tactic, they would have loaded this gratuitous contribution.

This strategy should enable your Agency to at least qualify for the list of candidates. And increase the possibility of becoming a finalist. Further, properly parlayed, your contribution will create a special relationship because of having tangibly indicated you relate to them. So serve the prospect *prior* to selection—and it could be you.

Thus, a basic process for Agency screening/selection should be developed and included in your new business arsenal. Then, attack with it as appropriate. While the other Agencies just *react* to the battle.

G. Prospect Using Consultant

Occasionally, an advertiser planning to switch Agencies will retain a consultant to provide direction in conducting the search and selection process. Supposedly, this introduces a new and complicating element.

No it doesn't. Your objective is still to land the account. Not the consultant.

Therefore, *don't change* your strategy from that originally considered necessary to score. However, with this ringer involved, you will have to be prepared for closer than usual scrutiny. This would include your appearance and behavior as well as claims and promises to be made. Because they are first looking for a cause to eliminate Agencies.

For that matter, it would be well to apply this discipline whether or not a consultant is on board. It will leave less to chance—and assure a more professional job.

So target on convincing the prospect of "Why our Agency is best for you." And don't compromise what it will take to win in an attempt to impress this guru.

H.   Travel with Prospect

After a prospect nets down to the finalists, the human equation often becomes the deciding factor in Agency selection. If the chemistry is a standoff, the Agency perceived as having greater knowledge of the advertiser and its market can be the tie-breaker.

This is what made the difference in picking the winner by a supermarket chain recently. Agency "A" went the full route in conducting both quantitative and qualitative research. And gave the impression of being intimately informed regarding this advertiser's operation and market.

But Agency "B" arranged to travel extensively with the chain's store supervisors. This also gave them considerable contact with individual store managers. A diary was kept of this experience, conclusions drawn, recommendations made—and photos taken. Of course, this hands-on experience was strongly merchandised throughout their presentation.

The upshot was that Agency "A" came off as having gone that extra mile. But Agency "B" gave the impression of having walked it in the prospect's shoes.

The moral of this story is: conducting research for the prospect is admirable. Doing so *with them* is likelier to land the account.

I.   Projects

Season your Agency with projects. Here is the recipe.

Since the awarding of new business has become less than an all or nothing proposition, if the total account can't be landed, find out what can be pried loose. Maybe it's an individual function (i.e., Creative, Media, Research, P.R.). Or a particular project (i.e., new product introduction, test campaign).

Then, ask for it. Don't rely on the prospect assuming you would be willing to settle for a foot in the door. They won't assume anything. You'll register only what is literally spelled out for them.

For example, here are two specific opportunities. Successful handling of either will enable your shop to progress from a "Project" to "Agency of Record" status.

First, your most potent strategy is to request producing their **Annual Report.** This is near and dear to their C.E.O.'s heart. (His picture is in it.)

This assignment makes possible regular contact with the advertiser's ultimate decision-maker. The relationship developed, and exceptional job done, could eventually result in your being awarded the entire account.

If this overture doesn't play, try to get their **National Sales Meeting.** In putting on this event, your key personnel can be showcased to their top Management. And if your treatment of this important function has the desired effect, their gratitude could be expressed via a Letter of Agreement.

For the record though, neither these or any assignment should ever be a gamble on the come. Your work is too good to be given away. In *all* instances, these are charged for—and priced to include a satisfactory profit. On this up-front basis, there is no doubt about how you operate— and the value of your work. Then, if you don't pick up the rest of their business, you still made out.

There is one more caveat. Since project work can be especially profitable, there is the temptation to skew your new business efforts toward them. And after a flurry of activity, a quantity of assignments are landed.

Then the Agency becomes immersed in these—at the expense of further solicitation. Upon completion, there could be a serious void in income— because provision wasn't made to replace it. That's why it is desirable to convert this type of client relationship from an affair to marriage as soon as feasible.

Summing up, projects can carry your Agency from rags to riches. And back just as quickly. If projects are to be an integral part of your operation, these four qualifications must be met:

1. Each project should be an independent source of profitable income.

2. Maintain a sound balance between projects and contractual accounts.

3. Recognize the uncertainty of project income and plan to be consistently aggressive in the new business area.

4. Realize that project work should lead to a contractual arrangement.

Now go ahead and have it both ways.

J.   Protection Against Theft

You have a missionary presentation coming up. (Not knowing whether or not the prospect can be had.) So it's just foreplay.

But your Creative types have come up with such a sexy idea that they want you to go all the way. They are certain that this will be the aphrodisiac that will enable you to score.

So although unsolicited, you attempt to seduce the prospect with irresistible comped-up layouts and storyboards. They become excited, breathing hard, but not being a pushover they ask if you will leave your proposition for their consideration. Then you become struck with the fear that they may try to steal what you conceived. However, they can't if you require a legitimate adoption procedure.

Here's how to protect your chastity. First of all, don't cool off your live one by putting a © on any evidence of what you have to offer. They've been around. And know that the U.S. has just about the weakest copyright laws in the world. ("Change a colon and I'm yours.")

Instead, street-wise Agencies are finding they don't have to surrender the family jewels. Rather, when emotions are running high, the Agency will righteously produce a wedding license. That is, a simple sheet setting forth, in effect, if you would love to use any of this desirable stuff, it has to be placed through our Agency. Please sign here.

In this way, they can't try it before they buy it.

So go ahead and tease the prospect by hinting just enough to get to the altar. Just so they understand you have a price: *Marriage*.

K.   Tour of Agency

Your podium presentation isn't the prospect's only opportunity for a head-to-head judgment of the Agency. In addition, there is the tour of the Agency—to which they attach considerable importance. The impression made has disproportionate influence in the selection process.

What are they looking for? In regard to your people, the prospect wants to determine whether they are 3-dimensional—or Social Security numbers waiting to get the day over with.

As to the appearance of your quarters, they are strongly opinionated. The prospect is sensitive to an Agency looking too posh. Because they assume you would play it loose with their money, too.

Yet, they are quick to counter with not wanting an Agency that looks ticky-tacky. So I've asked, "Then what are you seeking?" And they will reply, "One that looks successful." Probing further, I'll inquire as to what that means. And finally, the attitude that emerges is, "A place we'd be proud to bring someone."

Advertisers believe that in the Agency tour they can get a feeling of whether the Agency is extravagant or cheap, friendly or cold, imaginative or dull.

Thus, the tour should never be conducted as an impromptu event left to chance. It ought to be as well conceived and structured as a formal presentation. This involves what they will be told, what they will be shown—and whom they will meet.

Accordingly, your people who would be involved must be instructed to be present. And clued on the prospect's needs and interests—so they can come across as being particularly perceptive. So don't surprise your Media Director with a prospect, and then ask, "Gwendolyn, say something cost-efficient."

With this planned program you will control—rather than gamble on— the impression made.

Beyond achieving the desired effect on the prospect, this event provides an excellent opportunity to further explore what they *really* want of an Agency.

Here's how. Assign an individual tour guide to each prospect person. (If more than three of them, set up teams.) Those of your people to whom they would be introduced would be prepared to ask them a pertinent question regarding their Marketing and Agency needs. And their attitude toward these matters.

In this relaxed environment, the prospect is likely to reveal inner feelings which they wouldn't express under more formal conditions. Then after the prospect group departs, your guides would hold a debriefing session. This would identify insights received beyond official pronouncements. And also expose differences in what the prospect said—and what was meant.

Thus, by augmenting the prospect's corporate statements with their casual comments, you can present to them as people rather that functionaries. And with this discreet familiarity, they will be able to relate to your Agency more so than to the others.

Summing up, this occasion also offers a great means to distinguish your Agency from competitors. Because often the Agency tour elsewhere consists of just screening the TV reel—and giving the prospect a copy of their client roster. Obviously, you don't have to do much more to be way ahead of the pack.

L. Antagonistic Prospect

Occasionally, you'll come across an egocentric prospect who seems to work at being offensive. How much heat should you have to take? That depends on these three factors.

- the account's appeal: profitability, compatibility, growth, etc. (Are they worth your toughing it out?)

- this contact's importance (Is his/her conduct representative? Would others of your people be more appropriate?)

- your own sensitivity (Can you come into the kitchen?)

Rather than hastily taking a "T'hell with 'em" attitude, objectively consider these matters. You may conclude that they would be rough as a cob, but so desirable that it would pay to play with pain. If so, learn from how Jack Reynolds found that it is relative—and succeeded.

He and I started out together at Dancer Fitzgerald Sample, after WWII (the big one). Having been a Navy (U.S.) Beachmaster, he soon concluded that the Agency business wasn't rugged enough for him. So he got a job peddling space for *U.S. News & World Report.*

They had Jack doing grunt work in the office until it was felt safe to let him out in public. Then for his baptism under fire, the Midwest Sales Manager sent Jack to call on the most miserable sonofabitch he knew. And Jack went there to attack this person with the same ferocity as when he stormed beaches.

Little did he know that his boss set him up to prove it's a jungle out there. And as expected, he was brutally cut up.

Jack returned looking as if he had just been hit by a kamikaze. In reporting to his Manager, he said, "Y'know, maybe I'm not cut out for this business." And his boss asked, "Did he hit you?" Jack replied, "No, but he really worked me over."

And again his superior asked, "Did he hit you?" Jack repeated, "No—but he was ruthless." So pressing the issue, he was asked, "Yeah, but did he *hit* you?" Jack finally replied, "No dammit, he didn't *physically* hit me." At that, the Midwest Sales Manager said, "Then what the hell are you complaining about?"

As Jack came to think of it, he wasn't bleeding. He wasn't the walking wounded. Therefore, he could try it again without fear of risking permanent injury.

Jack learned his lesson well because he eventually replaced his boss in the catbird seat. And his rough indoctrination was literally compensated for. During all those years, he diligently squirreled away *U.S. News* stock. Then when the magazine was bought by Mortimer Zuckerman, it enabled Jack to live wealthily ever after. (I don't begrudge him this good fortune—even though he resisted all my attempts to be adopted by him.)

M. Buyer/Seller Status

I began this chapter by dealing with the advertiser's attitude toward new business solicitation. Just as important though is *your* attitude. For this reason.

Sometimes an Agency starts playing a cold hand, and isn't scoring despite what are believed to be excellent presentations. This often happens after a hot new business streak—when the Agency begins to forget who is the buyer and who is the seller.

For instance, there is an Agency in Minneapolis who was scoring so well they thought they had found the new business Holy Grail. They concluded there are two requisites for winning: (1) The presentation must be held at the Agency's office, and (2) a minimum of two hours must be granted. And they began specifying such to prospects.

Obviously, these factors are desirable goals—but never Agency stipulations. So despite the shop's meteoric rise, their growth flattened out just as quickly. Because as important as the environment and duration are to selling, the prospect needs to be *receptive* to buying your service. And since advertisers equate Agency terms with arrogance, setting ground rules is as far as you'll get.

Chapter 16

Claims and Promises: Pros and Cons

A. Perspective

There is a tendency to get so involved in the components of your new business program you somewhat overlook its purpose. Namely, convincing advertisers of *"Why our Agency is best for you."*

Every aspect of your prospecting, solicitation and presentation should contribute to proving this claim. Because that's all the prospect is interested in. Anything else is self-gratifying and distracting.

You may protest—thinking you certainly know this. But according to advertisers, Agencies do not totally hone in on what is most pertinent to them—and then stay on target throughout. Thus, to whatever extent you digress from justifying "Why our Agency is best for you" weakens your impact accordingly.

B. Identity

In an attempt to enhance and broaden their appeal, there is a trend by some Agencies to describe themselves as a Marketing or Communications firm. Supposedly, this implies offering more services than the conventional Ad Agency.

However, what an advertiser wants is an *Advertising* Agency. Sometimes, one which *also* has the additional services featured by those claiming to be an all-encompassing operation. But first there must be dynamic Creative work and a shrewd Media function before the advertiser will be attracted by support activities.

For instance, what started as a device by Agencies to distinguish themselves is proving counter-productive. To increase their stature, there are those who claim to be "marketing-driven." (Since every Agency should be, so what else is new?) Then as evidence of their dedication to this concept, they will insist to prospects, "We are *not* an Advertising Agency." Rather, they explain, "We begin by researching the prospect and its market—and then recommend what form of communication, if any, would be most effective." As an afterthought, it is mentioned that this might even include advertising.

If this approach is on the level, it is ill-conceived. Because it is negative. It isn't a matter of *not* being an Ad Agency. Instead, it is being *more* than an Ad Agency.

The moral here is that if advertising is sublimated for the sake of a positioning gimmick, the Agency will suffer two unaffordable consequences. First, a diffused image. And second, not being able to attract and keep desirable advertising personnel. As a result, it will have the veneer without the substance.

C. Promotional Material

Whether I am at an Agency for seminar or consulting purposes, invariably I'm asked for my opinion of their promotional material. They haul out their kid, with buck teeth and pimples, and hope I have the same paternal feeling.

Sure, I can play it safe and answer like the pediatrician, "Now that is a boy!" But there is one pattern that emerges across the board which can't be glossed over. Whatever the mailing piece, by whomever the Agency, they all have two faults in common:

1. It is an ego-trip on behalf of the Agency because its content does not pay off for the prospect (i.e., following through with, "this is the kind of imaginative creative work or shrewd marketing strategy you could count on if we became your Agency").

2. It does not involve the reader—giving them reason why it would be to their advantage to contact you.

A prospect will not interpret or draw conclusions from your message. They shouldn't have to extract cause/effect from it. Therefore, finish the job if you want them to start something.

These mailers vary from a folksy letter from the Agency C.E.O. to lavish 5-color heavy stock pieces in a variety of sizes and shapes. In all fairness, the art direction is usually excellent. But what happened to the message? It seems written to satisfy and receive approval from whoever necessary in the Agency. Not conceived to excite the recipient.

Instead, the only meaningful claims are those directed to the prospect's interests and needs. How many times have your achievements featured paid off for them?

Further, the communication should associate your Agency with the prospect throughout. And presented as your being such a desirable combination. How frequently do you refer to "we" and "us?"

Your greatest accomplishments are only as impressive as the degree to which the prospect can perceive benefiting from them. So stop assuming that a photo of your C.E.O. (usually on the phone), accompanied by a gut-wrenching exposition of the Agency's philosophy, is going to enrapture anybody. Rather, target on the only matter of interest to a prospect: *"What's in it for me?"*

Now for the treatment of your answer. Your Creative work is the most *obvious* evidence of what they can expect. And since clients are authorities in two areas—their business and advertising—Agencies will try to represent their talent in the most potent manner.

Unfortunately, in an attempt to convey dynamism, some Agencies confuse *startle* with *convince* in their promotional material. This occurs when using provocative descriptions of their Creative work for the sake of such. Like proudly referring to it as "outrageous." Hopefully, it is "challenging." But never described by cutesy words that implies its being off the wall.

So be innovative—not desperate—when promoting your Creative. The prospect wants their product or service described in an intriguing—not shocking—manner. Avoid the circus barker's vocabulary on behalf of yourself. Because the prospect doesn't want that language to represent them.

You can be as imaginative as possible when selling for your Agency—as long as it never casts doubt on your professionalism. As advertisers state, "The Creative we want doesn't come from 'flakes'."

This criticism needs to be strictly heeded because an Agency's appeal keeps coming back to what the advertiser is ultimately buying: *people*. Accordingly, since a person is the sum of his/her experiences, include a listing of all the accounts your Staff has worked on and the Agencies by whom they have been employed.

Invariably, Agencies compiling these lists are amazed at the extensiveness of their combined experience. This is an especially valuable device for Agencies of lesser size. Because even though they don't have the depth of larger ones, this itemization registers they have enough.

When developing your promotional material, don't naively assume the prospect will bother to think. They won't. Unless this reality is compensated for, some of your strongest selling appeals will be seriously weakened.

This applies to the use of client testimonial letters and press coverage in your promotional pieces. As proud as you are of this recognition, others aren't salivating to read it. And even if the prospect does, they may be happy for you—but won't make the effort to relate to it. To lure them into the tent, precede the reproduction of the letter or publicity with an intriguing statement. Then add a brief comment at the end explaining what this achievement means to them. Or else the recipient will lump these endorsements with all the other puffery received.

There is still another respect in which these promo folders are lacking. In effect, these are a presentation on paper. But unlike their human counterpart, they fail to ask for the order.

Admittedly, its primary purpose is to generate interest and pave the way for personal contact. Yet, why not use *all* of it to sell for you? This needn't violate any Creative esthetics. But it can convert this item from a promotional device to a *selling* device.

Finally, in regard to the closer, practically all Agencies use the same wrap-up. Each will conclude with the statement: "Please call John Doe, President, for further information. (987) 654-3210."

First, with this being a standard closer, its effect is a wash. Second, why should the prospect do so? Via this request, the Agency seems to forget who's who in this buyer-seller situation.

Instead, break the mold. Dare to be different. Show your respect for the prospect by wrapping up with the opposite tack: "You shouldn't have to call us. We'll phone you."

This deference will surely distinguish your mailer from the sameness of the others. Impressively so.

In the final analysis, here is the best reason to do yourself proud.

An Agency's ability to sell on its own behalf is a good indication of what it can do for clients. Thus, I recommend to advertisers that they request examples of promotional efforts by Agencies being considered.

Then they would critically assess whether it convinces that the Agency is preferable to any other. Or is it the usual warmed over Agency pablum? Does it create a desire for their work—or look and sound like most of the other pedantic ego-trips?

Your promo work can be either your beginning or end with a prospect. If you can't help your Agency, don't hurt it.

D.   Agency Philosophy

Agency philosophies are usually interminable, vague, pompous, eso-teric and pedantic—seemingly prepared by a Tibetan Maharishi. And presentation of this bores the hell out of a prospect.

It is assumed that, like office furniture and computers, some sort of statement of attitude is necessary. And coming from an Ad Agency, it should be bigger than life.

Instead of this wasted ego-trip, there are two approaches that can do you proud. Significantly, both are brief.

The first is provocative—and right to the point. Cite that you don't have an Agency philosophy. Rather, an individual objective for each client. Namely, to fulfill the ultimate responsibility of an Agency: *to best contribute to increasing client sales profitably.*

The other option is to set forth specific standards for operation in respect to performance and relationship.

In both instances, the appeal is based on what's in it for the prospect— as opposed to what you want to boast about. If you feel compelled to have an Agency philosophy, its intent should be to impress the prospect—not yourself.

And then, in presentation, don't belabor this. Even if you wrote it. Or your spouse did.

Any issue made of your philosophy is suspected of being a substitute for ideas. But here, too, watch your sense of proportion. Ideas are your second most valuable commodity. Your people from whom they came are first.

As you know, ideas don't make anything happen. People do. So when platforming your operation, keep your priorities in proper sequence.

E.   Why You're Preferable

Your objective is to convince the prospect that your Agency is preferable to the incumbent—or any other. The most impressive approach is most basic: The caliber of your work will enable them to operate more productively. They will be able to better apply marketing strategy because you can create more persuasive advertising. This benefit gets right to the heart of their needs—and is the first reason for hiring an Agency.

F.   Objection to Size

Unless you are Y & R, Dentsu or owned by a British firm, there may be concern about being smaller than your competitors in a new business situation. It is assumed this implies being less desirable in regard to personnel, services, and facilities.

By contrast, sometimes a prospect is reluctant to consider your Agency because of its being *too big*. It is feared they might get buried and receive short shrift. Then what to do?

Here is your strategy. The best way to defuse prospect objections to size is to constructively refute them *before* they occur. Proact rather than react.

Go beyond the usual impersonal claim of being "a full-service Agency." (As a client, who would they ask for: "Mr. Production? Or Ms. Media?") In addition, provide the prospect with a list of the specific people—by name, per function—who will be assigned to their account. And cite the back-up personnel ready to serve them. (Unless touting bodies for the sake of numbers, no other Agency can offer more than this primary and back-up team.)

This commitment, in writing, can dissipate the prospect's fear of being dumped into some humongous, or inadequate, operation. This action provides proof that there is already a designated team on line who would be held accountable for performance.

Anticipating this suspicion in either case, and dispelling it up front, is the most effective means to prevent the prospect's misconception as to the appropriateness of your Agency. Because the ultimate consideration is the caliber and depth of people assigned to their account.

G.   Combating Larger Agencies

Yet, except for possibly those Agencies ranking among the 17 largest (those billing over $1 billion), there is constant concern regarding the difficulty of pitching against larger Agencies for new business.

Admittedly, you're not going to hack it with transparent claims such as, "What we lack in numbers, we make up for in ideas." Or, "Just think, you'd be getting our first team." The advertiser has already yawned through these and a variety of other attempts by Agencies to compensate for being smaller than their competitors.

Instead, you can overcome the misconception that a larger Agency must be preferable in the most logical manner: the economics of the Agency business. An Agency can allocate only as much employee salary to a client as is affordable based on income received from them. And this applies to any Agency—regardless of size.

(As a result, some smaller advertisers are learning the hard way that the Account Executive they received from the prestigious big-name Agency selected, turned out to be a 14-year-old kid with pimples.)

Sure, some Agencies will over-promise. But eventually they will be confronted with the moment of truth: the balance sheet. Then the Agency will discover it trapped itself and has to start cutting time applied— particularly from the stars promised. Now it's only a matter of time until this wheeler-dealer Agency receives a "Dear John" letter. Because clients take a jaundiced view of being deceived in presentation.

Therefore, if necessary, explain that Agency size cannot be equated with the amount of attention they will receive. Anyway, that's not the criterion for determining preference. Rather, the difference lies in the *quality of personnel assigned*.

So you needn't be beaten in the numbers game. You can win by convincing the prospect that your people are better. After all, they wouldn't hire Goliath if they knew David was looking for a job.

H.   Financial Status

It is a generally accepted practice that clients are entitled to inspect the Agency's books *on their account*. This privilege does *not* extend to the Agency's finances.

By contrast, how much does a prospect have a right to know about your overall financial status? Only proof of your being acceptably solvent. Anything beyond this is proprietary information. And you needn't be conned into divulging it.

Yet, some Agencies will offer to reveal their books as an inducement in new business solicitation. It is assumed this tactic conveys, "We have nothing to hide." And it implies integrity.

But might this come across as a desperate move? Supposedly, running scared. The prospect wouldn't release their confidential data on their operation to strangers.

Thus, bare your soul—but not your money. However, if you are going to consider this device, as with any other come-on, use maximum discretion. Because as noble as your intentions may be, it could have the opposite effect.

I. Agency Location

The factor of Agency location is a two-edged sword. Local or otherwise, it can be used to your advantage—or need be compensated for.

Although Agency selection should be based essentially on compatibility and performance, sometimes proximity is a consideration. Since it could work for or against you, here are your recourses:

- If in your favor, cite your distance from the prospect in minutes and miles. (You needn't mention the substantial difference in distance that applies to any of your competitors. The comparison by inference is strong enough.)

- If location can be to your detriment, note that their objective should be to have the Agency of greatest value to them—irrespective of distance. Anyway, the substantial progress made in telecommunications significantly minimizes this matter.

Here, too, is another possible prospect concern for which you will want to be prepared to capitalize on or rationalize.

J. Successful Performance

Here is another respect in which Agencies are like shoemaker's children.

The ad you created for the Acme Company earned an exceptionally high readership rating in *Porno Age*. Of course, this remarkable achievement is called to the attention of the client. And hopefully their reaction is better than, "That's the kind of performance we should be getting anyway."

All right, you've promoted this super job to this lucky ingrate. But how about so many prospects who would *appreciate* this great work?

Consider this.   To those non-competitive advertisers in the same issue—or those you would rather have—merchandise this accomplishment to the hilt. The numbers are there. You scored 72% above the norm. How would they like results such as that?

This door-opener should at least get you an appointment. And since your Creative product is the most obvious evidence of your value, your dynamic ad should cause dissatisfaction with the disappointing one prepared by their present Agency. You have proved being able to produce much better results—and are available.

Therefore, whatever you achieve for clients should also be used to pay off for you with prospects. *Every* noteworthy achievement should be viewed in terms of how it can serve as an inducement to attract new business.

Agencies spend so much time trying to dream up cutesy devices. Usually just touting themselves. But what could be more impressive than your actual accomplishments—and what this could do for the prospect?

This approach is success-oriented.   And that's what the advertiser wants. How well are you merchandising being better able to deliver? It should be S.O.P. to parlay client success into Agency success.

K.   New Category of Account

Here is a major new source of business for you. It is the type of account you haven't had before. Here is how to go after them.

But first, what not to do. Don't go in defensively. For instance, if the prospect zings you with, "How can you pitch us? Your Agency doesn't have a bread account." And you counter with, "If we had a bread account, we wouldn't be here."

Admittedly, it is frustrating trying to determine if and how you can solicit an account in a category with which the Agency hasn't been previously involved. That is why an Agency will too often take itself out of contention for a desirable prospect—assuming this factor automatically disqualifies them.

Not at all.   The prospect isn't just buying your name.   Rather, it is your *people's experience* in their field—wherever obtained. And they are especially interested in the *Agency's marketing know-how*.

It could well be that even though your shop has never had a related account, your people may have the working knowledge in this area that can be very impressive. So while you may have to acknowledge a lack of involvement from a corporate standpoint, you can promote your Staff as having had a combined total of 128 years of experience in this area.

But don't expect this verbal claim to suffice. For credibility, document in writing the names of your people who have worked on related accounts, where, in what capacity, and for how long.

There are agencies who perform this function on a state-of-the-art basis. They have all this information for every employee on computer. For whatever type of account to be solicited, they push the magic buttons and come up with a specific list of the appropriate talent their Agency can offer. At the presentation, furnishing this printout is very effective and compensates for not being the Agency of record for a similar advertiser. Because in the aggregate, what the prospect is buying is *people*.

There is another reason why your appeal doesn't depend on having had a prospect's competitor as a client. It is possible that you have, or have had, an account with the same market as theirs. For example, if the prospect's thrust is to an upscale audience, and you are adequately experienced in this demographic area, then you are professionally qualified to service this business.

Further, there is still another reason for an advertiser to consider an Agency without an established reputation in their field. Your value can also be demonstrated convincingly via a related marketing experience.

Specifically, if the prospect has a distribution problem, and you solved one like it for a client, the category of account becomes incidental. If relevant, you could even use a high-tech case history in regard to food. What's most important, you already have the marketing know-how. You can always pick up product information.

Beyond your marketing capacity, there are also your functional qualifications. Particularly if you want to diversify.

For instance, let's take the case of Agencies whose clients' advertising is placed entirely in Trade media. These could be Business-to-Business, Healthcare or High-Tech shops. However, they want to start appealing to accounts who are also involved in Broadcast.

Your Agency being strong in one account category or medium needn't mean it is weak in others. Don't wait for a negative assumption to be raised—and have to scramble to convince them otherwise.

Here is how one Agency of this type in Silicon Valley handled this challenge. They didn't want to be put in the position of having to defend their presumed lack of Creative experience in the TV area. They prepared a storyboard on how they would promote this prospect's product in this medium—and routinely included it in their presentation.

This strategy enabled the Agency to platform its talent in a positive manner—and head off doubt being raised as an issue. The result is they are now in the finals—with the jury still out.

So you can broaden your base as desired. Begin by objectively determining the areas that prospects in industries new to your Agency might suspect your not being adequately qualified for. Then you take the initiative in dispelling this misconception—in an imaginative, constructive manner.

On this basis, you can not only reach for the brass ring—but also grab hold of it.

Thus, you needn't be at a disadvantage if you haven't sliced-rye-bread experience—or produced a string of CLIO-winning commercials. Your "smarts" on how to get it into the store, or what to put on the air, is of greater concern to the prospect.

Summing up, despite any seeming shortcomings, you do have the most important ingredients in the performance mix: qualified people and the necessary operating experience.

L.   Toughest Lesson

You felt real good about that presentation. And you should. Everything was right on the money. Your team were those likeliest to appeal to and impress the prospect. The pitch was relevant to their interests and needs. And the results promised were believable and better than they are presently getting.

Further, you were on a roll in both concept and execution. Because you flushed out the necessary information in your pre-presentation meeting with them so as to develop the most appropriate presentation. And your team came across as pros due to the discipline and confidence gained in rehearsal.

In fact, you felt euphoric about it—since this kind of preparation and conduct is what resulted in your having won the last three times.

Then came the cold gray light of dawn. A different Agency was selected. What particularly hurt is that they aren't as experienced in the prospect's field—and don't have your depth and caliber of personnel.

Where did you go wrong? You didn't. Apparently the chemistry factor wasn't right. And you can't do anything about the human equation.

Difficult as it might be to accept, as maybe Confucius said, *"Everybody ain't gonna love you, Baby."*

Therefore, don't panic into changing strategy that has proved successful. Rather, it is a matter of not becoming emotionally unglued because of not always being irresistible.

Recognize that even with everything going for you in presentation, your charm isn't going to work all the time. Hang in there—and don't let a downer that doesn't make any sense throw you off stride. Instead, have the faith to stick with the necessary basics mentioned above, and you'll get more than your share of new business.

Chapter 17

Compensation Caveats

A. Perspective

In simpler times, the method of compensation wasn't a factor in Agency selection. Everyone played the same game: 15% commission.

Then tradition gave way to negotiation. Because advertisers are now expecting the same cost-efficiency of Agencies as is required of them.

As a result of the demise of this status quo, compensation has become a key criterion. And since it is a consideration in many areas of solicitation activity, this is dealt with wherever appropriate throughout this book. There are certain matters, though, that warrant being singled out for special attention. You'll see why in this chapter.

B. Advertiser Attitude

As is being made amply evident, advertisers aren't buying the 15% commission system any more just because it is tradition. Few are willing or can afford to make this concession to sentiment.

This stand is being taken because of the increasing market pressure to operate more economically *in all areas*. This has resulted in their becoming more knowledgeable regarding Agency finances. Many advertisers now have a fair idea of what amount of service Agencies can provide based on income received.

If it is a Business-to-Business, Healthcare or High-Tech account—concentrating in Trade Pubs—they realize you can't break even on 15%. By contrast, advertisers primarily in Network TV, are aware that handling this kind of business for a straight 15% is a license to steal.

Contrary to the assumption by Agency cynics that advertisers are out to screw you, actually most of them want you to make a satisfactory profit. And for a basic reason: they want to be associated with a winner. In essence, the advertiser wants an Agency it can respect—not one that can be had.

However, they are concerned about—and intend to protect against—your making an unjustifiable profit. That's why the growing preference to pay on the basis of time charges for work performed—rather than the coincidence of Media budget. In support of this, advertisers use the analogy that their legal firm doesn't peg its charges according to their clients' sales. Rather, on services rendered. The crux of the matter is that advertisers want payment to be equitable: commensurate with output.

Thus, whether Agency compensation is based on time or work: fine. As long as the Agency can receive a realistic profit. And the advertiser can pay according to what they get—rather than what you fell into.

The bad news is that you won't get fat on this arrangement. But the good news is that you will be assured of an acceptable profit.

Most important, selling a method of payment geared to productivity rather than chance offers advertiser satisfaction in the most meaningful manner: value received.

C.   Method of Payment

There is an important development taking place in Advertiser/Agency compensation. A smart move, long overdue.

Because Agencies can no longer afford to get hung up on intermediate words like Commission or Fee. Having been deceived (and burned) by these front-end terms, they have come to realize that the only word that matters is *profit*.

As a result, these converts are evaluating prospects more realistically. Specifically, according to projected workload and estimated income. Then the amount of dollar profit deserved is established. Not some cockamamie formula. Instead, the exact number of dollars to which the Agency is entitled.

This net-oriented approach prevents being dazzled by an account's assumed size or appeal. Either they are affordable based on your requirements, or they aren't. If this concept seems too cut-and-dried, better bring into focus the purpose of your Agency: a profitable enterprise or a charitable institution.

The application of this discipline is contained in the following case history.

One of the most wonderful prospect inquiries you can receive after a presentation is, "In our particular case, what would be the most appropriate form of compensation?" Here is how Bill Biggs, majordomo of Biggs/Gilmore in Kalamazoo, handles it. Being exceptionally charming, he disarmingly replies, "Whatever will make you happy."

Bill isn't giving anything away. He couldn't care less what they call it. His only concern is that the account returns the predetermined amount of profit.

I've heard his own people ask, "But, Bill, what if some other Agency undercuts us?" His Socratic reply was, "We'll wish them the best of luck. We have a responsibility to serve our Agency as well as clients."

In the final analysis, charity begins at home. So develop a two-way-street mentality regarding compensation. Because you can only take care of a client if the Agency is adequately cared for.

D. Unsophisticated Prospect

There are all kinds of ways to make—or lose—money in the Agency business. The obvious factor is payment for services provided. However, your profit is directly affected by the amount of time needed to justify that which is developed.

If a client has a working knowledge of Agency operation and work performed, you can concentrate on what you have proposed—needing only a minimum of time for indoctrination. But if they are lacking in this experience, then the period spent educating them in addition to your presentation, can become unaffordable.

A key consideration in determining a prospect's profitability is their sophistication in dealing with Agencies. Because it is not only a matter of how much time you spend on work performed. It is also how long it takes to sell this to the client.

In order to realize a satisfactory profit from a naive prospect, you may have to build into your charges the time cost of bringing them up to speed.

So to whatever extent applicable, take this matter into consideration when negotiating compensation.

E.   Desirable but Unaffordable

Yet, don't arbitrarily turn away a prospect with acceptable billing because of assuming they couldn't be sufficiently profitable. Granted, based on estimated income and projected workload, they may seem unaffordable. Rather than writing them off though, present the amount of supplementary income necessary for you to realize a legitimate profit. (Sure you can be had. At your price.)

If they accept: great. This advertiser has just graduated from appalling to appealing. However, if they refuse, they will still respect your acumen. And you didn't offend by rejection of what might be a worthwhile prospect down the road.

So don't eliminate; negotiate. Sound out the prospect. Your value to them may be such whereby they would be willing to work out a financial arrangement that would accommodate you.

F.   Political Advertising

It is necessary to periodically bring political accounts back into focus.

Granted, this type of business is very tempting. It offers the opportunity for substantial income in a relatively brief period. Thus, some Agencies will salivate when the time comes for political campaigns to get underway. In fact, some will get so carried away as to forget the first law for compensation on this type account: **C.O.D.**

Even though aware of the considerable financial risk in handling a political client, on occasion this knowledge is compromised by idealism or greed.

For instance, there is an Agency head in Atlanta who was approached by a State Senator to handle his reelection campaign. Although the Agency had a policy against accepting *any* political advertising, this candidate happened to be a close personal friend. For that matter, the C.E.O. knew that his buddy was in such good financial shape that it wasn't necessary to stipulate pre-payment of charges.

This naivete ignored the nature of the political beast—and the ground rules for the game. As a result, six months afterwards, the C.E.O. was still trying to collect the $24,000 owed to the Agency. At this stage, he desperately stated to the deadbeat, "I never dreamed you would try to stiff me!" The State Senator vehemently denied this accusation and countered with, "I'd rather owe you this money for the rest of my life than renege on my word to pay you!"

Remember, for this type business, there is no exception to the rule born of bitter experience: *Get your money up front.* Because even if the politician may be honest in some respects, that's not the way the game is necessarily played with the Agency. Therefore, support your candidate at the ballot box—not out of your Agency's cash box.

Chapter 18

Blunders to Avoid

A. Perspective
B. The Two Major Causes for Coming in Second
C. Description of Agency
D. Role of Creative
E. Evaluating Prospect Advertising
F. Materials vs. Presenters
G. Gimmicks
H. No Written Commitment

A. Perspective

Sometimes the winning Agency is the one that made the fewest mistakes. The major reasons for being eliminated are:

- inadequate pre-presentation input
- insufficient rehearsal
- bad chemistry
- irrelevant presentation
- offensive conduct
- unsatisfactory handling of prospect zingers

Beyond these obvious traps, there are a variety of other pitfalls that could scuttle your being selected. We had better examine the more dangerous ones because any of these could do you in. However, since criticism carries with it the responsibility to contribute, also furnished is the alchemy to make a silk purse out of a sow's ear.

B.   The Two Major Causes for Coming in Second

Before we go any further, let's establish top-of-mind awareness of the two major causes for an Agency coming in 2nd—and what it takes to win.

First, there is the belief that who would know better than you how to develop a presentation. The strategy is based on the assumption that the prospect is holding still because they want to get to know you. Sure, they do—but only after you've satisfied what's in it for them.

So you sell hard rather than smart, concentrating on promoting the Agency—leaving dealing with the prospect's perceived needs as an afterthought. As a result, the pitch becomes an ego-trip—based on past performance and successes claimed. This unrelated nostalgia turns off the prospect because they can't associate themselves with it.

Instead, open with what you learned they want to hear about. Then devote the rest of the time to proving why your Agency is best able to satisfy their wants. This involves targeting as quickly as possible on what they consider their most important marketing needs—and the Agency functions most important to them. This is the best strategy for satisfying their expectations—and distinguishing your presentation from the routine typical ones.

Again, remember: the prospect is holding still to first find out what's in it for them. And then why your Agency can best provide it. However, bear in mind they are sold by the *benefits*—not the availability—of your services.

Second, upon developing a dynamic presentation, you assume it's so compelling that the prospect can't help but draw from it why your Agency is preferable to any other.

But the prospect becomes numb very easily. (How often have you seen that glazed look?)

Further, they will not make the effort to think. As far as they are concerned, it is a buyer-seller situation. And it is your responsibility to attract and hold their attention. Only what is readily apparent—and so intriguing—will penetrate and be absorbed.

How can this be achieved? First, critically appraise whether your presentation was developed to appeal to and satisfy the prospect—or your Agency. (Too often, the latter is the case.)

Then, invite a Devil's Advocate to the rehearsal. Someone not encumbered by pride of authorship. And who has the clout to be objective. It would be especially desirable if such person also has in-depth industry experience and advertiser knowledge of Agency presentations. Having these four qualifications, he/she becomes the most valuable person in your rehearsal.

This individual not only exists—but is probably available to you. He/she is a client, who by virtue of past or present involvement, is an authority on your prospect's industry and/or market. And of course, has a track record in choosing Agencies.

This action was taken by a Minneapolis Agency. They have a major bank client for whom merchandisable results have been produced. Thus, they decided to roll out and parlay this success among other non-conflicting banks.

Having a good relationship with the Ad-V.P. at their client, the Agency invited him to cut them up at their rehearsal. Result: the Agency credits the hands-on insight and objectivity of this Ad-V.P. with providing the clincher for winning.

Thus, when appropriate, capitalize on this secret weapon—prior to going into combat. It could provide your Agency with the added firepower that will enable coming out alive in a shootout.

Summing up, if your presentation can withstand the disciplines of a critical appraisal and Devil's Advocate, then you know that at least you are on the right track.

C. Description of Agency

Forgo the hackneyed sales ploy of claiming your Agency is different.

Regardless of philosophy, size, specialty or location, an Agency is an Agency is an Agency—with essentially the same problems and opportunities. Your potential for distinction lies in being *better*—not different.

Is this just a matter of semantics? No. Because this statement is just as irksome to a prospect as when they tell you, "You gotta realize, our business is different."

Anyway, "different" could be construed as being "odd." However, there is no doubt that "better" conveys "superiority."

D. Role of Creative

While advertisers want an Agency where creativity can flourish, they *don't* want an environment that functions to provide therapy for their Copy and Art people.

Specifically, an advertiser wants it known that their product or service—not the ad—is the star.

Thus, platform your Creative as being vital—not flaky. Registering that its role is to persuade for the client—not win awards for the Agency.

E.   Evaluating Prospect Advertising

Usually this function is initiated by the Agency—using it as a selling device. On occasion, a prospect will request this service.

The former tactic warrants little attention because you probably already know that it is suicidal. Specifically, regardless of how well your criticism is cloaked in the guise of a constructive contribution, nevertheless the impression conveyed is that they screwed up in having approved this inferior work. Then, having revealed their ineptness, their jobs are threatened. Now, how anxious will this prospect be to bring your Agency aboard—and risk being finished off?

Therefore, no matter how lousy their advertising, there can *never* be any justification for trashing it. Because this amounts to trashing the people to whom you are presenting.

It is not that their existing advertising is bad. Rather, that what you could provide is *so good*. So fresh, intriguing and persuasive. The prospect would be hiring you for what they perceive as being better—not because of what you accused them of—being worse.

The reverse situation is more complicated and requires being dealt with in greater detail.

When a prospect asks an Agency to evaluate its advertising, this may be sincere or a trap. But either way, it can be a heads-you-lose, tails-you-lose situation.

Don't get sucked into this supposed opportunity without having options. This is a gamble that serves the prospect's interests—however, it is usually stacked against you.

There are four reasons why you can get hurt—terminally:

1. You can't possibly be familiar enough with their marketing strategy and advertising objectives. Thus, not being qualified to pass judgment, there is bound to be an inadvertent blunder.

2. It is inconceivable that there wouldn't be anything critical in your analysis. Accordingly, those who have approved their advertising become instant enemies.

3. There is the risk of your judgment being used to resolve internal political differences. Then you are remembered as the hatchet-man—and have outlived your usefulness.

4. Your conclusions are bound to be suspect because your self-interest is involved.

Yet, you don't want to flatly refuse their request. Whether it's on the level or you're being conned, here is how to salvage the situation. But first, let's set the stage for the solution—with this nightmare.

An Agency President told me last week about a prospect having enticed him into a very tacky position. This involvement cost him much time, effort—and the respect of his peers at two prominent Agencies. He reluctantly wrote off this experience as a calculated risk—and couldn't have done otherwise.

Sure he could—and have made money. Here is what happened—and how you can benefit from this debacle.

First, let's protect this Agency President by referring to him by only his first name: Bob. Bob had been romancing the Sr. V.P./Marketing of a major package goods company—any portion of whose account would be highly desirable. It had been determined that this contact had the clout to hire or fire Agencies.

The opportunity to ingratiate himself with the prospect arose—however, in a dangerous way.

The Sr. V.P. offered Bob tapes of TV commercials just produced by the two incumbent Agencies—and asked that these be critiqued. Supposedly, this cooperation would provide the incentive for Bob's shop to be given active consideration.

Despite this devious tactic, Bob salivated—rationalizing that the potential was just too great to resist. In fact, rather than becoming just a little bit pregnant, he decided to go full term. Namely, Bob not only assigned his Creative staff to analyze these commercials from a concept and production standpoint, but also involved his Marketing people to identify objectives and determine the appropriateness of the approach taken. For further impact, Bob called upon the resources of his Agency's other offices for their input. Obviously, the combined time cost was brutal.

Needless to say, the report was very impressive. So much so that the Sr. V.P. sent copies of it to the presidents of his two Agencies.

They were appalled at this client subterfuge—and their competitor's acquiescence. But who are they going to get mad at? Sure as hell not their valued client. Instead, Bob became the villain. And whereas there had previously been a good fraternal relationship, the other two now froze him out.

To compound the injury, this favor wasn't enough to pry loose any of the prospect's business.

Sure, Bob was used—but there was no need to be had. He could have gained stature—and profit—by proposing to undertake the project on a fee basis. Specifically, instead of giving the store away, Bob should have submitted a recommendation detailing:

- the professional, objective approach to be taken
- the service to be provided
- the results that could be expected
- the direction for applying the findings
- a justification for the charge

This then makes the assignment a legitimate business deal—serving both interests. From the Agency's standpoint, it doesn't come off as being desperate. And if nothing occurs afterwards, at least you were compensated for an above-board job. On the prospect's behalf, this arrangement is clean—and they are not beholden. As a result, the prestige of each remains intact. And the Agency can continue to ethically solicit the account without any loss of face—or financially shafting itself.

What can be learned from this case history is best expressed by the credo of the Harvard Business School: "If you can't sell it, sit on it, but don't give it away."

F.   Materials vs. Presenters

There are probably as many ways for blowing a new business presentation as there are Agencies.

One of the more common causes is the attempt to impress the prospect up front by placing a portfolio of material where each of them will be seated. This usually contains a variety of information about the Agency and various examples of its work. It is assumed that this tactic will favorably pre-condition them.

Instead, the Agency is fighting its presenters. This is a distracting device that competes with what will be said and shown. Even reference to its content is difficult and confusing because people read at different rates. Finally, most damaging, it sacrifices eyeball contact.

This matter is so critical that it's hard to be tactful about it. For instance, like when Buzzy Killeen was C.E.O. at Fitzgerald in New Orleans and retained me to critique a forthcoming new business presentation.

He began by acknowledging, "I know the ground rules. Y'all role-play the prospect. Before I start the presentation, though, Jack, I want y'all to promise to be totally frank. Completely frank. Absolutely frank."

I said, "Okay Buzzy. I'll be frank, frank, frank."

He then got underway by placing a folder in front of me and exclaimed, "Now Mr. Matthews, just get a load of this fabulous 5-color reproduction, these fantastic client testimonials, such successful case histories . . ." I interrupted with, "Buzzy, I'll try to be diplomatic." He growled, "Jack, I asked y'all to be frank." I came back with, "Well, at least I'll be discreet." This time he barked, "Dammit, I asked y'all to be frank!" So I unloaded, "All right Buzzy, you just screwed yourself." And he stated, "Y'all didn't have to be *that* frank."

I then went on to explain the problems of competing with himself, varying reading speeds and loss of eyeball contact. I hope he became a convert. Otherwise, his pitch would have died without redemption.

You retain control by *presenting* whatever you want shown—in the sequence desired. Rather than an ego-trip in a packet, simply distribute a one-page agenda—whose brevity and ease of being read will not interfere with your program.

G. Gimmicks

Even the most sophisticated of Agencies keep looking for a by-the-numbers formula for winning. However, the prerequisite for scoring is the relevance of your pitch—in an environment conducive to the prospect being receptive. This eliminates any all-purpose canned approach.

The above premise is a truism, from which I won't get any flack. Just as it is conceded that playing the horses is a losing proposition because the odds are usually 8-to-1 against you. Yet, in both instances, there is a constant search for a "system" to beat the odds.

For example, here are a couple of "hooks" used by some heavy hitters in New York. Unfortunately, each has recently worked—once. As a result, both assume they found the new business Holy Grail. And are diverting their efforts from proved successful strategy to these cockamamie devices.

Hokey Approach

This consists of showing the prospect samples of exciting Creative work—and then informing them they can't have it because of your not knowing the prospect's business. That's being a lousy host. You invited the prospect over for cocktails—and then didn't serve any since you don't know what they drink.

This supposedly *realistic* angle is a letdown—and negative. A prospect wants to know what's in it for him—not what he can't have.

Actually, you *can* present "cause and effect" based only on input provided. Then there isn't any concession of ignorance on your part—and you've registered your capacity to satisfy their needs according to the parameters set.

Summing up, give the prospect the same thing they expect of their advertising: *A reason why to buy*.

Cutesy Approach

The Agency responsible for the other case history concentrates its activity on those accounts wanted. (Rifle-shot method.) Fine so far. Then, for this missionary purpose, a woman with a British accent and a sexy voice phones the targeted contact *every day*—until this person agrees to come over to the Agency for a get-acquainted luncheon meeting with its top management.

Ostensibly, this persistence will wear down the prospect's reluctance. And the curiosity of meeting the body that goes with this intriguing voice will be irresistible.

Granted, this woman is well-trained in telemarketing. And knows the right moves. But the concept is offensive. Although it may appeal to the voyeur type, it will antagonize most others. Further, this conduct will ruin the Agency's chances with this advertiser for as long as that contact is there.

Therefore, use a constructive door-opener that offers to increase this person's corporate value—rather than a one-shot gimmick.

The moral of this message is that *there isn't any single miracle, regardless of how different, that will provide a quick-fix for landing new accounts*. There is only the sum of all the necessary sound activity it takes to win.

You have a much greater opportunity for winning using a strategy based on synergism rather than an individual tactic.

H.   No Written Commitment

Some Agencies pride themselves on their handshake arrangement with clients. It is assumed this lack of formal commitment is indicative of the respect for their word.

This ego-trip can be a bummer. All it means to the client is that they are less obligated. And if that is the way you want it, good luck with the greater risk. Because why should they buy you if renting will suffice? In effect, you are living together, they are being serviced—but there are no vows to deter them from any other affairs. Or worse, desert you for someone who will promise them a better, more permanent home.

A lack of written agreement also denies you two vital opportunities:

Protection
This details how your Agency operates—and method of compensation. Then if any doubts arise regarding the type of service they receive, there is tangible evidence that you kept your word.

Promotion
Enables setting forth officially, rather than on a self-serving basis, the variety of functions your Agency can provide. And why it would be to their advantage to make maximum use of them.

Granted, to some advertisers, a contract is an anathema. Incongruously, though, that termed **Letter of Agreement** is semantically acceptable. Same content. Just a difference in connotation.

As to appearance, how you read this new client will determine whether it should be a printed or typed form. The former implies it is the standard accepted approach. By contrast, the typed version is less awesome—and indicative of the personal nature of your relationship. Thus, consider which tactic would be more appealing.

Summing up, this confirmation of claims and promises made should preclude any misunderstandings or unwelcome surprises. It is evidence of your operating on a professional instead of casual basis. This distinction has become increasingly important to advertisers. So after you ask for the order, give them a receipt—for signature.

Chapter 19

The Rational Reaction to Competition

A. Perspective

The subject in presentation is the prospect—not the other Agencies. And why your Agency is best for them—not why the others aren't. So don't distract the prospect. Your purpose is to create a winner—not a loser. Let the others defeat themselves.

Of course be concerned about competitive activity. Which Agencies; their strengths, weaknesses and tactics. And, if necessary, how to combat them. But don't waste time *worrying*. It is counter-productive and blows the situation out of proportion. Devote all your energies to proving that your Agency is the most desirable—and the other candidates will end up eating your dust.

B. Developments

First, here is an overview as to what's going on. There is currently more solicitation activity than can be recalled.

Significantly, the game has changed in the respect that Agencies are no longer limiting themselves to soliciting only the accounts of their peers.

Nor are they restricting themselves anymore to pitching accounts of prescribed size—or for that matter, appropriateness to their shop. Therefore, it has become open season on *all* your accounts—by *any* Agency.

A good example is the tactic being used by one of the top 10 Agencies. Their new business strategy has been expanded to include aggressively soliciting any prospect on which they believe they can make a satisfactory profit—*including yours*.

For instance, for smaller advertisers, their angle consists of revealing, "Did you realize that over 70% of our clients bill under $1,000,000?" I don't know whether that's on a monthly or quarterly basis—but it is proving to have considerable appeal to smaller advertisers who never thought they could qualify for so prestigious an Agency.

As further evidence of this mentality, another Agency in this category will go after any account on which they figure they can make 2.5 times the employee salary necessary to service it. (The national average is 3.0.) In the event any of you choose to dismiss this action as being irrelevant because of the size of these Agencies, you could be inundated by the trickle-down effect.

This sheer weight and type of effort is making your clients more vulnerable than ever. Further, with the traditional 15% commission system becoming an anachronism, Agencies are now wheeling and dealing like never before. And not only under the table; they are throwing in the table!

Therefore, you had better do unto others before they do unto you.

C. Size

To begin with, let's dispel this delusion. Unless an Agency is mammoth, there is a tendency to be defensive about its size. This self-deprecating attitude is defeatist, minimizes prospect impact, and infects your entire operation.

Now for perspective. There is no such thing as a "small" Agency. Only Agencies with people who think small. If, however, you have fewer employees than a competitor, and the matter of size comes up, you are never smaller. Rather, you operate *leaner*.

Granted, you may not be as big as some of your competitors from the standpoint of income. But you intend to become so. For that matter, you are already better than they are. Aren't you? Better believe it—or there is no reason to become a client of yours.

Therefore, get rid of any paranoia regarding larger Agencies—and the assumption that you are stymied because you can't fight fire with fire. You don't have to. Usually water will suffice. This is because all Agencies have the same common denominator: *people*. And even though a competitor may have more, they don't put on their pants both legs at a time.

For that matter, the prospect may not be looking for an elephant. They may want a tiger. Like you.

D.   Prestige

While we're at it, let's tackle any defeatism that exists regarding the advertisers supposed desire for the prestige of being with a big name Agency. Those shops assuming this are conceding accounts to the mega-Agencies. However, the Y&RS, Saatchis, McCanns, Ogilvys, etc. don't have a sure-win advantage. Nor are they invincible.

The most meaningful proof is the success achieved by Agencies formed not all that long ago. For instance, look at the track records of Hal Riney, Hill, Holiday and Chiat/Day/Mojo.

They didn't buy the negativism that it couldn't be done. Rather, they set about to convince blue-chip advertisers that they have better people, with better ideas, who can execute them better. By concentrating on what an advertiser buys: *people*, they succeeded in competing against the heavy hitters. And you can, too.

Actually, you are all starting out even, with the same thing going for you: *opportunity*. The winner is the one who makes the most of it.

Therefore, instead of falling into the cynical trap of assuming that presentations are rigged in favor of big-name Agencies, critically appraise yours to determine how it can be made more appealing. Because if those mentioned can do so well from ground zero you surely ought to make out due to already having momentum going for you.

Thus, get off the excuse of *why* you can't score. Instead, concentrate on *how* you're going to do it.

The most astute judgment of the matter of size came from Glenn Verrill who ran the BBDO office in Atlanta. At dinner there, he mentioned having receiving word that day of the name of the parent company for their three-Agency merger: **Omnicom**. I commented (unoriginally) that it sounded like they manufacture computer chips. Having a stake in it, he took this development more seriously. His concern went beyond the name to the operation itself. His conclusion was as brilliant in concept as in its simplicity. "Bigger isn't necessarily better. Only better is better." Here is a credo that *any* Agency should live by.

E. Treatment of Opponents

Agencies get so concerned as to who their competitors are when pitching an account planning to switch. Unfortunately, sometimes this goes beyond curiosity. It is assumed this insight provides a competitive edge. Namely, being able to promote why your Agency is preferable to the others being considered.

However, the extent to which you devote your presentation to combating the others is the amount of time sacrificed for convincing the prospect of why your Agency is best for them. And hardly any Agency can afford to concede this advantage to the competition.

Therefore, sell *for* your Agency rather than *against* the others. That is, concentrate on what it will take for you to win—instead of how you can cause them to lose.

Admittedly, though, sometimes it can be to your advantage to know who your competitors are. This will enable you to capitalize on your strengths and compensate for weaknesses. Of course, always positively and constructively. I'm not moralizing. Because if any attempt is made to instill doubt regarding your competitors, the environment created could boomerang to include your Agency.

However, your method of finding out will affect the impression made. Don't confront the prospect by asking who the others are. You're not entitled to know.

Instead, if appropriate, subtly inquire as to whether the names of the contenders will be released to the press. This finesse precludes offending the prospect—and your seeming worried. Then, if they are willing to identify the others, you will have flushed out this information without jeopardizing their opinion of you.

Then, in presentation, you can get as competitive as circumstances require—as long as you *never mention another Agency by name*. After all, this romance is between you and the prospect. Why acknowledge anyone else? You only afford them further recognition—while forfeiting your own objectivity. Worst of all, any negative implication impugns the prospect's judgment in considering any other Agency.

Moreover, don't get baited into passing judgment on another Agency. You may be able to knock them out of contention. But the risk of it backfiring is too great to take.

If the prospect presses the issue, you have a respected out—which will accomplish the same purpose. You can righteously state, "We're here to present our strengths—not their weaknesses. Our approach is strictly positive; being entirely prospect-oriented."

So don't dilute your effect by falling prey to this tempting but shabby tactic of sniping at competitors. You might wind up with the prospect's gratitude—but not the account.

Remember: It's a matter of why your Agency should be selected—not why the others shouldn't.

F. More Expensive Commercials

A desperate question was popped at me in a recent Agency network meeting. "In a competitive presentation, if you know that another Agency has better TV commercials than yours, what should you do?" I replied, "Don't."

The inquiring president snapped back with, "What the hell kind of answer is that?" This desired reaction enabled me to explain: "Their commercials won't beat you. Your defeatist attitude will."

Although a little heavy, the end justified the means. Because as I have previously stressed, the only way you can go into a new business presentation is as a winner.

After this explanation, he simmered down and asked, "Okay, since we are up against Coke commercials, how do we combat their advantage?" With his now being receptive to positive action, success is possible.

Here's the solution. You can overcome their seeming superiority in *appearance* of material by the *conduct* of your presentation.

Your competitor may assume that their more expensive commercials will speak for themselves—and rely on them to do so. By contrast, you finish the job by selling how the *strategy* of your commercials can fulfill this prospect's needs. This will compensate for supposedly more impressive work, since the prospect won't bother to associate the other Agency's efforts with their requirements.

Thus, *relate your performance to the prospect's operation—and how they will gain from it*. Because your vaunted competitor may be indulging themselves in the ego-feeding luxury of merely taking credit for their material. Upon comparison, your Agency will come off as being preferable.

So despite what may seem like insurmountable odds, stop whining and start winning.

G.   Cost of Presentation

Some Agencies will forgo upgrading themselves by soliciting larger accounts. It is assumed they can't afford to spend as much as needed on these presentations as can bigger Agencies. This misconception is caused by articles in the Trade press citing the astronomical amounts spent on major presentations. As a result, many Agencies have seriously limited their potential.

Apparently it is necessary to identify on *what* all this money is spent. It is not on the *physical* requirements for the presentation. How many slide or film projectors or VCRs can you rent? And the price for processing slides, tape or film is approximately the same for any Agency.

What runs up the cost is the content.   And if you feel that the audio-visual function of your presentation need look like a soft-drink commercial, you'll pay accordingly.

Beyond this, the heavy part of the expense you read about is accounted for by spec Creative: comped-up layouts and videotaped commercials. By contrast, the investment in the vehicle for presentation, the medium used, is just about a standoff.

Therefore, unless the production of your A-V message must be especially elaborate, or you are required to submit air-ready commercials, it *is* possible to compete against bigger Agencies.

So don't restrict your opportunity for significant growth by figuring you're at a disadvantage in this respect. Particularly, if you have the confidence you should have in your Agency's ability to persuade via the materials developed and your presentation of them.

Chapter 20

Selection of the Most Appealing Presentation Team

A. Perspective

Now you are ready to bring what you have conceived to life. For the birth desired, this depends on who can deliver it most effectively.

B. Strategy

There has always been a dichotomy regarding the composition of the new business presentation team.

Some Agencies maintain that the team should be composed of only those who would work on the account. Namely, the ability and experience the prospect would actually receive.

By contrast, others hold that since the objective is to land the account, your participants should be those who can sell best. Then, the group who will be assigned to service this new client would be responsible for ingratiating themselves to such an extent that the original charmers will be forgotten.

The tie-breaker is a simple one: the prospect's attitude. As far as they are concerned, anyone present from the Agency will be involved on their account. If not, why are they there? The prospect isn't shopping for an Agency logo. Rather, for the specific people who will become theirs.

Granted, sometimes the "swat team" concept can increase your rate of scoring. However, it can also result in a higher incidence of account losses. Because if ever a client discovers that one of your new business presenters by whom they were smitten isn't available, they will always believe they were deceived in the pitch. And after that, the Agency is on borrowed time.

So be as honest in your use of presenters as you should be in what they say. Otherwise, you too can get caught in the "revolving door" syndrome. And remember how expensive it was staffing up for this ex-client?

C. Size and Participation

The chemistry factor requires that the size and composition of your team be based on those comprising the prospect team.

Obviously, you don't want to outnumber them. Psychologically, they would feel placed at a disadvantage. (Or as the prospect expresses it, " . . . ganged up on.")

Further, every member of your team must have an active role in the presentation. You can't afford any observers. Otherwise, it is suspected that you brought along empty suits to compensate for whatever was lacking in the Agency's message.

I'm asked, "Well, then, how else will a young Account Executive learn?" Easy. By attending your rehearsals. It's too risky trying to train them while in combat.

D. Composition

Create a presentation team as you would create an ad: for its impact on their market.

To begin with, seek personality balance. Besides the dynamo, it should also include your solid citizen. (The one who wears white socks to the office.) This person is likely to have greater overall appeal.

Agencies wrongly believe that each member must be cast from the same sensational mold. But the prospect selection team isn't comprised as such.

Without sacrificing putting your best feet forward, build in the variety of characters the prospect can most associate themselves with. All else notwithstanding, there must first be rapport between the presentation and selection teams before there will be acceptance of the Agency.

If you were to have 20 presentations coming up, hypothetically they could require 20 different combinations of your people.

E.   Qualifications

The most important criterion for selecting your presenters is their ability to communicate. Regardless of how well qualified in their function, if they can't register this clearly and persuasively, it will seriously weaken your effect.

However, they can be only those of your people likeliest to appeal to and impress that individual prospect.

F.   Star Presenter

Despite Agencies having learned the preceding truisms early, most have forgotten it long ago. This is evidenced by Agencies continuing to feature their same star presenter for every prospect. This is the person who earned the reputation of being dynamic on his/her feet.

But hold it. It may have been discovered in the pre-presentation meeting with the prospect that they are the laid-back type, and being such, your dynamo would overwhelm and possibly offend them.

Therefore, your star isn't a designated hitter for use in any situation. Rather, your best presenter is always the one most appropriate for the prospect involved. He or she may not be as articulate or charming as your star—but more important, this person is that prospect's kind of people.

G.   Anyone Objectionable?

Since an Agency must cover itself for any eventuality, even concerns such as this surface, "Is there any type person who might be unacceptable to the prospect as a member of the Agency presentation team?"

No. None. For any Agency members there is built-in acceptance because the prospect assumes the team consists of those who can best represent your Agency.

However, they are accepted for admission only. Your objective, though, approval, still needs to be earned. And this is achieved by their evidence of professionalism and vitality—at which no one excels or is lacking because of race, religion, nationality or sex.

Consider this. Psychologists claim that any individual appeals to only 25% of the others. The feelings of the majority 75% range from apathy to hostility. When soliciting new business, there is no such thing as a man for all seasons. It takes a person for each.

Chapter 21

Team Conduct Likeliest To Impress

A. Perspective
B. Appropriate Dress
C. Necessary Behavior
D. Use of Humor
E. Evidence of Teamwork
F. Effect of Taste
G. Profanity
H. Speaker Stature
I. Prospect Questions
J. Unexpected Interruptions

A. Perspective

The ideal situation would be if all you had to concern yourself with was the quality of your work. Then you could be as misanthropic as this business causes a person to be.

However, while an advertiser realizes they need the best performance possible, they *want* the very best relationship. Which is more important? A want is always stronger than a need.

A prospect must first buy you before they will buy your work. Only after having convinced them of your compatibility can they be impressed by your performance.

You tried to provide for the right chemistry factor in the selection of your presenters. Thus, they should *conduct themselves* as being the prospect's kind of people.

B. Appropriate Dress

Let's start with the first basis by which a prospect forms a judgment of you: your appearance. What's right? You can best decide that by honestly answering for any presentation, "Do I look like a winner?" That's your objective, isn't it? Then *dress* like a winner! And that means dressing in a manner to show your respect for the prospect.

This is not only desirable. It is essential. Emery Lewis felt compelled to punctuate this point during my seminar at his McCann-Erickson office in Louisville. And justifiably so.

He said, "Let me tell you about the time we came in fifth out of four Agencies." At the time, they were doing collateral work for Kentucky Fried Chicken. On one occasion, Emery's client contact mentioned, "I meant to tell you that our co-op account for West Virginia is open. Although we're down to three finalists, I can still get you in. It bills about $1,000,000. Want a crack at it?"

Upon Emery acknowledging that they would be delighted, the KFC contact admonished, "But remember: We're dealing with the State of West By God Virginia. These are good old boys. So don't make your grand entrance in your usual swallow-tail coat, ascot and spats."

Emery agreed and thanked him for this perceptive advice. I was then told, "So the five of us went there dressed in nice plaid sports jackets, clean golf slacks, etc.

You can see what's coming. The other three Agency teams all showed up in 3-piece blue pin-stripe suits. As Emery put it, "We looked so different, we were eliminated right off the top. We couldn't have *given* the Agency away."

This experience proves the importance of evidence of Agency respect for the prospect. Without it, there can't be a relationship—or your being selected.

C. Necessary Behavior

Your behavior during presentation has a much greater influence on its effect than realized. All your professional qualifications notwithstand-ing, sometimes the final criterion for selection could be as arbitrary as, "Would I want to have these people to my home for dinner?" So mind your manners.

The best strategy is to conduct yourself throughout as if you were ap-plying for a job. In this context, here are two tips for making a better impression.

The first is based on a question that was frequently asked of Vince Lom-bardi: "How come your teams are always so great?" And he would reply, "Because the players have such respect for each other."

Well, the quality of your team's relationship is every bit as important. And should be made apparent by their interaction at the presentation.

Further, beyond claims and promises made, you're scrutinized for vi-tality, attitude and professionalism. How? Consider this. Only 20% of communications is by words. The balance is accounted for by listening, facial expressions and body language. Therefore, in addition to the job you do at the podium, the selection team is directly affected by the other 80% of you afterwards.

However, I can appreciate there is an emotional letdown when you finish. Further, this is compounded by the fact that you've heard your next speaker 39 times before—and not only do you know his part word-for-word, but could probably deliver it better anyway.

Your reaction is vital, though, since it sets the pace for the prospect. Thus, throughout the total presentation, you need give the impression of momentarily expecting the Second Coming. Remember: even when you're not at the podium, you are on just as much as the speaker.

As proof, think back. You couldn't help but notice how those from the prospect surreptitiously eyeballed each of you during the presentation. And their level of attention was no higher than that of the least interested Agency person.

How can the necessary absorption be exhibited? Here is a tactic for giving the impression of being totally enraptured by the speaker. Listen for the first word used beginning with an "A." When this occurs, move on to one starting with "B," then "C"—and so forth. Then, for each of your speakers, see how far you can get through the alphabet. This game will not only serve the purpose of conveying a high intensity of interest—but will help keep you awake.

This device, of course, could also cover for you in rambling client meetings.

D. Use of Humor

The first impression sought by the prospect is one of buttoned-down professionalism.

The initial meeting is your first chance—make sure it isn't your last. They want to experience a sense of confidence and trust in you—not be entertained. So be careful that the last laugh isn't on you. Here's why. I've been told by advertisers, "There have been presentations that we've heartily enjoyed. But that's not how we select an Agency."

This is not meant to imply that the use of humor is forbidden. Only jokes for the sake of such.

When relevant, it can make your point in a more appealing, memorable manner. Further, the use of humor can create a relaxed environment—one in which the prospect will be more receptive.

For instance, Rumrill-Hoyt in New York uses a delightful ice-breaker for this purpose. They open their presentation by mentioning, "Before telling you anything about ourselves, let's first check on whether you can pass our fitness test for clients, namely, whether you can qualify for our shop."

Then, after coming on this heavy, they quickly admit, "Actually, no advertiser has ever flunked this test." This is because the "test" turns out to be the Agency's qualifications—as they would benefit this prospect. So, of course, they always pass. This has proved to be a great warmer-upper—getting them off to a friendlier start.

But again, humor is to your advantage only if appropriate to the prospect's interests. And only if delivered by those of your people who have a knack for doing so.

E. Evidence of Teamwork

A prospect is more impressed by deed than word. Verbalizing your intent to fulfill their expectations is worthwhile. But it doesn't convince until actually demonstrated.

This concept was proved in a novel manner recently. I was working with an advertiser who decided to switch Agencies. They went through the cattle call/questionnaire/screening presentations.

Upon selecting the short list, they stressed to both finalists that they will be strongly influenced by the capacity for Agency teamwork. (The apparent dissension at their previous Agency caused loss of client confidence in their performance.)

Both finalists took this prospect direction literally. Agency "A" voiced their dedication to teamwork throughout their pitch. Agency "B" didn't make any mention of this. However, they *demonstrated* their belief in the importance of teamwork via the planned interaction of their presenters.

Thus, Agency "A" came across as offering contrived lip service while Agency "B" was convincing due to actual conduct. And the latter was clearly the winner. Therefore, what you *do* in presentation speaks louder than what you say.

For that matter, even if the advertiser desire for this attribute isn't specified, Agency evidence of teamwork is impressive. Because as a client it is assumed that if you can get along well with each other, there is a better chance of your getting along with them.

F.   Effect of Taste

If the human equation is satisfied, then the impression made is based on two factors: professional qualifications and presentation skills. Beyond this, though, there is an intangible that, of itself, can wipe out your credentials. It is the matter of *taste*.

Playing it safe to avoid offending doesn't require being rigidly programmed. Or self-righteous. Rather, it amounts to not taking anything for granted. This includes anticipating the unexpected. Otherwise, here is how even a rigged opportunity can be ruined.

An Agency was contacted by a substantial advertiser via an intermediary. This prospect's President was smitten by one of this Agency's campaigns and wanted to set up a one-to-one meeting with their C.E.O. The "John Alden" confided that if the chemistry was right, the Agency would be home safe with an upper 7-figure account.

The Agency C.E.O. came in well-prepared, was totally relevant, highly persuasive—and couldn't give it away. Afterwards, he reported to the intermediary that he was baffled by the President's fickle about-face.

The third-party mentioned, "You're not very observant." He went on to explain, "His office is liberally decorated with pictures, busts and statues of J.C. Nevertheless, you repeatedly sprinkled your pitch with 'Jeez' or 'Keerist' or a combination of both."

The advertiser's President was a born-again Christian! And he was infuriated by these irreverent references. End of prospect.

Thus, be loose, confident—but never so relaxed that you overlook this being a buyer-seller relationship.

G.   Profanity

Even if the selection team swears like Art Directors (usually misspelled), this does not give you the license to use such language. Initially, they consider themselves to be a private club—and resent such familiarity on your part. So for openers, play it safe. Express yourself as if they were your mother.

This isn't a matter of being so proper; just realistic. For instance, recently there were three finalists for a very desirable account—with one of them being given indication of having the inside track.

After the final presentations were made, I ran into one of the participants from the Agency seemingly wired in. I asked how it went and he said, "If we don't score on this one, we never will. Because we really related to them."

However, when it came down to the bottom line, a different Agency was selected. By now I was quite curious regarding this turn of events. Knowing the advertiser involved, I phoned to find out why they decided otherwise. My contact mentioned, "On the surface the preferred Agency was certainly more appealing. But, in the final analysis, we concluded that we just couldn't risk having our Company represented by such foul-mouthed bastards."

Therefore, an Agency should never blow a fine opportunity by conducting itself as if it's already one of them. It is not. And won't be if it does.

H.   Speaker Stature

Although hardly appropriate anymore, Agencies are still defensive about their blue-suede-shoe image. Yet, most advertisers with any degree of sophistication don't perceive Agencies as ranking somewhere between a real estate firm and a used car dealer. Despite this, Agencies attempt to compensate in new business presentations by bending over too far backwards to establish an "aw shucks" image. Usually at the expense of denigrating themselves.

For all the reasons you should know only too well, Agencies can be very proud of their function. Nevertheless, there is the obsessed concern to counter this assumed negative advertiser attitude.

This was proved again at an Agency presentation I was critiquing recently. After an excellent demonstration of their advantages, they platformed their heavy hitter for the closer. His credentials were remarkable—and he was very charismatic. Seemingly, everything going for him.

Even so, this person sent in for the kill felt the need to develop acceptance via a Mr. Humble approach. He opened by announcing, "I'm not going to be modest." And then he paid off this attempt at credibility by quoting Golda Meir: "Don't be modest. You don't have that much to be modest about."

This angle brought a few chuckles. Mostly at him; not with him. Then, to try to ingratiate himself, he conceded some apprehension. This was illustrated by drawing upon Winston Churchill, who said, "Never speak to an audience that knows more than you do."

After that second personal putdown, it was obvious he lost the selection team. Because they concluded that if he was lacking to that extent, and was representative of the Agency, it was not for them.

False humility is as transparent as your tissue roughs. Most often, it takes comp art to sell a prospect. So come in with your best shot. What you can be proudest of: your own self.

You didn't get where you're at by being wimpish. Rather, it was the result of obviously conveying ability and dynamism. Don't ever sacrifice what was responsible for your success by minimizing its value. You've proved what works. Encore!

I.   Prospect Questions

You're on a roll in the presentation. It has that undefinable rhythm that inspires confidence.

Then the prospect hits you with a question requiring some thought. It could probably be answered—if you just had a few moments to think without dead air time. But they seem to be expecting a profound reply—now.

Don't panic. Instead of blurting out an answer for the sake of such, ask them a question about their question—or for some elaboration on it. This will buy you the time to formulate a knowledgeable answer, acceptable to them.

However, if your response would require preparation, don't risk an off-the-cuff remark. (For instance, if they ask, "We have committed two-thirds of this fiscal year's Media budget. How would you handle the balance?") Mention that the importance of this matter requires analysis. Then inform them of how soon you will return with your recommendation.

Yet, how about when the prospect confronts you with, "How much do you recommend we spend?" Expecting you to pull a budget out of left field is a loaded request. Because regardless of how well this assignment is performed, it is based only on assumption and desire.

You've been placed in a no-win situation. Yet, in your eagerness to score, you scramble to come up with figures that are bound to be vulnerable. Obviously, you can't develop a meaningful proposal from scratch without any input.

So you've been baited. And seemingly stymied, since there is no way in which you can conjure a defensible amount.

However, you don't want to concede being unable to fulfill their challenge. Therefore, go on record regarding your capacity and willingness to deliver—if provided with the basis for developing an ad budget. Specifically, *their sales figures*.

It is improbable they will release this proprietary information. But you will have called their hand. If they are on the level, this "how much" zinger will not be used as a factor in considering you. Otherwise, you will know they are just playing games.

Do these tactics seem like gamesmanship? No. It's the pragmatism necessary to win it all. And that's the only way to compete. Because in the new business Olympics, there is no such thing as a silver medal.

J. Unexpected Interruptions

Even with these protective measures, though, there can be an unexpected interruption. And it will produce the amount of cold sweat that deodorants aren't made to overcome. Such as the slide tray being dropped. Or the prospect's decision-maker being called out—and asking that you wait until he returns.

In both instances, you are confronted with a maddening void. The way you handle these calamities will indicate your resourcefulness—or lack thereof.

Prepare a transitional filler for use in the event such a situation occurs. Where do you get this material? You will discover in rehearsal that your presentation well exceeds the amount of time allotted. The portions that need to be cut become your filler in case of emergency. Then, whatever said is relevant—and no one from the Agency has to come up with an impromptu soft shoe number.

In the event the opposite happens, and their decision-maker says, "Keep going"—that's okay, too—unless you're the only one remaining in the room.

Chapter 22

Presentation Skills Beyond Those Taught

A. Perspective

It is worth the risk of offending you by bringing up something as elementary as your vocal delivery in presentation. To the prospect, though, this is a forecast of a strength sought: The power to persuade. And it is viewed as indicative of your ability to convince on their behalf.

As proof of the importance of this attribute, Motorola conducted an in-depth study of the effect of their sales training programs. They learned that of all the factors involved (i.e., location, format, content, timing, etc.) that having the greatest influence is the speaker. It was found that the impression made is what determined subject appeal and retention.

Significantly, this aptitude will also fulfill the prospect's personal objective of having an Agency with the charisma that will make them look good.

B. Fear

Agencies are usually comfortable with the value of the *content* of their presentation. But they invariably have misgivings about its delivery. The feelings experienced by most presenters could provide a field day for psychotherapists. These range from inferiority to paranoia—capped off by fright. In addition, you are physically hampered by a dry mouth/cold sweat reaction.

I didn't realize how universal this hang-up is—and its intensity—until coming across a startling study on this subject. The findings, which reveal the solution to the speaking problem, can immediately improve your performance.

This survey was conducted among top Management of the Fortune 500 Companies. The sum of their response was, "Second only to death was their fear of having to address a group."

Upon probing further, it was discovered that the cause of this fear is that *they are not adequately prepared.* Therefore, plan and rehearse enough so your energy can be devoted to your talk rather than fighting stress. Having this control, you can come across as being able to fulfill whatever the prospect's needs.

Thus, you *can* do something about this mental block. And all it takes is preparing to the extent necessary to do yourself the justice deserved. This breeds confidence, which in turn produces empathy—resulting in acceptance of you and your message.

C. Nervousness

The most charismatic speaker I have ever heard was Bo Kreer. As to who ranks 2nd, no one is close.

He honed his skills when serving time at such institutions as J. Walter Thompson, Campbell-Mithun, Clinton E. Frank, Young & Rubicam, etc. And he became so good on his feet that people were either totally captivated by him—or they resented his exceptional ability.

For a while, I fell into the latter category. Because too often, I had to follow him in new business presentations and client sales meetings. And this was undertaken with a deep feeling of inadequacy.

After one of these humbling experiences (and a few Beefeaters with him at dinner), I said, "Bo, it would be awfully easy to hate you." This confession was startling—and not conducive to job security—since he was my Management Supervisor when I was an Account Supervisor.

So I went on to explain, "Presenting comes so goddam easy for you. You're always so cool up front." His response: "You're not very observant." And then he went on to explain, "Regardless of how hot a summer day, if I have a talk to give, I always wear a winter suit. Otherwise, in a summer suit, it would be apparent to the audience that I perspire right through it."

But Bo wasn't complaining. He felt this nervousness was one of the greatest things he had going for him. Because it gets the juices flowing— and reduces the possibility of a mental lapse. And he *used* it to get up for the event and keep him at the level of intensity necessary. He summed up by saying, "If ever I get to the point when I can address a group in a summer suit, I'm in trouble."

However, Bo realized that the charge generated can become self-defeating if not harnessed. He found this can be achieved via the control provided by confidence. That's great, but what is the formula for creating confidence? Bo believed that the clue lies in your *knowledge of the subject*. If familiar enough, you can handle whatever the situation.

Yet, this doesn't absolve you from preparing your material. Even though being authoritative, you still need to develop how you are going to express it. Assuming you can wing it gives the impression of taking the audience for granted. And then you will have plenty of reason to be nervous.

D. Assumption of Inadequacy

In weak moments, top Management of some Agencies will describe their performance in presentations in terms ranging from, "We're nice mice" to "We're so boring!" And they are somewhat resigned to these afflictions because "That's the kind of people we are."

They aren't alone. Most people deprecate themselves as speakers—selling short their ability and appeal. This borders on masochism—assuming they lack the innate magnetism required. ("I'm just not the flamboyant type.")

That isn't the problem. Most often, a presentation is dull because it is irrelevant—and/or delivered in an unenthusiastic manner. Both of these causes of boredom can be overcome if you are willing to apply the discipline necessary to land accounts.

Specifically, your presentation should be a stimulant—not a sedative. This will be as convincing as its pertinence to the prospect's interests and needs. Yet, regardless of how fabulous your materials and ideas may be, if not communicated in a fired-up, inspiring way, you aren't going to create the *want* for your Agency.

This calls for coming across as really believing in what's said—and being truly excited about working with this prospect. Conveying this impression isn't difficult. Because emotions don't have to be memorized.

E.   Control

Your big picture in presentation is only as good as its strokes.

In new business activity, there is no room for assumption. This particularly applies to the presentation. Because the winning Agency can be the one who made the fewest errors. Being on a presentation team is like working on a bomb squad. You don't get more than one mistake.

Due to the precariousness of this event, Agencies are coming to realize that they must prepare themselves in every respect. The goal being to exercise optimum control—thereby leaving the least to chance.

Protection, then, begins with the basics. This especially consists of the mechanics. Having been through them many times before, you are inclined to take them for granted—and become careless. However, since advertisers eliminate rather than select Agencies, no detail is too small—or can be speculated on.

That's why when I am conducting seminars and consulting for Agencies, they are now grilling me on nitty-gritty. No conjecture. Instead, they want to know what I'm finding works or doesn't.

For example, here is a matter that seems so elementary that the question belies its importance. "Is it best to deliver from a standing or seated position?"

Don't brush off this factor as being inconsequential. Because it establishes *who* is running this event. Therefore, unless there are so few people involved, or the environment precludes it, *the presentation should always be delivered from a standing position.*

By creating a focal point, it provides a visual reason for the prospect to pay attention to your speaker. And as significant, this format establishes authority.

Admittedly, to some people, being this prominent seems more difficult. There are Agencies who will rationalize not bothering to be more effective by claiming, "We're more of the laid-back type. And best when just seated around the conference room table, talking informally."

Although they may feel more comfortable, *it forfeits discipline.* Being at the prospect's physical level, you don't seem any more important than they are. This makes it more difficult to attract and maintain interest—and deter them from rudely talking among themselves during your pitch.

So take command by at least *appearing* to be in charge. While the prospect may set ground rules, they expect you to take over from there. And they will place much emphasis on how well these are implemented. Therefore, the method by which you *conduct* your presentation will have a strong influence on its outcome.

Yet, what if you have a person, vital to your presentation—who can't get up in front of a group? It is probable that this key individual can communicate well—but only on his/her terms.

Here's proof. I was called in by an Agency to critique a presentation they lost—and smoke out why. It was decided to go through the entire pitch exactly as performed for the prospect.

However, in the interest of determining what it would take to win next time, anyone could interrupt with questions and suggestions.

As it happened, I sat next to their Creative Director. I was immediately struck by how valuable and interesting his comments were. And in particular, how well these were articulated.

When it came time for his turn at the podium, the President proudly platformed him. The C.D. leaned back and said, "We all know what I did. Let's move on to the next presenter." The President objected with, "Now look, we agreed to reconstruct this for Jack. Let's do it right."

The C.D. snapped through gritted teeth, "Awright, goddamit. But you know what happens when I stand up to present—I freeze!" At that, he stomped up to the podium—and froze. His white knuckles clenched the podium, he became livid—and speechless.

Obviously, the presentation of Creative is critical. In this case, especially by him. Because this C.D. had everything going for him—except his mental block on speaking from a standing position.

The solution was to stage his delivering while seated—representing this as a change of pace. This alternate provided the C.D. with the necessary comfort and confidence—and enabled unleashing his extensive abilities. Result: he blossomed into a dynamic presenter. And the Agency's rate of scoring increased substantially.

Summing up, plans for every presentation, regardless of size, need to be totally buttoned up—with all fail-safe precautions applied. And then each opportunity should be orchestrated for maximum impact.

F. Comfort

Agencies are becoming more sophisticated in the preparation of their new business presentations. In particular: more research; more ambitious, expensive presentation materials. And significantly, substantially more time is being spent in its development.

Seemingly, this greater thoroughness accounts for every conceivable factor. All except that most critical: the *presenters*.

Can they relate to the concept? Are they confident with the visuals? Because a presentation is not only show. It's also tell. And if they are ill at ease with either, in any respect, the finest-conceived presentation will be like the dodo. A wonderful bird—but it couldn't fly.

Here, too, this isn't an academic assumption. It was inspired by an Agency who recently had this experience.

The President told me that their Creatives had come up with a delightful (not cutesy) cartoon approach—to be delivered in a whimsical manner.

Management loved this fun tactic for dealing with otherwise heavy matter. It communicated why their Agency was preferable to any other in an especially clever, distinctive style.

Then came the moment of truth: Performance. In the dry run prior to actual use, his people discovered that the presentation wasn't *them*. Great in theory. But not implementable by *these* presenters. Nobody had caught it, because the presentation wasn't wrong. It just wasn't right for *this* Agency.

He concluded, "The materials cost a bloody fortune. However, my people just weren't *comfortable* with it. And there is no sense in trying to convert them into something they are not. So we're biting the bullet and going back to square one." Sadder but wiser.

There is a moral to this story. Whatever the presentation created, it is meant to be delivered. Thus, while in the conceptual stage, apply this acid test: Is it appropriate to *our* presenters? Because your objective is to achieve the most effective blend of speakers and message.

G.   Preparation

A presentation can be only as good as the thoroughness with which it is planned. If any portion is relegated to "winging it," that becomes a crapshoot. And no Agency can risk this built-in handicap.

Acknowledging the necessity of whatever preparation it takes to win, participants will write out their part of the presentation. Fine. This discipline gives the matter the thought it deserves. As a result, you will register being well organized and authoritative on the subject. And this control precludes any repetition among speakers.

However, one caveat. People don't talk the way they write. And if you deliver from a written script, you will seem stilted and what's said will sound canned. So that you speak to them rather than at them, translate your formal message into "people talk." By speaking their language, it's more understandable—and you become more acceptable.

Then, make the effort for your presentation to be as *effortless* as possible for the prospect. (The selection team expects the Agency to work; not themselves.)

Avoid any lengthy dissertations on slide or poster card. No Lord's Prayer on the head of a pin.

Agencies attach a spiritual quality to their philosophy. Whatever the medium used, it is filled from top to bottom, side to side, with this deathless message.

What do you do? Insult them by reading it word for word? Or shift around during this dead air time hoping they will read it.

Instead, use a few buzz words and/or illustrations to intrigue them—while you just tell them about it. Because the most impressive presentation is one that is conversational. Yet, throughout this casual scenario, remember: if you're not selling, you're being sold.

H.   Use of Presentation Materials

There is a relationship between a presenter and the support material used. These visuals are only as good as how well you employ them. Further, regardless of how appealing these are, they can't compensate for a dull speaker.

Therefore, don't ever count on audio-visual materials to carry you. The effect of your message begins with your delivery. It depends on your enthusiasm, and the relevance of your message—and its value.

So be constantly aware of your respective roles. It is your responsibility to sell—and the function of the presentation materials is to assist you and enhance the impression made.

I.   Content vs. Conduct

When I first started critiquing new business presentations for Agencies, I assumed my concern would be essentially with its *content*. Is the message and communication of it relevant—registering what's in it for the prospect? Are the graphics doing your Creative talent justice—so the prospect would want it to represent them? (Obviously, it would behoove you to also role-play this mind-set and do whatever is necessary to satisfy it.) Beyond this, I figured that unless the Agency's *conduct* was offensive, its importance was secondary.

Then came the greening of Jack Matthews.

Because on the other side of the street, in working with advertisers on Agency selection, I found they have a different set of priorities. It all stems from the fact that *you're in a people business—and that's what the advertiser is buying*.

If they are willing to hold still, they want to get to know you. They wonder: "Are you our kind of people?" And, "Could I live with you? Would you be good for me?"

Becoming privy to these criteria, I began evaluating pitches from a different, more realistic perspective.

With all due respect to the significance of the content of your presentation, it begins with the prospect's vibes. Only after establishing a rapport they would be comfortable with can they be impressed by your ability and experience.

J.   Performance

Now, being psyched to do yourself proud, let's deal with performance.

There are various strands in the tightrope you walk during a pitch. Specific provision is made for demonstrating the quality of operation and relationship they could expect. But the prospect is also scrutinizing you closely for *attitude*. They are trying to determine in advance how your Agency would be to live with.

It is paramount to convey your *respect* for the prospect in the conduct of your presentation. (So don't lounge on the podium—or blow smoke at them.)

Of course you want to come across as being confident—to instill such. And register your dedication to challenge them. However, there is a fine line between this conduct and arrogance.

Convey conviction and you're respected. It is evidence of your commitment to selling—which the prospect feels so strongly about. If, in the heat of presentation though, you become too heavy, you seem domineering. And no advertiser, as a client, wants that. So be sensitive to getting carried away.

To further prevent any misconception of arrogance, guard against these two common pitfalls:

- acting too familiar
- being adamantly right—all the time

Although the perils of both are well known, Agencies will inadvertently drift into this behavior. Unequivocally, any such lapse offends—and thus is a handicap you can't afford.

By contrast, here is how you can especially ingratiate your shop. Maybe because of being so basic, this strategy is usually neglected. Namely, evidence of *your willingness to listen*. The prospect's opinions should be sought—and your interest in them made apparent.

Too basic to bother with?   I know of a high-scoring Agency that attributes much of their success to positioning themselves as seeking prospect input—and then hearing them out.

K.   Relevance to Prospect

Media and Research people express a common frustration regarding their role in the new business presentation. It is assumed they come off poorly by comparison with those presenting Creative work.   Because all their functions have are dull numbers and charts—while Creative has bells and whistles.

Not so. Actually, any function is only as interesting as its relevance to the prospect. If numbers are used solely to tout the Agency's ability, of course they are dull. But these same numbers become exciting if *related to the prospect's operation*. Because they can then associate with the benefits promised.

For instance, if you're talking Media, what could be more important to them than how *their money* is invested? And as to Research, whatever is communicated regarding their product/service, industry or market is crucial to them.

It's not the subject or visual effect that turns on the prospect. They are impressed only by what is said or shown that is geared to fulfilling their needs.

Summing up, you will be as vital as you are pertinent. It's that easy to be a star presenter.

L.   Technique

Don't resort to any of these crutches which seriously lessen being able to convince prospects:

1. Don't *read* to them.   This approach forfeits eyeball contact—and implies that you are not adequately prepared.
2. Don't *act* out your part in the presentation.   Namely, delivering in a manner assumed to be expected of a presenter.   This role-playing sacrifices sincerity.

Even though the previous admonition is self-evident, it warrants elaboration.

Again no theory. Because I lived this experience, too. And that learned about delivery was invaluable.

This happened after I finished critiquing an Agency presentation in rehearsal. The Agency C.E.O. wrapped it up by observing, "We're probably as ready as we will ever be. Yet, I have a gnawing apprehension." He went on to explain that this is by far the biggest account they have ever gone after. And they are spending substantially more money on this pitch than ever before.

Then what had been welling inside him erupted. He fired off, "Look Jack, we didn't bring you in to win a popularity contest. If you have any reservation whatsoever about anything we've said or done, for God's sake, do me a favor and level with us."

Apparently this challenge triggered a concern I was harboring for some time. Being given this license was the incentive I needed.

I let loose with, "Okay, I had breakfast and lunch with you people. You are delightful, impressive and stimulating. Tell me, what happened to you on your way to the podium? You had a complete personality change. You became robot-like, mechanistic. Certainly not yourselves. But that's who the prospect wants to meet."

I wound up by offering a two-word recommendation: *"Don't change."* And paid it off with the following direction: "Let the prospect get to know you for who you are—rather than having to interpret what exists behind the facade of a programmed reciter.

Therefore, to improve your odds for being preferable, present according to the best of *your* ability—not that of a stereotype.

3. Finally, don't deliver from a *memorized* script.   It will sound canned—and if someone interrupts, you're wiped out.

If appropriate, and you're comfortable with it, work from a series of buzz words. This will allow you to talk for understanding instead of effect. Further, it will keep you on target, prevent rambling—and require you to think.

This organized spontaneity will then enable you to come across in the most believable, authoritative manner: Remember: *The advertiser wants a persuader—not a reciter.*

M.   Being Understandable

It's incongruous asking, "Are you understandable?" Supposedly, that's a prime requisite for being in this business. But there is a fair amount of comment by prospects to the effect, "We don't know what the hell the Agencies are talking about."

You're not dazzling a selection team, comprised of those with varying degrees of exposure to Agencies, by proposing, "We fractionate your demographic quintile." Instead, it is a putdown. And no one will be receptive to considering your Agency after having experienced that.

This risk always exists. Because there is one member of the selection team who may not be the decision-maker—but who can scuttle your being chosen.   This is the person responsible for the sales function— whether his title is V.P.-Marketing or Sales Manager. In all likelihood, he is not as familiar with your vernacular—and will be alienated if unable to comprehend all that you say.

A specific example is the case of three finalists being judged by a five-member selection team. Four of the five thought Agency "A" should be picked because of clearly having the best ideas. This preference was voiced to the fifth person: the head of Sales.

Now he couldn't understand all the Agency said—but wasn't about to admit it. So he agreed that the preferred Agency has great ideas—but followed with, "It's a shame we can't use them." When asked, "Why?"— he made his point by delivering the ultimate karate chop: "Because their ideas won't work in the field." And nobody is going against that indictment.

Therefore, to prevent shooting yourself in the foot, it is imperative that you speak to his level of understanding. Not down. Just communicate clearly.

Use people talk—not "addy" talk. Spare them any reference to your efficiency in buying G.R.P.s. Or your strategy in negotiating a broadcast roadblock and then describing the cost of the campaign as "200 thou" or "two mill."

As far as the advertiser is concerned, there is never anything frivolous about their money. Thus, you can persuade only if you are understandable and sensible.

Since this matter is so basic, it is often taken for granted. For instance, at a recent Agency seminar, their President punctuated this point by stating, "Y'know, Jack's right. We use too much obfuscating patois."

N. Level of Communication

A common Agency concern in presentation is the risk of offending the prospect by talking *down* to them. Even so, at least they know what you are talking about. (Actually, a putdown occurs only if you deliver in a patronizing manner.)

By contrast, you will suffer much more if you speak *over* anyone's head. If there is a single word used that any individual can't comprehend, they will tune you out thereafter. And scratch one vote for your Agency.

It is not that an Agency will purposely try to impress by playing mind games. But it can be derelict in assuming that *everything* said is intelligible to all. Be constantly sensitive to this matter—with provision made to guard against such oversight in your rehearsal.

Here is what can happen. I was critiquing a run-through for one of the top Agencies in Canada. These heavyweights did a great job. Particularly the person proposed as Account Supervisor if awarded the business.

He covered the Agency's marketing capacity in a remarkably knowledgeable manner. And without a single note. His only prop was one poster card containing nine numbers—which he eloquently brought to life.

As this spellbinder was wrapping up, he felt compelled to justify these figures. So for credibility he announced, " . . . and these mnemonics were extrapolated from empirical sources."

That set my head to shaking—sideways. He stopped and asked, "What's the matter?" So I told him, "I don't know the hell you're talking about."

He was amazed. Because this erudite language wasn't an affectation. Rather, I found he is just that articulate. And expressing himself in what was for him a normal manner.

If this hadn't been caught in rehearsal, and he had rattled off this series of mind-boggling words in presentation, the selection team would have gone blank. And an Agency is never chosen in a vacuum.

Thus, speak for understanding—not effect. Remember: your purpose is to convince not dazzle. Otherwise, your Agency may be an easy sell—but a tough buy.

O. Expressions

Consciously or otherwise, Agencies pepper their presentations with trite phrases. These are used in an attempt to convey humility and honesty. And thereby gain acceptance for claims made. These include asinine prefaces such as:

- "Frankly, to tell you the honest truth . . ."
- "Trust me."
- "Please bear with me on this one."
- "This can't be proved but . . ."
- "Would I lie to you?"
- "You can check anyone on this."
- "I'm not sure of this, however . . ."
- "Don't take my word for it, but . . ."
- "As everyone knows . . ."
- "May God strike me dead if . . ."

Advertisers find these ploys, at best, annoying. And they detract from the effect desired. Therefore, in rehearsal, make a point of stripping these qualifying prefaces from your style of speaking. Otherwise, they will make all else said suspect.

P. Qualifying Phrases

Here is another common weakness in expression that I find across the board. It is in style, not substance.

In delivery, Agencies seem compelled to qualify their claims by prefacing statements with the phrase, "We think . . ." Or justifying a recommendation by preceding it with, "We believe . . ." And for sincerity, starting the conclusion with, "We hope . . ."

Actually, the prospect prefers that your justifications are based on a broader, more authoritative source. Not just your humble assumption.

And these qualifying phrases instill some doubt because of implying lack of certainty on your part.

Therefore, to convince prospects, sell without these restrictions. It is not a matter that you "believe" this is the best marketing strategy for them. You *know* it is the best marketing strategy for them. And it is not only that you "think" it is best. It *is* best.

So don't lessen your power to persuade by backing into your claims and recommendations. Sell with conviction—without reservation. Because that is how a prospect expects an Agency to sell on their behalf—and are sensitive to evidence of such.

Q.   Offensive Characters

Regardless of how dynamic a speaker may be, no one can impress a prospect if there are blunders in conduct. This could range from coming across as being arrogant or patronizing to distracting characteristics. For instance, tapping your pen on the podium or jingling coins in your pocket—or scratching yourself like a baseball player.

Particularly annoying to the selection team is sloppy delivery.

This is evidenced by speaking too softly, mumbling or letting your voice trail off. It is assumed you don't think they are worth the effort to be understandable.

Offensive attitudes or mannerisms can wipe out what would otherwise be an acceptable, convincing presentation. Don't turn off a prospect before you can turn them on.

Incidentally, I'm often asked if it looks all right to talk with your hands in your pockets. It's okay—if you don't move them around.

R.   Knowledge

With all due respect to delivery, though, heed these pearls of wisdom from someone in the best position to know.

I had lunch recently with Brian Palmer, Director of the National Speakers Bureau. He said, "The importance of presentation skills is a given. But first, *you better know what you're talking about*."

This point was never made better than when Bob Noble of Springfield, MO, asked to be included in the Agency search by Tyson Chicken some years ago. This request seemed incongruous because Noble's total billing at the time was $2,500,000—and this advertiser's Media budget was $6,000,000.

Nevertheless, Noble persevered because they were already doing the collateral work for Tyson. And their rationale was, "What Agency could know more about your operation than we do?"

Even though selecting Noble seemed so improbable, Tyson acquiesced. They assumed they could afford this gracious gesture because Noble would be eliminated in the screening presentations anyway. Since based on the competing Agencies, they were so far out of their league.

However, not only did Noble make the cut, but even more amazing, they wound up as one of the two finalists. This time, though, the odds against them were insurmountable. Because their adversary was one of the top ten Agencies in the U.S. So, no horse race.

Yet Noble concluded that they had already invested so much time and money, they might as well see it through—in the event a miracle might occur. It did.

Inasmuch as Noble would be an afterthought, the big-name Agency was scheduled to go first. And of no surprise, the amount they spent on their presentation was comparatively overwhelming. Like the difference between lunch in New York City and Springfield, MO.

Unbelievably, to customize, the heavy-hitter Agency kept referring to Tyson *Turkeys*. Tyson didn't have a single turkey! Only chickens. Thus, without taking anything away from Noble's efforts, all they had to do was show up. And after this fiasco, they were awarded the account.

Of itself, this object lesson is enough. However, there is more to be learned from this experience.

Because of its financial impact on the Agency, (staffing up, adding space, etc.), Bob Noble phoned Harry Paster of the 4 A's to find out the first thing that needed to be done now that he had quadrupled the size of his Agency.

Speaking to the money maven of the Agency business, he expected financial direction. Instead of "debits-credits" counsel though, Harry came back with some of the most valuable advice that can be given in this business. He wisely said, "You'd better get more aggressive than ever on soliciting new business to compensate for when this dominant account leaves."

This warning was in no way due to a lack of confidence in Noble's operation. Rather, it just acknowledged a cold fact of Agency life: you begin to lose an account the day you get it. Think not? Clients have all the characteristics of a dog—except loyalty

Chapter 23

Benefit from Hindsight in Use of A-V

A. Perspective
B. Function
C. Production Techniques
D. Narration
E. Multi-Media
F. Equipment
G. Lighting
H. Protection

A. Perspective

Yet, as appealing as your presentation team and material may be, when appropriate, intriguing use should be made of audio-visual techniques to attract and hold attention. However, remember: If the prospect is willing to hold still, they want to get to know you. Therefore, *the degree of use of A-V depends on the extent to which it is worth sacrificing eyeball contact.*

While this medium can substantially improve the impression made, there are some situations where it can cause you more harm than good. You're familiar with these—but let's flush them out anyway. Because if overlooked, the damage can be irreparable.

B.   Function

Many Agencies go into a presentation with everything *selling* for them—except their visual aids. However, your presentation is only as good as its weakest link.

There are two tactics that lessen your impact:

- Visual aids are annoying and a diversion if used as a substitute for your notes. This code is only meaningful to you—and distracting to the prospect. Therefore, these aids should be prospect- rather than presenter-oriented.

- These visuals also fail to pay off if used just to *identify* the subjects. Actually, their function should be to *persuade* on behalf of whatever is being covered. In particular, use action words rather than passive ones.

Thus, just as with what was verbalized in presentation, the purpose of what is shown should be to convince them. So put whatever visuals you've planned to this test: Are they working as hard as you are to land the account?

C.   Production Techniques

Your use of A-V should not be so fascinating as to be more memorable than the message. Rather, it should support and enhance your presentation—not be a substitute for it.

I've been told by advertisers of instances in which they were so mesmerized by production techniques, they couldn't recall anything that was said. So in regard to the relationship of technique to message, usually less is more.

D.   Narration

It is axiomatic that your new business slide, tape or film presentation should represent the Agency in the most impressive manner. The production should be indicative of your creativity. And register the vitality of your people.

Beyond all else, its ultimate objective is to convince a prospect of why your Agency is best for them.

As a final touch, a professional announcer is often hired to provide the polish desired. But this surrogate presenter isn't one of you—causing your message to lose credibility. Instead, it is some paid stranger making claims and promises—rather than being a commitment from an actual Agency person.

Therefore—if you are comfortable with it—"Why don't you speak for yourself, John?"

So forgo a Rex Harrison delivery. Replace this formal narrator with one of your own Agency executives who will talk *to* the prospect instead of *at* them. He/she may not be as much of a smooth talker—but will be more believable because of the authority with which this person can speak.

This tactic is not considered amateurish. Rather, as a sincere, real approach.

Remember: One of the severest indictments an advertiser will make of an Agency pitch is that it is "canned." By contrast, selling on your own behalf removes this stigma from a produced presentation—and enables better transition to the "live" portion.

E. Multi-Media

Agencies assume that presentation impact depends on the quantity of slide and film projectors and VCRs used.

Undoubtedly, this can have a very desirable effect. However, in developing a multi-media program, apply this three-word criterion: "Will it travel?"

If not, you're severely limiting its potential. Because too often, the prospect will require that the presentation be held at their office. Whatever your presentation, it should have the versatility for optimum effect—wherever it is used.

F. Equipment

Don't leave anything to chance in regard to equipment. The best conceived program can go down the drain if a mechanical problem occurs.

Further, regardless of circumstances, any foul-up is considered your fault. Therefore, *bring your own* (and if appropriate, your own person to operate it.) You're more familiar with this equipment—and will have checked it out in advance to assure it is operating properly.

Then don't relent and get trapped by good intentions. This happened when an Ad Manager told a soliciting Agency that they would provide the A-V equipment.

The Agency demurred, stating they would prefer to bring their own. The Ad Manager, to assure them that this arrangement would be risk-free, said,

"Not to worry. We'll even furnish an experienced technician to operate it."
Seeming safe enough, and simplifying matters, the Agency acquiesced.

The Agency was then notified of the ground rules. They were to supply
their slides, films and tapes prior to the meeting. The client's operator
would have everything set up and ready to go at the designated time. Then
the prospect's President would be informed that the group was assembled
and ready for his grand entrance.

Upon entering, his majesty signaled the operator to begin. But nothing happened. And despite the operator's desperate fumbling with the
switches and dials, still nothing.

After a few minutes of this frustration, the President turned to the
Agency team and said, "If you people can't even handle a presentation,
you can't handle our advertising."

Some prospects aren't as pompous as that. Even so, it is generally felt
that putting on the presentation is your show. And accordingly, you are
liable for its success or failure.

So play it safe, safer, safest. Despite all the precautions taken, there is
always the risk and fear of something going wrong. Therefore, prepare an
emergency kit for presentations that would contain all possible life-saving
items.

To begin with, provide for any contingency by bringing along spare
parts, bulbs, reels—and the all-important extension cord. And of course,
a 3-way plug plus an adapter plug. In addition to those mentioned, this kit
could also include Valium, screwdriver, tape, vodka, etc. For that matter,
a person at the Agency who has the N.R.A. account suggested, "A gun."

It hurts enough losing to a competitor. Being beaten by A-V equipment,
though, makes the pain almost unbearable.

I know of some Agencies who would no more leave for a presentation without this tool box than they would take off without their Creative
material. Besides, it's a great security blanket. However, don't *use* any
equipment that could be counter-productive. Obviously, circumstances
determine the type and amount of equipment to be used: i.e., presentation
strategy, size and configuration of room, number of attendees, etc.

Yet, except for unusually extenuating circumstances, *don't include an
overhead projector*. Because invariably this type of equipment is misused.

This presentation starts and continues with the speaker placing the
cells on crooked—and spending the rest of the time trying to straighten
them. Then, instead of using some form of notes, the visuals serve this
purpose—and the obvious is drolly read to the audience verbatim. Finally, this deadly performance is compounded by being delivered with the
speaker's back to the audience. And to all: Good night.

The National Rifle Association maintains, "Guns don't kill; people do." Analogous to this, overhead projectors don't screw up; people do.

Thus, due to the human element, if any of your people insist on using an overhead projector, confide that it is suspected of causing genital herpes.

G.   Lighting

Understandably, there is the desire to screen your films, tapes and slides in the most impressive manner possible. This can best be achieved by killing the lights. But that's also a sedative. Further, the prospect may want to make notes about your Agency. Hopefully favorable. Don't deny them—and yourselves—this opportunity.

Thus, compromise on the showmanship somewhat by just dimming the lights. This will enable their doing the necessary writing, does not totally sacrifice eyeball contact—and reduces the risk of their minds going out with the lights.

H.   Protection

You are only too well aware of the cost of developing a presentation. This includes time, material and equipment. And they are escalating in quantum amounts.

All of the charges incurred are an investment. Unless something goes wrong. Then it becomes an unaffordable expense.

That's why heads-up Agencies are now bringing two sets of equipment. And for further safety, each is transported separately. Then if there is any foul-up, the alternate set can fill the breech.

For additional protection, Agencies are also bringing along duplicate material. Because the cost is incidental when compared to the disaster of your visuals having disappeared.

Therefore, considering what's at stake, this is a paltry premium to pay for this back-up insurance and peace of mind.

Chapter 24

Necessary Organization of Presentation

A. Perspective
B. Entrance
C. Introduction: Agency Team
D. Introduction: Presentation
E. Opening
F. Show-and-Tell
G. Closer
H. Exit
I. "Leaver"

A. Perspective

This brings us to the moment of truth. The payoff for all your efforts and expense: The presentation.

The prospect assumes this represents the best you can do. It must be the most conclusive evidence of your performance and compatibility. Because it is intended to create the most favorable impression of your ability, experience and chemistry. Therefore, it is interpreted as the best they can expect.

The prospect is further sensitive to how well your presentation is organized. The logic of its sequence. How well it builds, convinces and pays off. Here, too, this communicates the caliber of people and work they will get.

Since the new business presentation is the most stressful activity in the Agency business, the following is how to function in a calmer, more confident manner.

B.   Entrance

The most uncomfortable time begins with your entrance—and lasts until the opening of your presentation.

What can be done to reduce the awkward factor? Can this period be choreographed? The extent to which this phase can be controlled depends upon your knowledge of the following circumstances:

- **Location:** your place or theirs—or a neutral spot
- **Environment:** size and layout of room
- **Facilities:** conference table, theater style or informal seating
- **Time:** beginning, middle or end of day
- **Sequence:** first to present or following other Agencies
- **Arrangements:** able to set up beforehand or have to do so while they are present
- **Familiarity:** degree to which prospect people in attendance are known

Having this insight enables planning on how you are going to conduct yourself under these conditions. And plan you must. Because it will distinguish your Agency from the fumbling uncertainties exhibited by the others. By contrast, you can come across as being more confident, organized and professional.

For instance, being aware of the logistics, you can orchestrate the transition from entrance to presentation. This would include:

- handling introductions
- creating acceptance for your people
- generating interest in your presentation
- arranging location of presentation and selection teams
- establishing procedure for getting underway

With this programming you can control rather than react to the situation. Therefore, what had been a tacky phase, can actually pave the way and enhance your presentation. Further, with this awkward phase planned for, you can open from strength—able to concentrate on convincing the prospect of why your Agency is best for them.

C. Introduction: Agency Team

With this perspective, let's go into the meeting room. Your team enters as strangers. The quicker this status can be changed, the sooner the necessary rapport can be developed.

Thus, instead of the usual practice of withholding identifying each member until their turn on the program, introduce all of them at the outset. This should include their present Agency function—and proposed involvement if awarded the account. This way, the prospect group can immediately begin to relate to them.

The importance of this tactic is due to a ridiculous reason. The prospect plays a silly game when your people come in: trying to guess what each does at the Agency. To whatever extent you delay in informing them introduces a distracting element—which detracts from your presentation.

Yet, upon arrival, the situation usually consists of a fast round of sweaty handshakes—with both parties anxious to get this amenity over with. Thus, due to this environment, the Agency formally introduces their people—but seldom platforms them. This procedure only identifies your team. To their disadvantage, it does not create the authority and acceptance of them for prospect receptivity.

The next acknowledgement of each Agency member occurs when it is their turn on the program. And then they are thrown to the wolves with not much more than: "Now to tell you about Creative, here's Charlie."

Then poor Charlie begins that long trek to the podium—during which the silence is deafening. Next, he has to begin building stature and credibility for himself—which is tough for an individual to do on his own behalf. And valuable selling time is lost while he attempts to ingratiate himself. Obviously, this could be accomplished much more effectively by someone else.

Instead, *pre-condition the prospect to each of your presenters*. This will eliminate the dead air interval—and enable each member of your team to hit the deck running by devoting its entire time to selling for the Agency.

Further, *platform them intriguingly* to generate interest. For instance, introduce whoever is presenting Creative by parenthetically confiding: "There is something you should know about Charlie and his staff. They can't be bought from their wrists down. They have the marketing vision to see past their drawing boards and typewriters. This is the totality of creative involvement you can expect."

Subsequently, if this is to be followed by the subject of Media, Charlie can set up Gwendolyn by revealing: "Are you aware of her reputation? She is recognized as one of the shrewdest negotiators in the business. Reps know that if they haven't an especially attractive buy, at an exceptionally economical cost, don't bother coming to our office. That's the kind of hard-nosed handling of your money you can count on."

Remember: The prospect is buying the team they believe can best fulfill their communications needs. Therefore, to whatever extent your people can be represented as being preferable to those of any other Agency will provide a potent competitive edge. This people-oriented tactic will also distinguish your shop from the impersonal impressions made by your competitors.

Summing up, most Agencies fail to make the most effective use of participants in their presentation strategy. Specifically, having their presenters function as the medium for the message. In this situation, Marshall McLuhan was right when he said, "The *medium* is the message."

For that matter, how well do you promote the proposed account executive/team? After all, this is who would actually represent the Agency.

Do you shoot your charm and leave them as an afterthought? If so, you'll be failing to adequately satisfy the prospect's desire to know the Account team's qualifications and compatibility.

Therefore, create acceptance for them going in. Because the prospect's judgment of the Agency will be strongly influenced by their impression of those with whom they would work directly.

D.   Introduction: Presentation

Upon establishing acceptance for your participants, the next objective is creating interest and understanding for your presentation. Again, right from the start.

To begin with, distribute an Agenda—whose appearance and content will represent the Agency in the most appealing manner. And because of its effect on the impression made, it should be accorded the importance of a full-page introductory ad for the Agency.

Then, preface your presentation with the announcement that it is based on information they provided. This protects you in the event of having received any inaccurate or misleading input. (If so, your misguided approach still provides evidence of your ability and willingness to follow direction.) Further, this tactic establishes its relevance and identifies where you're coming from. And it precludes the prospect's wondering, "How the hell did you ever come up with that?"

Finally, pave the way for your opening by intriguing the prospect with a brief highlight of each feature to be covered. (Coming attractions.) This will put them in an anticipatory frame of mind.

E.   Opening

The opening of your new business presentation will establish the amount of prospect interest and receptivity thereafter. Here is a four-step sequence that will immediately attract and hold their attention:

1. First, in your pre-presentation efforts, you flushed out what they need from an Agency—and the reasons why. This insight forms the basis for your most logical and effective introductory statement. One that identifies and brings into focus the purpose of this meeting: their Agency needs—and why yours can best fill them.

   Therefore, your most compelling opener is, "As you informed us, what you need from an Agency is . . . , because (the reasons . . .), and we're going to prove why our Agency is the most appropriate for you."

2. From there, you get into describing your Agency. (Of course, only as relates to this prospect.)

   This should take only as much time as necessary to establish the authority and qualifications for the claims and promises to be made. If you belabor the point, you come across as I-I-I, me-me-me—which doesn't include them.

3. Now proceed with creating the prospect frame of mind desired. One that will immediately start tracking with you. This prelude should also jolt them out of their lethargy.

   Set the tone by announcing, "We will start by dealing with your most important marketing needs—followed by the Agency functions most important to you." This will promptly establish an environment pertinent to their interests—one in which they will be more receptive to your presentation.

4. Then you better get right to the point with the answer to the prospect's ultimate question, "Why should we hire you?" Any approach short of supplying specific, relevant reasons will make your efforts a long run for a short slide.

   They shouldn't have to discover or assume why your Agency is preferable to any other. That's your responsibility.

Therefore, sell early by spelling out up front, "Here are the six reasons (or five or seven) why our Agency is best for you." And not just general puffery. Rather, your claims should directly identify with their needs.

Start winning with your opener—and clinch it with the rest of your presentation.

F. Show-and-Tell

Now let's get into the show-and-tell phase of your presentation.

The *promise* in your solicitation activity has gotten you this far. Now you have to convince the prospect you are able to *deliver*.

Here's how. Provide an insight to their company, industry or market hitherto unknown—and what to do about it.

Then substantiate your proposals with successful, pertinent case histories. In doing so, though, go that critical step further and translate how the strategy of these achievements can fulfill this prospect's needs.

Yet, remember: Your track record is an opener—not a closer. Beyond all else, they are expecting the same thing of you as of their advertising: *A reason why to buy*.

And what is the reason? Your brilliant Creative work? Or shrewd Marketing strategy? Not quite. These are the means—not the end. What the prospect will actually buy is *the Agency they believe can best contribute to increasing their sales profitability*. Therefore, lead from strength by featuring your attributes—and then pay it off with how their business will gain from these.

For instance, you give much emphasis to your TV reel in presentation. You're proud of it. And justifiably so. But as such, it merely entertains unless you explain what it can do for them. Thus, use this most interesting medium as proof of your ability to serve—not amuse.

On occasion, exception is taken to this direction at one of my Agency seminars by someone who asks, "But isn't the purpose of the reel to demonstrate our ability to produce outstanding commercials?" That's half right. Because the purpose is to demonstrate your ability to produce outstanding commercials—*for them*. So finish the job. Spell out how they will specifically benefit from your particular know-how.

Here's why. Agencies will select six to ten of their commercials they are smitten with, rack them up—and zip-p-p, run them off. The prospect's only reaction is, "I wonder what they meant by that."

Instead, turn on your projector or VCR, switch it off in 30 seconds—and announce, "This is the kind of exciting Creative work you could expect if we became your new Agency." Then flick it on again, turning it off in another 30 seconds, and mention, "Here is our type of shrewd marketing strategy you could rely on." And so on.

This screening procedure answers what's in it for them, establishes mutuality—thereby creating a climate for receptivity.

Further, be consistent with this strategy for Print ads and collateral material presented and exhibited for the prospect. Explain why this is relevant and important to them. Otherwise, these are just decorations. And the desired visual effect is wasted—because they will not make the effort to relate it to themselves.

For example, Agencies will totally cover the cork board in their Conference Room with ad proofs and sales promotion items. However, to the prospect, this is just an art contest. Upon mentioning this fact at Agencies, someone will take offense and insist, "Just a damn minute, Jack! This is evidence of our ability to do outstanding print work." Granted. But the prospect is only interested in what pertains to them.

Thus, a smorgasbord display will just confuse matters—and you will end up competing with yourself. Therefore, exhibit only what you are going to tell them about. Otherwise, this will be a physical extension of your ego-trip.

Summing up, the criterion for whatever shown is whether it will be actively used to convince the prospect of why your Agency is best for them.

G.   Closer

It is no end of amazement how an Agency will go the full route in development and execution of a splendid presentation—and then quit with victory in sight. Upon completion, they are reluctant to ask for the order. That's like spiking the football on the five-yard line!

There are those who feel it is in poor taste or beneath them. As a result, their bells and whistles climax will consist of a grabber like, "Well, there it is." Or, "The gang at the shop is really excited about this." That isn't a finale; it's a fizzle.

And then the Agency wonders why their nights and weekends of work on this pitch didn't pay off. (The Creative, Research and Media plans were brilliant, profound and shrewd respectively.) Here's why. You got the prospect all excited—and then left.

Other Agencies are aware of the need for some sort of "closer"—but are uncomfortable with it. So they will apologetically state: "I guess at this point we're supposed to ask for the order. Well, we're doing that." (Then, it is followed by an insincere chuckle). This matter-of-fact, lighthearted approach is intended to remove any stigma of seeming crass.

This thinking is 180 degrees off target. Because an advertiser wants an Agency that will forthrightly sell the way they do. Particularly, with conviction. They feel if you can't sell boldly and imaginatively on your own behalf, how are you going to do so for them?

And watch out for that third characteristic. The prospect is nearly as turned off by commonly used trite expressions like, "We're ready to go to work for you right now!" Or, "We're really anxious to become members of your team!" The prospect figures you surely ought to be able to come with something more intriguing than that.

Let's wrap it up with this situation. Agencies wince when there is news in the trade press about an account change—and their being mentioned as a runner-up. Actually, the advertiser doesn't view this as your having failed. Rather, they relate—construing this as your being out hustling as they do. And instead of having a negative effect, you're respected.

Finally, the matter is this basic. The reason the prospect is in business is to sell their product or service profitably. Thus, they are most impressed by an Agency that is demonstrably selling-oriented. Beginning with itself.

Such being the case, base your asking for the order on the ultimate reason for selecting an Agency: "Did we convince you that our Agency can best contribute to increasing your sales profitably?" This registers that you realize the extent of the Agency's responsibility—and associates yourself with increasing sales and profits. What more could the prospect want?

If this doesn't get a rise out of them, state: "Obviously, what you want is an Agency who will ask for the order. We are. What do we have to do to become your Agency.?"

If you're not comfortable with either of these, and can carry it off, lighten up. Admit that, "After we leave here, the first thing we'll do is ask each other: 'Well, how did we do?' Whatever our assumption though, it's worthless. Because the only opinion that counts is *yours*. Therefore, instead of this exercise in futility, would you please tell us how we did?"

Finally, all of your activity up until now has been geared to build to this high. Don't blow it because of an awkward exit. A planned "closer" will prevent this from happening—and your being left in limbo.

H.   Exit

You won't have to wonder about the prospect's reactions to your presentation if they hint at, or worse, inform you that it is time to leave. Because if they say goodbye first, it's your last goodbye.

To prevent overstaying your welcome, *you* take the initiative. This provides advance evidence of your respect for their time—and that as a client, they would not be taken for granted.

Therefore, prior to the farewell lull, acknowledge that they have a tremendous responsibility: selecting the Agency that can best contribute to increasing their sales profitability. Then mention, "And since this dedication is the basis of our operation, we will get back to our clients now. However, we'll also keep the champagne cold in the event we're awarded your account."

Then, leave gracefully. Here's how.

Your dynamic presentation is followed by the mundane function of packing your material and equipment. It is sort of embarrassing coming down to this menial task after having operated in the lofty areas of how you would solve their insurmountable marketing problems and revealing incomparable advertising applications.

However, the prospect isn't anywhere near as sensitive to this situation as you are. It is an expected procedure; part of the package.

Yet, it is still desirable to minimize this wrap-up—and conduct it as efficiently as possible. To do so professionally, include planning for the departure in your rehearsal. Most Agencies break down the set in an obviously disorganized manner. But by orchestrating this procedure, with responsibilities assigned, you can prevent coming off as the Three Stooges. Rather, you will give the impression of being the follow-through Agency that knows what it is doing—all the way.

I.   "Leaver"

Finally, there is a pre- and post-factor that will make or break the impression made. The first has already been covered: your *rehearsal*. The latter refers to the "Leaver" furnished the prospect after the presentation.

As with the rehearsal, the "Leaver" should also be accorded as much importance as any component of the presentation. No pitch, of itself, is so fantastic as to suffice. After a series of presentations, the prospect's impressions of the various Agencies begin to blur. Further, this summary is essential because it is used for reference, review and comparison.

Therefore, the criterion for developing the "Leaver" should be how well it can represent the Agency in your absence. This applies to the vitality of its content and the appeal of its appearance. In essence, whatever you leave should be so compelling as to tip the scale in your favor.

Here is why this deserves your best shot. In the Agency selection meeting held after all presentations have been made, the "Leaver" in effect *becomes* the Agency.

A member of the selection team will hold up a copy and ask, "What do you think of this one?" Another will toss a copy across the conference table and say, "How about that one?" These are the *Agencies* they are displaying and throwing back and forth! And as such, when the prospect is attempting to arrive at a decision, the "Leaver" is the final impression received.

Therefore, while your objective is to develop a winning presentation, you still need the clincher: a winning "Leaver." That is why your Creative staff should be involved in its preparation from inception—to assure that the "Leaver" is most likely to be opened and read.

What will it take to accomplish this? Glad you asked. First, let's consider the circumstances. When an advertiser decides to change Agencies, whoever is responsible for organizing the search (i.e., Ad Manager) becomes by far the most important person they have ever been. Thus, he/she will turn this assignment into a make-work project. And will drag it out as long as possible until someone from on high hollers down, "F'Chrissake, Fred, you've been screwin' around for 11 weeks. We can't afford any more downtime. Let's pick the Agency—*now!*"

This edict makes for instant panic. All the presentations have probably been made by this time. All that is left is the tie-breaker: the "Leavers."

Here is what you need to know regarding its content and appearance to make the difference.

CONTENT

This is how your Agency can come across as being more desirable than the others. To begin with, though: what *not* to do. Because of the amount of work and pride, Agencies will reproduce the entire presentation—assuming they will impress the prospect by the pound. However, because of the pressure to resolve the matter, the selection team has neither the time nor inclination to sweat out what looks like a Master's thesis.

Instead, your "Leaver" should contain only what is critical to remember: communicated telegraphically. This does not mean that you are restricted to a limited number of pages. Only to the discipline of preventing its content from looking overpowering. If, however, the situation requires a thickness which could be intimidating, preface it with an "Executive Summary."

In particular, the "Leaver" should recap:

- why your Agency's functions and qualifications are better for fulfilling their requirements
- pertinence and value of the talent/experience of the Agency team to be assigned to their account
- claims and promises made
- how the ideas and solutions offered will serve this prospect's specific marketing needs
- how you would operate together
- method of compensation
- checklist/timetable of action to be taken upon being awarded the account ("First 100 days")

He should then ask for the order, and, if appropriate, include a Letter of Agreement.

If you are an Agency known to have fewer employees than your competitors, you will want to give the impression of nevertheless having sufficient depth.

Here is how to combat their numerical advantage. Include a listing of all the Agencies your employees have worked for. And itemize all the advertisers they have served. It will be amazing how substantial and impressive both these lists will be. And how well they can help compensate for any quantitative disadvantage. (For that matter, if appropriate, use this upgrading strategy in your next promotional piece.) Actually, even if size isn't a concern, this tactic is worth considering.

APPEARANCE

The "Leaver" is considered a vital insight to your Creativity. Therefore:

- The cover should be intriguing enough to encourage being opened. Conveying class, your being imaginative—and the kind of people they would want to know.
- As to the contents, each page should be treated as an ad for your Agency. Laid out attractively—and easy to read. And like good copy, providing the incentive to read further.

Above all, your "Leaver" must give the impression of having been developed especially for this individual prospect. Thus, the prospect's corporate name and logo should appear on the cover—plus the person's name for whom it is intended. Beyond this, their corporate name should be sprinkled throughout the subject matter. This device will preclude any suspicion of your "Leaver" being a stock item.

As to *when* it should be furnished: first, here are two caveats:

1. Never, repeat never, distribute the "Leaver" *before or during* the presentation. It is assumed this is a valuable tactic because it involves the prospect. However, you actually lose them because people read at different rates—and you sacrifice eyeball contact. And, in effect, the Agency winds up competing with itself.

2. Some Agencies surmise it is a better maneuver to mail the "Leaver" the next day. Supposedly the cumulative effect provided by this additional shot at the prospect will compound the Agency's appeal.

   But this strategy also reduces the amount of time the prospect can spend with it. Even worse, you may be slated on the last day of presentations—and they might hold their selection meeting right afterwards or the next day. Then this lack of presence could cause your being eliminated.

   So don't gamble on the benefit of another exposure. Because it might occur after the decision is made.

The only right time for supplying the "Leaver" is immediately after the presentation.

Summing up: The "Leaver" is accorded much more importance among the mix of factors for choosing an Agency than realized. It is your ultimate "closer." Therefore, it should be so convincing that—of itself—it will register that your Agency is preferable.

Chapter 25

Presentation Strategy That Has Proved Most Effective

A. Perspective
B. Objective
C. Angle or Hook
D. Capabilities/Credentials Presentation
E. Emotional Appeal
F. Style vs. Substance
G. Move Prospect to Presenter's Offices
H. Ask for the Order—Throughout
I. When to Feature Creative
J. Team Proposed
K. Prospect Involvement
L. Seek Prospect Reaction
M. Duration
N. Gimmicks
O. Concluding Gamesmanship

A. Perspective

The previous chapter set forth the step-by-step procedure for conducting your presentation. This includes not only what should be contained—but also how to achieve the reaction desired.

Now here are the smarts to be applied. Techniques that will compound the potency of your efforts.

The direction is based on this crucial development. The combination of advertiser attitude and economic circumstances is causing a much more critical evaluation of Agency presentations. Thus, you can't count on last year's strategy anymore.

Rather, it needs to be now-oriented. This pertains to the two basic factors that comprise a presentation: its appearance and content. Visually, it need be obviously fresh. And in content, it must relate to the prospect's current and projected marketing needs. Beyond this, it must answer: what's new, what is vital to them and why.

This may not strike you as being all that earth-shaking. But by being fresh and relevant, it could make your presentation unique by comparison. This approach will also prevent the indictment of it being: S.O.S. Same Old Stuff.

B. Objective

Based on my working with at least one Agency each week, I sense a growing need to bring back into focus the function of a presentation. Somehow, conception of its purpose has been obscured and Agency efforts misdirected.

Possibly due to taking the path of least resistance, some Agencies are lapsing into presentation strategy short of what their objective should be. For instance, there are shops putting on full-scale presentations to create familiarity. Or for cultivating purposes. That's ridiculous!

There is only one reason for a pitch: *to land the account.* Therefore, only apply this time, effort and expense to going for the jugular—rather than just holding hands. With an Agency's margin of profit, anything less than the intent to score is unaffordable.

Further, Agencies will then make abstract promises like building the prospect's brand awareness or improving its image. This is just fluff compared to the advertiser's ultimate want. All else notwithstanding, your mission for them is to persuade people to buy their product or service. That's the kind of bottom line attitude sought by advertisers.

C.   Angle or Hook

Agencies are constantly seeking an angle or hook for their presentation. An approach that will fascinate the prospect. However, the angle or hook is so obvious few notice it. *It is the prospect.*

As far as they are concerned, there is nothing more fascinating than themselves. Therefore, the only strategy that works in promoting your Agency is that communicated within the framework of the prospect's concerns. Anything less than totally relating what is said and shown to their interests was developed to appeal to the Agency—not the prospect.

Thus, there aren't any gimmicks; only the prospect's wants and needs. And the prospect is impressed only by those of your advantages that pertain to them.

Therefore, this is not a matter of two separate entities: the Agency and the prospect. Because their basic concern is with the impact of your mutuality. And not just that one plus one equals two. But that your combined effort will produce the synergism for one plus one to equal three.

D.   Capabilities/Credentials Presentation

It has become trendy for advertisers to ask for a "Capabilities Presentation" or a "Credentials Presentation." Don't get thrown off-stride by this misleading request, because it is incomplete. What they actually want is a capabilities or credentials presentation that *relates to them.*

However, as a result of how this request is expressed, the Agency mistakenly presents itself as a separate entity—exclusive of the prospect. And since they aren't included in context with yourself, they don't associate you with themselves.

Therefore, the generic presentation on behalf of the Agency as such doesn't work anymore. The prospect must now be given specific reasons why your Agency should be selected—developed and customized for them.

At a recent seminar, it was brought up to me, "Oh hell, Jack, we just produced an expensive slide presentation on behalf of the Agency. Does this mean it can't be used?"

I asked him, "Can you afford one more slide?" He replied, "Of course." So I said, "Fine. Then put the prospect's name on it and drop it in the first slot in the tray. And if you're flush, make up a couple of dupes—and put one in the middle and the other at the end. This shows your respect for the prospect—and the importance attached to the presentation."

Therefore, prepare the reasons why your Agency is best for this prospect—and give the impression that the presentation was created especially for them.

For instance, here is a very effective yet economical means for doing so. For whatever the medium used (slide, poster card), subtly place the prospect's logo in the lower right hand corner. This gives the impression that everything said and shown was developed expressly for them.

If the prospect isn't worth this basic effort, you're just spinning your wheels. Instead, concentrate your activity on those sufficiently desirable—with whom you want to get traction and get going.

E.   Emotional Appeal

Essentially your presentation approach is factual and tangible—directed to the prospect's intellect. But logic will get you only half way there.

In addition, provide for an organic appeal—to their heart and gut. In a competitive situation, if all other matters seem equal, the prospect's emotional reaction can be the tie-breaker. In fact, if the *impression* made is powerful enough, it could induce the prospect to dump the formal criteria for Agency selection and defer to their own good judgment—and select you.

This impact can be achieved by establishing the following goal for your presentation. *Its effect should make the prospect wish they had been getting your caliber of people and work all along.* How? Get *up* for this. Come up with ideas the prospect would wish they had thought of.

By instilling this envy and regret, it can transcend all other considerations—and Agencies.

So compound their need with want. Since the latter is the deciding factor.

F.   Style vs. Substance

As important as it is to be personally appealing to your prospect audience, demonstrating how you would fulfill their marketing objectives is just as vital. Your own attraction must be matched by proof of how your Agency's experience and ability can best satisfy their needs. Thus, your compatibility is meaningful only if there are the qualifications to produce the results desired. And the prospect wants to be convinced *of both*.

Therefore, don't get carried away with style at the expense of substance. Assuming that sensitivity to them as people will suffice. And then use an obviously blatant device as evidence of such.

For instance, I know of an Agency specializing in high-tech accounts who got the jump on competition when learning of a German company intending to open the U.S. market in a big way. To indicate how well the Agency could relate, they delivered the entire presentation *in German*. And they lost; right then.

If language was much of a consideration, the advertiser could have set-tled for an Agency in Germany. Rather, they were seeking an American Agency because of wanting one that is U.S.-oriented in their approach to the market. Thus, instead of ingratiating themselves, this shop served as a reminder to the prospect of what they don't want in an Agency.

So sure, speak their language—but not literally. Instead, figuratively put out the sign: **MARKETING SPOKEN HERE—YOURS.**

G.   Move Prospect to Presenter's Offices

There are three negative factors with which an Agency is confronted in every presentation:

• The prospect is not accustomed to holding still.

• They have a short attention span.

• There is the tedium inherent in any pitch.

Why hope that your devastating charm, of itself, will overcome these obstacles? Rather, here is a tested idea to combat these forces fighting you. This applies if the event is held at your place—and if the facilities are conducive.

Instead of the usual practice of bringing all your presenters to the conference room, take the prospect to the presenters' offices for that por-tion of the presentation (i.e., open in the conference room; next, present Creative in their digs; and then move on to the Media Department).

This will provide a refreshing change of pace for the prospect—and break the mold of the stereotyped presentation. This tactic will also contribute to a more relaxed environment—and a more alert audience. (Not incidental, your participants will be more confident and effective performing in their own surroundings.)

Thus, when appropriate, use this memorable presentation technique. Yet, remember: the logistics make adequate rehearsal even more essential.

H.   Ask for the Order—Throughout

Asking for the order is thought to be a function performed at the end of the presentation. Thus, your attempt to inspire a favorable decision is postponed until it becomes an afterthought.

However, you are soliciting their business beginning with your opening statement. Then why not start landing the account at inception?

Your "closer" should be the most compelling reason for appointing your Agency—now. Sure, it's the climax for your pitch. But its potency shouldn't be sublimated to sequence. So don't hold your trump card until the game is over.

Rather, develop variations of this payoff appeal. And sprinkle them throughout. In effect, use the *entire* presentation to convince the prospect to act on your behalf.

This strategy will assure a *total* selling effort—which is what it takes to score.

I.   When to Feature Creative

One school of thought staunchly assumes it is best to open with Creative—to get off to a roaring start. Others prefer to close with Creative—guessing that a bells-and-whistles climax would be more impressive.

They are both wrong! The only *right* opener is what the prospect told you they want to hear about. Not the format you prefer.

The wrong choice can weaken the impact of the soundest Creative strategy and its execution. Because there is not one standard positioning that is most effective for every situation.

Rather, the only consideration for locating Creative in the program is the prospect's perceived needs. If they indicated in pre-presentation contact that their major concern is with Creative, of course that is what you start with. If they expressed greater concern regarding some other function, then Creative should be slotted according to how it will compliment the Agency service most important to the prospect.

Summing up, the prospect is holding still to find out how their needs can be best fulfilled. To whatever extent you delay in satisfying this want is the extent to which you lose them. Thus, if your presentation is anything less than totally prospect-oriented, it becomes Agency-oriented. And you can't award yourself the account.

J.   Team Proposed

When an Agency pledges its troth to a prospect, the size and caliber of team promised is limited only by their imagination. And in retrospect, the claims made by Agencies are often so extravagant that they cancel each other out. Even worse, if not just suspect, they can be unbelievable. And though *your* intended commitment of personnel is legitimate, you suffer guilt by association.

Under these circumstances, how can you make your offer credible? Obviously, you can't bring along all of your staff who would be involved.

Instead, there is the device used by J. Walter Thompson/Atlanta. At the end of the presentation, with a flourish, they present to each member of the selection team a handsomely wrapped, jewelry-size gift box. Obviously, this pulls them forward in their chairs—and causes suspicion of impropriety. Having totally captured their attention, JWT invites the prospect to open "The best gift our Agency can give you."

Upon doing so, it is discovered that it contains a stack of the business cards representing all the Agency people who would be assigned to their account. This imaginative approach has proved to be very impressive. It is accepted as physical evidence of a bona fide commitment. One that can be trusted. **NOTE:** If your agency isn't too big on the use of business cards throughout its operation, offer an album consisting of snapshots of these back-up people.

There is a worthwhile conclusion that can be drawn from this tactic. For whatever the promise made, if feasible, deliver it in an idea-oriented vehicle. It's more intriguing, memorable—and indicates that your Agency can produce beyond that expected.

K.   Prospect Involvement

Having your game plan in place, it is unlikely you'll be too easily startled. For instance, it is not unusual for a prospect's participation in the presentation to consist of opening with the statement: "Go ahead." And then not saying anything until concluding with: "Next."

In between, the Agency conducts a monologue—gambling that of itself this will be sufficiently compelling to win the account. However, no agreement is ever reached without communication between the parties involved.

Therefore, structure your presentation to be a dialogue, so that you can speak with the prospect—rather than at them. This can be achieved by building some questions into the presentation to involve the prospect.

Preferably those with which they would agree—thereby developing the desired rapport.

Importantly, these questions should be directed to specific individuals—*by name*. Then, to further impress them, casually intersperse at least one fact obtained on each. Make a key point by stating: "Janet, since you have an MBA from Harvard, you certainly know that . . ." And, "Phil, you knew back when you were a Division Manager in Cleveland that . . ."

This tactic confirms that your presentation was developed especially for them, it's flattering—and commands attention. And while you are at it, make the members of the selection team look good. Compliment them on the astuteness of their questions and comments. The interaction generated will enable them to better relate to—and favorably remember—your Agency.

This involvement should consist of no more than asking them to confirm simple truisms with questions like, "Isn't that right, Phil?" This way, you don't put anyone on the spot. But you did serve notice that they will be involved in your presentation. Anyway, all you want is their agreement—not a speech.

Then, since involvement begets interest, invite them to interrupt with questions at any time. This indicates that apparently you must know what you are talking about—and proves that yours isn't a canned pitch.

As further evidence of its not being canned (which is one of the worst criticisms made by an advertiser), also bounce some questions off your own people to corroborate claims made. The spontaneity this injects will, of course, be well planned in your rehearsal. But don't surprise any of your people with a question and expect a profound reply.

L.   Seek Prospect Reaction

You led the prospect to water. Now get them to drink.

The purpose of your presentation is to obtain a favorable decision in the shortest period of time. To succeed, this requires seeking a commitment—rather than the usual practice of submitting it for the prospect's eventual consideration.

Therefore, how about having the courage to occasionally inquire during presentation as to their reaction to it? For instance, "Is this the kind of exciting Creative work you're looking for?" "And is this the type of shrewd marketing strategy you expect?"

This is a catalyst to start them thinking immediately—and is conducive to a spontaneous expression of judgment. No time is wasted speculating on their reaction while they vacillate. This way you will fairly well know where you stand, right then—and what to do about it.

M. Duration

When an advertiser is planning to move, and to interview a quantity of Agencies, a length of time for presentation is usually specified. For screening purposes, one hour is generally set. If that duration is needed, then make it a full 60 minutes of selling time. To whatever extent you digress, that amount of advantage is given to your competitors. So skip the extraneous warm-up patter—and be strictly pertinent throughout.

Because the duration stipulated is usually exceeded—much to the prospect's annoyance—here is an ingratiating device. This will also increase your memorability—favorably. Open by announcing that your presentation will not take any longer than 57 minutes. This rare cooperation will pull them forward in their chairs. (Of course, this also makes adequate rehearsal all the more necessary.)

Since this matter of timing is so important, let's clarify what the prospect means when they specify 60 minutes. It is simply that you are not to go beyond 60. By contrast, it is not expected that your presentation must go *up* to 60.

Thus, if it's determined that for a certain prospect you can be most effective in 35 minutes, do so and get out. Don't be like the Agency who had everything going for them—except they couldn't take yes for an answer. In particular, don't sell for so long that you end up buying it back.

Finally, here is the best reason for complying with the timing set forth. Prospects interpret violating this requirement as fighting them—and as indicative of the type of relationship that would exist if such an Agency were awarded the account. Thus, ignored timing is one of the first and easiest means used to eliminate Agencies.

N. Gimmicks

Nowhere is it inscribed in stone that you must spring some oh-so-clever device in presentation. Actually, if the substance of your program is impressive enough, there is no need for any sort of gimmick.

I am not philosophizing. Here is cold, hard proof.

Dennie Davidoff invited me back to her shop in Fairfield, CT. I was looking forward to congratulating her because it is not often a $9,000,000 Agency lands a $5,000,000 account. The new client was the regional co-op portion of Domino Pizza.

Upon offering my felicitations, she humbly countered with, "Thanks, but we just got lucky." I wasn't buying it. Nobody falls into that kind of achievement. However, Dennie insisted they lucked out. Since I still objected, she revealed what happened.

Whatever her Agency did right to become a finalist seemed like it would no longer sustain them. Because the other shop was five times bigger. And they had everything going for them to justify their selection. Plus, as feared, they put on a smashing show—which of itself easily sufficed. But Dennie's competitor wouldn't let it go at that. They had to get creative.

At the end of what had been a winning presentation, they had a huge cake wheeled in, smothered in frosting. And covering the top was inserted a Domino Pizza!

The selection team found this to be the most nauseating sight they had ever seen. At that, they called in Dennie's team with the instructions, "Do your thing, and if you don't screw up, you've got the account.

The moral here is *don't force a gimmick*. Certainly not one playing games with the prospect's product. Instead, make the message and the communication of it so good that you're not tempted to hokey it up with something cutesy.

O.   Concluding Gamesmanship

Sure, you want to wind up your presentation in a blaze of glory. But don't ruin a fine performance with a hokey finish.

This happened to an Agency who was actually wired in—yet couldn't resist the temptation of a cutesy clincher. Get this.

In critiquing their pitch recently, I was tremendously impressed with what they said—and how they did it. It looked like they confirmed the prospect's preference for them.

However, as it drew to the conclusion, I was told, "Now Jack, get a load of this wrap-up. It will blo-o-ow your mind!"

The concept was based on the fact that an annual fee of $100,000 had been negotiated.

As evidence of the Agency's integrity, they planned on having a Brinks guard enter at this time carrying a canvas sack. And he would dump its contents on a table in front of the presenter: $100,000 in cash.

Then the presenter would announce, "In the event we fall short of fulfilling the advertising objectives established, we will rebate a pro-rata share of the money to you." This statement was accompanied by grandiose gestures depicting the money being returned. Afterwards, the Agency President bubbled, "Dynamite, huh Jack!"

I winced. Hard. And with whatever calmness I could muster, explained, "You've shot yourself in the foot not only once—but three times":

- "First, this device is negative—suggesting you probably won't fulfill this responsibility.

- Second, there is nothing more appalling to a client than the specter of their Agency playing with its money.

- And finally, you've demonstrated what you are. Now it's just a matter of negotiating price."

I hope the Agency didn't use this gimmick. If so, *they* will end up holding the bag. Empty.

Instead, when you get to the end of the presentation, use this gamesmanship as further proof of why your Agency is best for them. Casually mention having complied with whatever their ground rules were for presentation. Because in all likelihood, to some degree, your competitors will have disregarded the prospect's wishes.

This reminder will confirm your compatibility—and subtly imply that the others are lacking by comparison.

Chapter 26

Inducements: As Rebuttals and Clinchers

A. Perspective

There are four basic excuses used by advertisers for not changing Agencies. Here is what you are confronted with—and how to overcome them.

There are also four factors by which a prospect is most influenced. Their favorable reaction to any one of these could persuade them to come around.

B. Four Excuses for Not Changing Agencies

1. How many times have you put on a fine presentation, with the prospect seemingly very impressed, only to be informed that, "Actually, we have no cause to drop our present Agency."

Obviously, this type needs to be given *a reason to change*. This can be accomplished with some finesse by furnishing them with a list of vital criteria for performance and relationship that should be expected of an Agency.

If for nothing other than curiosity, this will instigate evaluating their present shop. Such action is bound to reveal some inadequacies—and even problems. By contrast, having supplied this service, it implies that these desirable standards represent *your* method of operation.

Euphemistically, this could be described as creating constructive dissatisfaction. If you have any concern as to the advisability of this tactic, the way the new business game is being played now, Leo Durocher was right when he said, "Nice guys finish last."

2. Causing particular reluctance to change is the momentum factor. Advertisers estimate that changing Agencies causes them to lose one year of marketing momentum.

   To minimize this apprehension, register how smooth a transition you can provide. Your ability to maintain marketing stride for them should be stressed.

3. Another reason for hesitating is the matter of training. Advertisers worry about how long it will take a new Agency to become functionally familiar with their account.

   Put their mind at ease by assuring them that you could be on stream from the moment you're awarded the account. As evidence, provide a timetable detailing the specific dates as to when ideas will be created, plans developed and materials produced.

   I've seen a few instances in which Agencies wrap up their presentations by revealing a big bar chart. And then they announce, "If we are awarded your account by March 15, you will receive copy and layout by April 1, first proofs by April 15, etc." To the prospect, this graphic visually confirms that these people are set to go.

   In fact, that is how Ketchum in Pittsburgh got Westinghouse. After going through this bar chart, they were interrupted and asked to leave the room and wait outside. The Agency's reaction was, "How the hell did we screw up?" However, after a brief period Westinghouse called them back in and inquired. "Can you spend the rest of the day here?" Ketchum, puzzled, replied, "Sure, but why?" And Westinghouse informed him, "Well, apparently you're ready to go to work right now. So you've got our business."

4. There is the emotional factor. The prospect wants empathy, under-standing—and assurance that they would be doing the right thing by switching Agencies.

Thus, when an advertiser seems inclined to change, but you can't quite get them to the altar, help justify why this action should be taken. Yet remember: even if convinced of the need for a new Agency, you still have to *create the want for yours*.

By contrast, what if the prospect digs in his heels and snaps, "We'll switch Agencies when there is an earthquake here." Okay, take out earthquake insurance on them—with your Agency as beneficiary—and send them the policy. The Agency that did this didn't score right then. But one year later, when the account was ready to move, this Agency was the first one contacted.

C. Desire

The variety of inducements offered advertisers by Agencies is probably infinite. All striving to be so unique and appealing as to be irresistible.

However, anything other than telling them what they want to know most clouds the issue. Instead, as I have recommended, spell out up front in presentation: "Here are the six reasons (or five or seven) why our Agency is best for you."

Then pay it off in the wrapup with: "Here are the six reasons (or five or seven) why we want your business." Because a prospect doesn't care how much you know until they know how much you care. They view this explanation as indicative of the desired attitude and effort they could expect if you were awarded their account.

Besides whatever reasons you may want to cite, your list should include these two basics:

- Make a point of the prospect being especially *desirable* to you. There is much to be said for being wanted.

- Stress their *importance* to you—with specific reasons why for credibility.

Emphasizing these two matters can be very impressive because a key cause for client dissatisfaction is the assumption of being taken for granted.

Therefore, rather than the usual Agency practice of concentrating on why you should want us, this additional flip side approach sets forth your incentives to be more valuable to them. And this desire provides another justification for selecting your Agency.

D. Client Endorsement

The most impressive tactic in presentation is proof of client satisfaction.
Regardless of how great a job you've done for a client, a prospect considers
it only as good as the client's reaction to it.

Client endorsement can be communicated in a variety of ways.

1. That most often used is the **testimonial letter**. This is the usual
   evidence. The prospect assumes you must have garnered some of
   these by now. Thus, this standard impersonal approach is the least
   influential.

2. The next generation is the **slide-audiotape** technique. Projecting
   the client's photo on a screen, accompanied by a voice-over pitch
   extolling your virtues, is a good make-shift means for conveying
   authenticity.

3. Today, however, that proved to be most impressive is a **videotape**. Depicting the client actually expressing their pleasure with the Agency
   is much more effective—and believable.

4. A client's **direct participation** in the presentation on your behalf
   can have considerable impact if staged properly. (Yet, remember:
   The prospect's main concern is with who will be working on their
   account.)

   The state of the art in the use of clients is that applied by a Los Angeles Agency. The highlight of their pitch is called, "Meet the Client."
   This consists of installing a closed-circuit TV hookup at the offices
   of three key clients. At a predetermined time in presentation, the
   prospect is invited to ask any of them why they selected and continue to retain this Agency. In turn, these straw men will presumably
   follow the script provided.

5. Finally, here is how you can best capitalize on a client's respect for
   your Agency.

   The usual practice is to offer the prospect a copy of your account
   roster and say, "Call any of them. They all love us." But why would
   the prospect do so? The burden of proof is your responsibility.

   Instead, here is an intriguing alternative. Ask the prospect if you
   can have three of your clients *phone them*. (No bother for the
   prospect). Sure it's rigged. But it is assumed that so is *any* client
   testimonial.

   This strategy registers that you have clients who think so highly
   of your Agency that they are actually willing to promote it to other
   advertisers. What greater evidence of their satisfaction with you!

One important warning, though. If you are going to use a client personality to tout your Agency, be sure this person isn't controversial. Or one who might antagonize the prospect. I ran into this just recently. The client endorser was outstanding. But unbeknownst to the soliciting Agency, the prospect hated him. And the advantage backfired.

In the final analysis, to what extent can you exploit client influence? Obviously, that depends on the status of your relationship with each. And using the option appropriate to the circumstances—in a logical, least contrived manner.

E.   Agency Team

The most appealing inducement you can offer a prospect is your willingness to assemble the best team for their needs—consisting of their kind of people. The promise to take such action not only fulfills the requirement of proficiency—but also satisfies their desire for the right chemistry.

This has been proved time and again in Agency selection sessions in which I have been involved. Afterwards, I always ask the reason for the choice made. At first I'm told, "They seemed right" or "They felt good." The advertiser answered, but didn't say anything until explaining, "I think I can live with them." Then this is usually followed with the final justification: "I believe they'll be good for me."

It boils down to this: You are in a people business—and that is what the advertiser is buying.

Now for the application of this concept—and why.

A prospect being pitched may be vulnerable, or planning to change because of dissatisfaction with the type and amount of service received.

Granted, a client will usually assume that they are not getting enough attention. However, they may also have misgivings about the caliber of Agency personnel assigned. And their turnover. Or worse, suspect that their account is being used as a training ground for young staffers.

The advertiser believes they invest in their Agency team becoming functionally familiar with the account. When achieved, and satisfied with the relationship and performance, the client wants *stability*.

In essence, they are buying an Agency. And feel entitled to whatever personnel, functions and facilities are needed.

But first, the prospect is concerned as to who are the *specific* individuals to be assigned to them. *Who*, per function, will be responsible for their account. Not *representatives* of each—sent into the presentation for the kill—that they will never see or have access to again.

Therefore, in presentation, assure the prospect that those present from the Agency are *their own team*. Not your swat team. Because the prospect is sold by the team you have for them—not that for your Agency.

For the impression desired, identify your people at the outset *as theirs*. Introduce Gwendolyn Reach-Frequency as *your* Media Director. And Mario Mastocelli as *your* Executive Art Director. Further, Sam Shapiro will be *your* Copy Chief. Then be proud to offer J. Fairfax Ney as *your* Account Executive.

This matter may seem minor. But not to the prospect. Because this tactic registers who they will actually get—rather than evidence of what might be available. So make this commitment desired by the prospect—if you want them to do likewise.

F.   Compensation

Agencies will use a variety of financial inducements to attract new business. This could be due to:

- needing cash flow when first starting out
- wanting to break into an industry or medium with which they haven't been previously involved
- being anxious for an account that would showcase the Agency
- the rugged competition for new accounts

It is assumed the most appealing come-on is money. Seemingly, this is likeliest to make the difference. But it is also the most dangerous.

Specifically, sometimes I am asked, "Should we offer the inducement of working on a break-even basis for the first year? This recognizes that an Agency has to go to school on them for that period."

Never! First of all, this concession has a negative connotation. Further, it is an admission of inadequacy. And finally, by this act, you are establishing what you are—and now you're just negotiating price. Then, a year later, it would be tough to hit them for enough of an increase in income for you to achieve a satisfactory profit. Because you have already demonstrated your willingness to sacrifice profit. Now it's just a matter of the client determining the extent to which you will shaft yourself again.

The ultimate variation on this theme was recently tried by an Agency in the Southwest. The bait used in promotion was: "We will prove our worth by performing any project that costs up to $2,750—free!"

What happened? The Agency reported that it generated "considerable awareness."

How about new business? None. Because the Agency didn't specify to prospects *what* they could do for them. And worse, it established a value for their work: Zilch.

Whatever the income-cutting device, it characterizes the Agency as being desperate. Advertisers think of it as one that can be had. However, as a client they want to be associated with a winner. Thus, while you may land a few small fish, there won't be the catch desired. Because the overall impression made is that of an Agency whose work isn't good enough to be priced accordingly.

Remember, your appeal to an advertiser begins with the *quality* of your work—not your willingness to give it away. Therefore, any investment spending should be in the people you provide on their behalf—not in cutting legitimate charges.

G.   Know Recipient

Finally, for whatever the incentive considered, it is essential that you have a sense of the person to whom it would be offered. What is likely to impress or offend that individual?

Here is why you need to know in advance how he/she would react to your bait. It is based on the overture by the head of a New York City Agency to a wavering prospect. His shop was one of the two finalists. Having exhausted all rationales to break the stalemate, the Agency President decided to appeal to his contact's professional pride. The dialogue went like this.

Agency: "If you select us, how would you like to write copy on the account?"

Prospect: "I don't know how to write copy."

Agency: "You know how to write an invoice, don't you?"

Prospect: "If that's the case, why don't you just pay me in cash?"

Agency: "What the hell do you take me for?"

The offer left little doubt. Yet, the Agency President vehemently defended his pristine integrity—right through Chapter 11.

Chapter 27

Post-Presentation Activity That Pays Off

A. Perspective
B. Discussion Following Presentation
C. Critique
D. Misgivings/Regrets
E. Pre-Finals Promotion
F. Pre-Finals Inducement
G. Post-Finals Activity
H. Gimmicks
I. Post-Winning Devices

A. Perspective

One matter has become increasingly evident in working with advertisers on Agency selection. There are certain aspects of the new business operation to which they attach more importance than you might expect (i.e., tour of Agency, presentation graphics). Of themselves, these might not seem that crucial. But if a tie-breaker is needed, the prospect's impression of any of these factors could tip the scale either way.

One phase in particular is the discussion that takes place after the presentation. Advertisers are strongly influenced by the way the Agency handles itself. They believe that the spontaneity of this phase strips away Agency veneer—exposing its actual personality and method of operation.

To prepare you for this, let us deal with the three matters of greatest consequence—from which most conversation will emanate.

Advertisers are also very sensitive to Agency activity between presentation and selection. Agency conduct during this white-knuckle period can either improve their chances—or blow them. Thus, it is necessary to set forth what succeeds or fails during this critical period.

B.   Discussion Following Presentation

GRILLING

It is axiomatic that your objective is to sell—and that of the prospect is to select. They realize that their responsibility exceeds relying solely on your presentation. Thus, they will probe—and even bait—to assist in arriving at a decision.

The Agency's best strategy is to expect a trapping effort—and be prepared for it. Because this book can't be endless, I can't give you an extensive list of zingers to watch out for. Like when they zap you with, "What do you consider to be your Agency's worst fault?" Or, "Explain a recent failure of yours." Or, "Other than yourselves, if you were us, which one of the following Agencies would you select?"

These are cheap shots. And despite the temptation to counter-punch, keep cool. Give them a straightforward answer and you'll be home safe.

As to identifying your worst fault, don't be a masochist. Or assume conceding some shortcoming will make all else said more believable. Dead wrong!

Don't ever bare your soul by admitting to anything that could cause the prospect to doubt the value of your Agency.

In regard to confessing to a failure, you have a legitimate response in, "If this occurred, it would involve confidential client information which we could not reveal. This is the same protection we would afford you as a client." If this answer isn't acceptable, neither are they. Because there isn't a court in the country that would require you to testify against yourself.

As to which Agency *you* would select, you can logically state: "Much of the judgment would need to be based on their presentations. Not having seen any of them, all we can offer is a subjective opinion. And you need one better qualified than that."

Your best incentive for these honest answers is that if a single reply smacks of double talk, the finest performance will have been just that.

For that matter, if you even hesitate, you'll be more than proverbially lost. That is what happened to the Agency who was informed of being the front-runner for the Cadillac Dealers Association account in a major market.

Seeking final evidence of the Agency's good faith, the Association Chairman asked the Agency the toughest question with which you might be confronted. He began by acknowledging, "We realize our account is desirable from a prestige standpoint. But we are also aware that the Chevy, Ford, Toyota and Honda Dealer Associations spend a helluva lot more money than we do." Then he turned the screw with, "If as a result of the fine job you do for us, the opportunity arises for you to get one of them, would you drop us?" The Agency President snapped right back with: "Well, we-uh-er-we . . ." And the Chairman said, "Don't call us . . ." You know the rest.

Obviously, the only answer to that is an honest one. Namely, "As long as our relationship continues to be satisfactorily profitable and desirable, we would have no interest in a competitive account."

Significantly, in addition to *what* is said in your response, the prospect is also affected by *how* you answer their questions. This indicates to them whether they would be getting a cohesive team—and how well organized it would be. As opposed to individual prima donnas who shoot from the hip.

Thus, prepare for this "informal" phase as diligently as you do for the structured presentation. Specifically, all prospect inquiries should be accepted by the same person, (usually the Agency C.E.O.), who would hand them off to the team member best qualified to reply.

This procedure precludes any unauthoritative answers being blurted out. And it prevents contradictions. Both make the Agency seem like it doesn't know what it's doing.

So don't win the game at bat and lose it in the field. Practice. There is much to be said for defense, too.

AGENCY INVOLVEMENT

Much is made by the prospect of wanting more Agency involvement. And in your eagerness to get the business, you heartily concur—and say something real profound like, "Oh yeah!"

Okay, you registered your good intentions. Now you better find out precisely what is meant by this vague phrase. It could range from being available when phoned to having an office on their premises.

Then, based on estimated income, projected workload and dollar profit goal established, determine the extent to which you can *afford* to become involved. Further, decide on whether any additional involvement will generate enough extra income to be worthwhile. This insight will also enable you to convey more believably how much you *can* do for them.

COMPENSATION

The tenderest matter that will come up in post-presentation discussion is that of payment for your services.

Recognize that the advertiser has become more knowledgeable regarding Agency finances. They know fairly well what services you can afford to provide for the amount of income received.

So when negotiating compensation, while being aware of their growing insight, constantly bear in mind that *your objective is to create profitable income as capably as you create advertising*. Thus, whether the compensation is based on straight commission, or a combination of commission and fee, or fee only—there is only one kind of good marriage for an Agency. And this doesn't mean just marrying for money. It means marrying for *enough* money.

C. Critique

Agencies estimate they should close on approximately one out of nine solicitations. After receiving this input, though, I am told your hit ratio can be tripled to one in three.

A very important practice for contributing to at least the projected record is conducting a thick-skinned critique after every presentation. This should be scheduled soon, while all matters are still fresh in mind. Imperative to its value is the realization that this is not a witch hunt. Rather, it is a means for objectively determining how your future presentations can be improved. What is sought is twofold:

• Better reaction to subjects and materials
• More effective use of team members

Usually, these sessions consist of the participants congratulating each other on their outstanding performance. This ritual is conducted for job security. Keep it short—and get on with evaluating this presentation experience. Then, since this is not intended to be a bull session, provide for the application of what was learned by assigning responsibility for follow-through.

The findings of this post-mortem, implemented as necessary, can significantly increase the potency of subsequent solicitations. This discipline will also preclude your becoming complacent or stale.

This procedure is the second half of the 1–2 assessment of your presentation. In your first phase, *rehearsal*, it was critically evaluated prior to actual performance. And improvements made beforehand—while it could still do you good. The payoff punch, *post-mortem*, will reveal what need be done to strengthen the impression make hereafter.

Therefore, pre- and post-test your pitch as if it were an ad campaign for your most important client. Because it is.

D. Misgivings/Regrets

In the post-presentation critique, the warts and wrinkles show up. Invariably it is discovered there were some sins of omission and commission that lessened your effectiveness.

Then regret sets in. And a lot of sentences begin with, "If only . . ."

The next reaction consists of wondering whether a letter should be written to the prospect to compensate for these shortcomings. Or request another shot at it—for whatever contrived reason.

Never. Both tactics are negative. The letter calls attention to something being wrong—which the prospect may not have perceived as such. And as to a repeat performance, it's suspect. Thus, your follow-through activity should not cast any doubt whatsoever on the worth of your pitch or Agency.

If, however, your misgivings are that strong, any subsequent effort should be strictly positive and constructive. Further, whatever your communication, it must be of value to the prospect. Otherwise, it is considered just a self-serving gimmick—resulting in a loss of respect for your Agency.

Any supplementary activity should come across as leading from strength—not compensating for weakness.

E. Pre-Finals Promotion

Congratulations. You just made the short list. Is there anything you can do between now and the final pitches to improve your position? There sure is.

But first, let's consider the circumstances at this time. Upon selecting the finalists, the prospect may speculate (with some justification) that little difference could be expected in performance.

Now the chemistry factor comes into play. Which Agency would wear well? Who would make them look good?

At this stage, the matter of relationship becomes increasingly important. Therefore, at this point, greater emphasis should be placed on the team to be assigned to their account. In particular, their appropriateness to the prospect. And especially, their compatibility.

Of course, your people will be platformed in presentation in the most appealing manner. Further, they should be highlighted in your "Leaver"—in a warm, pertinent way. Featuring them as persons rather than functionaries.

Beyond this, develop means for creating preferences for your people during this sensitive period. For instance, here is an idea that will particularly impress the prospect.

Provide them with a videotape (approximately 10 minutes) to be delivered several days prior to the final presentation. (Loan them a VCR if necessary.) This would feature your forthcoming participants, each of whom would answer the theme: "I asked to work on your account. Here's why." In addition to the desirable effect of this message, it will establish familiarity and acceptance for your presenters in advance.

Since the prospect's attitude toward the finalists is skewed more toward the human equation, satisfying this concern is bound to influence them in your favor. Having softened the prospect with this warmer-upper, you will want to take whatever other action will enhance your appeal as a finalist.

Circumstances may trigger an idea that is a blast—and begging to be used. However, for any promotional device, the more imaginative the greater the risk of it back-firing. Thus, for a favorable reaction, it is essential that you know the character of the prospect people for whom it is intended.

There is no better evidence of the validity of this advice than the experience of Della Femina Travisano when pitching Kohler Company. Upon being selected as one of three finalists for this $5,000,000 account, the Agency came up with a hilarious thought. What materialized was an ad in the Sheboygan Press; (Kohler's headquarters city). It contained a photo of Jerry Della Femina in a bathtub (assumedly a Kohler product). The headline featured this prospect's theme, "The bold look of Kohler." And was followed by, "The bald look of Della Femina. They belong together."

Anyone with the remotest sense of humor would have to love it. But Kohler is very straight. Straight-straight. So before the ink was hardly dry on the ad, Kohler notified this Agency not to return for the final presentation.

Summing up, if you are inspired to run a "courtship ad," don't make a pass at the prospect unless you know they don't insist on waiting until after they get married.

F.   Pre-Finals Inducement

You have just survived the baptism of fire in the screening presentations. Now comes the shootout: the finals. Having made the cut, now make the difference. Wouldn't it be great if you could skip O.K. Corral and just put another notch in your gun?

You can—by tantalizing the prospect with your having developed a marketing idea so dynamic that it shouldn't hold until the scheduled series of final pitches to be held later. In fact, further lure them on the basis that waiting until the formality of the other Agency presentations would result in sacrificing substantial potential sales. Then inquire as to how soon you can present this irresistible opportunity. (Of course, your idea had better be plenty damn good.)

Here is one that met this standard—and aced out their competitors.

The co-op account for a national fast-food chain in a major market opened up. After the make-work procedure of a cattle call, they netted down to four finalists.

Being worth several million in billings (which could pay for a lot of hamburgers), it was worth going the extra mile. But how without violating the traditional ground rules?

It so happened that the prospect's major push—a breakfast promotion—wasn't getting off the ground. Coincidentally, one of the remaining candidates had the morning newspaper as a client.

What could be more of a natural than a free copy with breakfast at any of these outlets? The newspaper was delighted to participate because of the heavy advertising exposure and sampling this tie-in would provide. And the fast-food co-op flipped. So much so, they awarded their account to the Agency taking this initiative—while the others were still preparing for the finals which never occurred.

So sure, play the game. But you control it by supplying the bat and ball.

G.   Post-Finals Activity

The time between final presentation and selection is the most delicate period in the solicitation process.

To the prospect, your activity during this phase can be the final influence as to whether your Agency rates thumbs up or down. From the Agency standpoint, you want to do something so impressive that it will clinch your being chosen. However, because there was a fine reaction to your presentation, you don't want to risk an impetuous device that might queer it. Since your pitch isn't over till the fat prospect sings, here is what your reprise shouldn't and should do.

Employing a do-nothing approach to be discreet, will accomplish just that. Yet, a prospect doesn't like to be hustled. (This is because he doesn't want to appear to his associates as being on the take.) Thus, while more than silent prayer is necessary, don't resort to any subterfuge in using their people—or any transparently clever devices.

Rather, here is a safe yet potent three-phase plan that can be applied. These tactics can particularly distinguish your Agency from competitors—and compound the favorable effect of your presentation.

The first phase is based on the advertiser's belief that an Agency's ability to sell on its own behalf is the extent to what they can do for clients.

To provide this insight, *produce an ad as to why your Agency is best for them*. The medium is the prospect. Thus, have proofs delivered to all those who might in any way influence Agency selection.

This type of aggressiveness will be respected. And the ad is the most pertinent indication of your creativity. Therefore, it should be prepared with the same dedication as for your most important client. Because again, your Agency is.

If this tactic seems prosaic to you, here is proof of its impact. I know of an Agency in Silicon Valley who never came in worse than 2nd. But they did so consistently. Upon adding this idea to their new business procedure, they scored on seven of their next nine pitches. Since nothing else was changed, the Agency credits the ad with tipping the scale in their favor.

The second phase consists of your assuming that all presentations wound up in a tie. Now, what kind of tie-breaker can you come up with that will make you preferable to the others? Nothing cutesy—or that might demean your Agency. Rather, at your critique of the presentation, determine what was the prospect's hot button. What tender nerve did they reveal? Then take whatever ethical action to register final proof of your sensitivity to their needs—and that your Agency can best satisfy them.

Finally, during this critique session, also objectively identify what aspects of your presentation received a favorable reaction. And follow through by capitalizing on these strengths in a letter to the prospect: briefly, imaginatively and in a business-like manner. The payoff is that you are confirming the soundness of their judgment.

Of course, personal contact with the prospect can be especially valuable—but only if geared to what seems vital to them.

H. Gimmicks

Usually, gimmicks should be forbidden. However, there are exceptions. These can be justified when they make your point in an especially appealing manner—as interpreted by the prospect. Also, the concept needs to be relevant, in good taste—and a sense of humor helps. Like this one.

It involves a major account that was loose which was coveted by an Agency clearly too small for consideration. This "David" Agency felt that, while not having the size, they had the firepower. Therefore, the "Goliath" account was worth their best shot. Afterwards, although the prospect was very impressed—and liked them—there was no way of rationalizing awarding so large an account to an Agency of such modest size.

Yet, even though rejected, the reception was so good, the Agency couldn't accept defeat. Anyway, landing even a portion of this account would be great for them. Thus, after all the presentations had been made, and the advertiser was getting the selection process underway, the Agency sent them a freshly baked pie with the enclosed note: "Save us a piece."

No mistaking the message. Nothing suspect about it. And it is both figuratively and literally in good taste. There was a happy ending: the Agency got a "piece" commensurate with their size—and have been living with this client happily ever after.

I. Post-Winning Devices

Granted, you begin to lose an account the day you win it. But this shouldn't actually happen the first day.

Yet, there isn't any grace period during which the Agency is safe. You're on probation from the outset. So don't mistake a new client's surface cordiality for acceptance.

Since an Agency's conduct determines the duration of the honeymoon, think twice about using any device to launch your relationship. Such as assuming that a final shot is necessary to confirm the soundness of their judgment in having selected your Agency.

This was learned the hard way by an upstate New York Agency. They were jubilant on landing a major baking account, because it became by far their biggest client. The victory wasn't enough for them, though. They felt compelled to further prove their desirability.

Thus, upon receiving the good news, the Agency decided to immediately deliver evidence of their devotion. And to no less than the new client's C.E.O. Unfortunately, they got "creative." The vehicle was appropriately a box of biscuits. However, the message inserted cost the Agency its dough, "We'll work our buns off for you."

The new client C.E.O. was appalled by the Agency's bad taste and promptly notified them of being persona non grata. And within 24 hours, the Agency went from the pinnacle to the pits.

There are a couple of overlooked lessons that need be relearned:

- Never risk a gimmick with someone you hardly know.
- If it would be construed as cutesy, this is disastrous with anyone.

Summing up, upon winning, if tempted to follow through with a post-clincher, heed the astute advice of Mies van der Rohe: "Less is more."

Chapter 28

How the Selection Process Works—and Your Options

A. Perspective

This brings us to the bottom line: Agency selection.

How does this process *really* work? I am not going to give you the published scientific procedure. Usually that is just given lip service.

Rather, here is what actually happens, what to do about it—and your options if you don't score.

B.   Sum of Activity Required to Win

But first, there is a deadly strain of new business myopia against which you need to be inoculated. Here's why. The most frequent question I am asked about the new business operation is, "What is the best presentation?"

This presumes that, for all practical purposes, Agency selection is based entirely on the presentation. But:

- If your initial contact isn't sufficiently intriguing
- and then there isn't persistent follow-through
- and the pre-presentation meeting isn't conducted in the most impressive manner

there won't be any presentation.

Further, if there isn't the will to prepare to win in respect to:

- prospect research
- presentation graphics
- selection team involvement
- and rehearsal

you won't make the cut.

Of course, the best presentation is the one most appropriate to the prospect and the circumstances.

Even so, it still takes:

- a compelling "Leaver"
- an appealing tour of the Agency
- and shrewd post-presentation activity

in order to win.

Therefore, as dynamic as your presentation may be, if the other components of your new business operation don't measure up, your show will close on opening night—in Peoria.

C.   Prospect Criteria

Despite the makework questionnaire forms sent you by advertisers, Agency selection nets down to the prospect's gut response to these four questions they ask each other—in the following order of importance:

1. "Did you believe them?"
2. "Are they our kind of people?"

3. "Do they know our business?"

4. "Can they create more persuasive advertising?"

This sequence may strike some of you as being heresy. But if you don't first satisfy the prospect in regard to honesty, compatibility and expertise, they won't *believe* you can create more persuasive advertising.

D.   Actual Procedure

After having applied these criteria, do you know how advertisers select the winning Agency?

They don't. It's too tough for them to pick # 1. Instead, the losers are methodically eliminated—from which the winner coincidentally emerges.

That is why sometimes the winning Agency is the one who made the fewest mistakes.

E.   Alternative to Losing

If the worst happens, and you don't make the cut, ask for another chance. Or if you are eliminated in the finals *before* the winner is selected—again, ask for another crack at it.

Are you above this? Y&R isn't. In both instances, they ask. And sometimes they get this concession—and the account. They are not too proud to make this second effort.

This tactic was spawned by believing you can only be defeated if you accept it. And the application of this attitude has contributed to their consistent success in new business activity.

F.   Learn from Losses

If you don't score, this needn't be a total loss. There must be something that can be learned from this experience which will make your Agency more appealing next time.

For this purpose, whenever a presentation is lost, try to flush out why the winner was preferable. Here is an easy and productive tactic for doing so. Contact and congratulate the prospect—acknowledging you respect that they did what was in their best interest.

Having established this favorable environment, inquire as to the reason for the selection made. Because of pride in judgment, they will generally reveal enough to provide the insight needed.

By contrast, *never* probe as to why you lost. This creates an adversary situation in which they become defensive—and either refuse to answer or provide misleading information.

In the follow through, remember: your motive is not to find an excuse for losing. Rather, it is to seek that key clue for winning.

G. Stay in Touch

Even so, this needn't mean the end for this prospect. You're down—but not out. There needn't be a finality to another Agency being selected. When this occurs, your first course of action should be: *stay in touch.*

Even though advertisers prefer to believe they are infallible in Agency selection, sometimes they discover three months later that a bum choice was made.

When this occurs, it is impractical and unnecessary for them to go through the entire Agency search process again. Rather, being unable to afford further down time, they will move fast and pick from the previous finalists. And since each has already given the prospect their full treatment, this now comes down to just a beauty contest.

However, by your maintaining top-of-mind awareness and interest in them during this traumatic period, the prospect will be more comfortable with your Agency. And they will love you even more on the rebound.

Chapter 29

Recap of Components of New Business Program

There you have it: The top-of-the-line set of clubs I promised. However, as I mentioned, you still have to play them. Now, in order to win, let's recap the set you need to have in your bag to go out on the new business course.

I'll admit to having taken some license. Because I am recommending sixteen clubs—and the U.S.G.A. only allows fourteen. But on your tour, you can't afford to miss a single shot. So here goes. Fore!

- Set goals: for dollar growth and consistent missionary presentations.
- Select New Business Manager.
- Institute total Agency team concept.
- Prepare Marketing Plan.
- Survey employees for their perception of Agency strengths and weaknesses in regard to personnel and operations.
- Create Unique Selling Proposition.
- Implement rifle/buckshot strategy for prospecting.
- Institute system for keeping informed of advertisers becoming susceptible to change.

- Assign responsibilities and set target dates for planning New Business Program, developing prospects and exploiting leads.
- Prepare introductory letter for getting initial appointment.
- Establish format for conduct of pre-presentation meeting.
- Decide on content for Prospect Factbook.
- Design Agency "look" for presentation, leaver and agenda.
- Plan procedure for tour of Agency.
- Prepare an emergency kit to be taken to presentations.
- Develop post-presentation critique.

Being this organized and prepared, you won't have to default on a desirable prospect because you're too busy to make the 100% effort required. Having these basics on line, now it is mostly a matter of *customizing* rather than starting from scratch.

Thus, you should never have to forfeit a game due to lack of equipment.

Now that you have landed the new account as I promised, the most important client you will ever have, your Agency—it is fittingly the end of this book.

But it is the beginning of your opportunity. If you take advantage of this input, it can be one of the best investments you can make in your Agency's future. Otherwise, this has been an expense.

Therefore, since experience is the comb that life gives you after you've lost your hair, use these "street smarts" *before* going bald.

J. L. Matthews Corporation
Beaverdam Run, 16 Stony Ridge
Asheville, NC 28804
(704) 251-0501

HUNT/KILL SELLING

SALES SECRETS OF THE PROFESSIONAL PERSUADERS

The only magic in sales is what *you make happen.* And this requires an aggressive, total plan — consistently applied.

Selling plans are the shark's teeth of the advertising/marketing professionals. And everyone in business has to work with, for, or against these "professional persuaders" — the true Hunt/Kill sellers.

By showing you how and why these hunters succeed, this book will empower you to win all the business you want — and fast.

With the proven strategies and tactics he has learned from the front lines of selling, veteran ad man Jack Matthews replaces crapshoot selling approaches with surefire techniques. And you'll especially enjoy the "war stories" that make this book so much fun to read.

Whatever you sell, you'll gain solid selling smarts from the pros who sell *selling.* Included are hundreds of tips from:

- Advertising agencies
- Sales promotion agencies
- Public relations firms

- Institutional promotion and publicity departments
- Direct marketing agencies
- Corporate marketing/advertising agencies
- Media: TV, radio, magazine, newspaper and outdoor

Knowing how the "professional persuaders" work will allow you to use their unique insights to your advantage. This insider's glimpse into the cutthroat world of Hunt/Kill selling will make all the difference between winning and being a runner-up.

Go for the jugular! *Hunt-Kill Selling* takes you on a safari through the selling jungle where you'll learn how to survive and thrive with this unique guide for the successful sales "kill."

La Mont DeBruhl

About the Author

Jack Matthews, a twenty-five-year veteran of the ad agency wars, has counseled over 390 agencies on landing the best accounts. He also heads an international management consulting firm that advises businesses on how to select the ad agency that's best for them. He resides with his wife in Asheville, North Carolina.